Nietzsche's Machiavellian Politics

Nietzsche's Machiavellian Politics

Don Dombowsky

palgrave
macmillan

First published 2004 by
PALGRAVE MACMILLAN
Houndmills, Basingstoke, Hampshire RG21 6XS and 175 Fifth Avenue, New York, N.Y. 10010
Companies and representatives throughout the world

PALGRAVE MACMILLAN is the global academic imprint of the Palgrave Macmillan division of St. Martin's Press, LLC and of Palgrave Macmillan Ltd. Macmillan® is a registered trademark in the United States, United Kingdom and other countries. Palgrave is a registered trademark in the European Union and other countries.

ISBN 1–4039–3367–7

This book is printed on paper suitable for recycling and made from fully managed and sustained forest sources.

A catalogue record for this book is available from the British Library.

Library of Congress Cataloging-in-Publication Data
Dombowsky, Don.
    Nietzsche's Machiavellian politics / Don Dombowsky.
        p.   cm.
    Includes bibliographical references and index.
    ISBN 1–4039–3367–7 (cloth)
        1. Nietzsche, Friedrich Wilhelm, 1844–1900 – Political and social views.   2. Machiavellianism (Psychology)   I. Title.
    JC233.N52D66   2004
    320'.092–dc22

                                                    2003064665

10   9   8   7   6   5   4   3   2   1
13   12   11   10   09   08   07   06   05   04

Transferred to digital printing 2005

for Milanka

Elle se répand dans ma vie
Comme un air imprégné de sel,
Et dans mon âme inassouvie
Verse le goût de l'éternel.
　　　　　　—Baudelaire

Contents

Acknowledgements

For support, conversation and assistance, I would like to thank the following individuals: Richard S. G. Brown, Daniel Tanguay, Douglas Moggach, Denis Dumas, Hilliard Aronovitch, Milanka Stojadinović, Frank Cameron, Michael Pelias and Philip Dombowsky.

List of Abbreviations

[A]	*The Anti-Christ*
[BGE]	*Beyond Good and Evil: Prelude to a Philosophy of the Future*
[BT]	*The Birth of Tragedy out of the Spirit of Music or: Hellenism and Pessimism*
[CW]	*The Case of Wagner: A Musician's Problem. Turinese Letter of May 1888*
[D]	*Daybreak: Thoughts on the Prejudices of Morality*
[DL]	*Discourses on the First Ten Books of Titus Livius*
[EH]	*Ecce Homo: How One Becomes What One Is*
[GS]	*The Gay Science*
[GM]	*On the Genealogy of Morals: A Polemic*
[H; Vol. II: AOM, WS]	*Human, All Too Human: A Book for Free Spirits.* Vols. I and II (*Assorted Opinions and Maxims* and *The Wanderer and His Shadow*)
[KSA]	*Kritische Studienausgabe*
[PTG]	*Philosophy in the Tragic Age of the Greeks*
[P]	*The Prince*
[Z]	*Thus Spoke Zarathustra: A Book for Everyone and No One*
[TI]	*Twilight of the Idols: Or How to Philosophize with a Hammer*
[UW]	*Unpublished Writings: From the Period of Unfashionable Observations*
[UM]	*Untimely Meditations*
[WP]	*The Will to Power*

Introduction

Virtually all treatments of Nietzsche's political thought today are concerned with its posthumous appropriation, how it has been used and how it can or should be used. The principal imperative guiding this study, conversely, is to situate Nietzsche's political thought in relation to the political issues, critiques and movements of his own period.

Of works in this vein, Peter Bergmann's *Nietzsche, 'The Last Anti-political German'*, a work of political biography, is one of the most extensive treatments. But Bergmann's view, a view that I dispute, is that of 'all Nietzsche's contemporaries, Nietzsche's position most closely resembles that of the anarchists'.[1]

In spite of the fact that Nietzsche considers that politics and economics 'are not worthy of being the enforced concern of society's most gifted spirits' (D 179), and in view of the fact that he refers to himself as the 'last *anti-political* German' (EH WW 3), whatever that may mean, Nietzsche's antipolitics constitutes a politics. All of his works contain political commentary, and some of them even commentary on political economy, which consists primarily of antidemocratic polemics. In turn, this political commentary has its basis in political theory, whether Platonic or Machiavellian. Nietzsche does have a political theory, a theory of what politics is and what it should be (which makes inequality the condition for the production of the exemplary type). He is antipolitical, strictly speaking, because he does not foresee the end of violence. If there is a problem with this theory, it is not a problem of consistency or contradiction, but rather a problem of insufficient detail and a style that tends towards propaganda rather than argument. Nietzsche's political theory is attenuated through lack of detail, but his antidemocratic polemics are prosecuted with resolve. To read Nietzsche without politics, with exclusion or censorship of his political commentary, represents a massive omission of vital signs.

To read it, also, without attunement to the positions of the political forces of his own period is equally inadequate. For example, reading Nietzsche's criticism of the German Chancellor, Otto von Bismarck (taken in its most comprehensive sense), in a way that would dissociate him from National Socialist ideology overlooks the obvious fact that Nietzsche's criticism of Bismarck comes from the Right. With respect to Bismarck's *Machtpolitik* policies, Nietzsche rejects them because they carry 'German culture' with them.

It should be noted that reading Nietzsche without politics is in the history of Nietzsche reception something of an aberration. I think of the symposium held around the turn of the last century, 'Is The British Policy in South Africa a Consistent Exemplification of Nietzsche's Social Philosophy';[2] or of Randolph Bourne's *Atlantic Monthly* article from 1917 on the *Good European*;[3] of the use of Nietzsche's concept of will to power in apologetics for French imperialism, namely in the work of Jules Harmand and Ernest Seillière;[4] of the National Socialist readings, particularly of Alfred Bäumler, who refers to Nietzsche as a 'politician' and asserts that 'the philosophy of the will to power is the philosophy of politics';[5] of the readings of conservative revolutionaries such as Ernst Jünger and Oswald Spengler;[6] of Martin Heidegger's reading of Nietzsche between 1937 and 1940, where Nietzsche's will to power is cast in terms of the technological 'will to will' and the 'programme for planetary domination . . . the operational and controlled manipulation of all beings';[7] of the Italian Fascist reading;[8] of his status as a 'master thinker for the royalist fringe of the radical right' in France;[9] of the reading of Gyorgy Lukács, who sees Nietzsche as 'the leading philosopher of the imperialist reaction', engaged in an 'ideological war against the proletariat';[10] or of the reading of Frantz Fanon, who invokes the will to power 'in the context of a minority struggle for independence and the assertion of suppressed identity'.[11]

This study is concerned with the question of Nietzsche's political identity or identification. In part, it constitutes opposition to and criticism of efforts in contemporary Anglo-American political philosophy to read Nietzsche as consonant with liberal democratic pluralism. Such readings claim a fundamental discontinuity between Nietzsche's Dionysian philosophy and his aristocratic, authoritarian politics of hierarchy and domination. They assume a necessary connection between Nietzsche's antifoundationalism and a liberal democratic politics. In hermeneutic practice, this means reading the will to power in terms of the processes of self-constitution (as *power for* rather than as *power over*) and Nietzschean perspectivism in terms of agonistic pluralism, with an egalitarian subtext, exorcising the ideological motifs of domination and exploitation in Nietzsche's formulation of these doctrines, and rejecting or excluding the Nietzschean figure of the philosopher-legislator or philosophical lawgiver.

They read as if Nietzsche's commitment to the finitude of all regimes, or perpetual overcoming, were incompatible with any consolidation or durability of power (formations of domination). Following Karl Jaspers (and Georges Bataille and Gilles Deleuze are conduits of this view), they see contradiction as the organizing principle of the Nietzschean corpus, whereby it ceases to be a closed system capable of legitimating an authoritarian politics and becomes, rather, a mode of thought continually receptive to new possibilities. But instead of concluding that this would mean that Nietzsche resists political codification, as Deleuze, for example, does, they translate this mode of thought into a form of government, or governmental ethos, making it clear that the only kind of political machinery appropriate to Nietzsche's basic outlook is that associated with liberal democracy.

The general position of the radical liberal democratic reading of Nietzsche is that Nietzsche misunderstood the implications of his philosophy and that his work contains a latent politics. Thus the project, as Mark Warren formulates it, is to free 'Nietzsche's philosophy from its political straitjacket' and adapt it to its latent liberal democratic political identity.[12] In other words, following the metaphor, they want to restrain Nietzsche's political *insanity*. But where does Nietzsche's philosophy stop and his politics begin? – especially for a philosopher like Nietzsche, who holds to the classical political conception, following Plato in *The Republic*, that the body resembles the polity, for whom there is a necessary connection between action and social organization, individuals and practices, practices and historically given structures; who describes in political terms, in terms of domination and exploitation, always legitimating inequality and order of rank, even the most fundamental biological activity. The post-Nietzschean liberal democratic reading has no recourse, as it admits, but to 'continue to bracket the political residue in Nietzsche's choice of words'.[13]

I will argue that Nietzsche may be more accurately associated with conservative or aristocratic liberalism (Alexis de Tocqueville, Jacob Burckhardt and Hippolyte Taine) and its critique of the results of the Enlightenment and the French Revolution; that the aristocratic liberal critique of democratic society lies at the basis of his political philosophy. The aristocratic liberals, like Nietzsche, ascribe the highest value to liberty, diversity and a form of individuality which is opposed to the bourgeois liberal preoccupation with personal interests and ends. Like Nietzsche, they express a general disdain for the masses and reject universal suffrage (although de Tocqueville was ambivalent but not adamant on this point). However, unlike Nietzsche, they are not unconditional opponents of democratic equality and democratic ethics or social justice.

I will argue that Nietzsche radicalizes the aristocratic liberal critique in so far as he takes as absolute what its proponents merely take for the potential dangers of democracy, advocating its subversion and manipulation through the figures of the free spirits and the philosopher-legislators, and a conception of the masses as passive material for manipulation and command. Nietzsche is engaged in antidemocratic class warfare and is ultimately committed to the reversal of the process of democratization and to laying the groundwork for an alternative radical aristocratic ideal of political organization which he sees as the condition for the production of the exemplary human being. Nietzsche is also more radical than the aristocratic liberals in his conception of the state and of the individual, the latter inspired by the individualism of the Renaissance, by the concept of the political artist who is characterized by Machiavellian *virtù*.

Nietzsche's philosophy of politics and power is informed by Machiavellian principles. He consistently holds, for example, to the distinction between the ruler type and the ruled type, elite and masses, master and slave, to the doctrine of the necessity of social rankings and subordinations, at least where *higher* culture is concerned. The ruler type, the founder of states, possesses *virtù*, while characteristic of the ruled type (the majority) is passivity. Of course, there are other similarities between Machiavelli and Nietzsche, such as anti-Christianity, the subordination of morality to politics, the emphasis on power in political analysis, the need for opponents or enemies and the view that the state has its foundation in immoralism and violence.

When I say that Nietzsche's philosophy of politics is informed by Machiavellian principles, this is meant to encompass neo-Machiavellian elite theorists of Nietzsche's generation such as Vilfredo Pareto, Gaetano Mosca and Gustave Le Bon. All of them are connected to that aspect of the aristocratic liberal critique which seeks to demonstrate the dangers of mass democracy. Like Nietzsche, they believe that rational action plays a minimal role in social and political transformation; they view the foundations of social change in mass behaviour manipulated by elite leadership; they believe in the necessity of mythic formulas; they view society as a pyramid, holding to the Machiavellian division between the *few* and the *many*; they are antiliberal, antidemocratic and antisocialist, but they argue that there can be no absolute commitment to any particular political programme or ideology.

This latter point is crucial to consider because the contemporary radical liberal democratic reading (unlike the Straussian reading) tends not to recognize its possibility in Nietzsche and thus does not consider that he may be tactical (esoteric and dissimulative) rather than merely contradictory, a view for which there is not an insignificant amount of evidence in the Nietzschean corpus. For example, in his notebooks, Nietzsche writes: 'Our true essence must remain concealed, just like the Jesuits who exercised dictatorship in conditions of general anarchy' (Nachlaß 1881 KSA 9 11[221]).

Nietzsche's radicalization of the aristocratic liberal critique is primarily informed by a reading of Machiavelli's *The Prince*, that treatise on statecraft which allows Nietzsche to think in terms of political control techniques and a spectral-syncretic or perspectival art of governance, a willingness to use whatever ideologies are at hand in the interests of deeper goals. Given this, Nietzsche's political thought may be more accurately situated in relation to the antiliberal and anti-democratic neo-Machiavellian elite theorists of his generation who radicalize the aristocratic liberal critique in supporting the idea of the manipulation of mass behaviour through elite leadership use of political technology. This proposition is opposed to the position that Nietzsche most closely resembles the anarchists of his period.

I follow Charles Andler in this: Nietzsche was a disciple of Machiavelli.[14]

So why does Nietzsche gravitate towards Machiavelli? Machiavelli complements Nietzsche's anti-Platonism, his anti-Christianity and his naturalistic morality. There is no evidence to suggest that Nietzsche read any work of Machiavelli's other than *The Prince*, in an 1873 French edition, although he certainly read commentaries on Machiavelli. One of the earliest references Nietzsche makes to Machiavelli, quoting B. G. Niebuhr, is in a notebook entry from 1873. Given the nature of this entry, it may be said that Machiavelli allows Nietzsche to think in terms of political technique and a perspectival art of governance. It runs as follows: 'At times you have to hold each single human being sacred, at other times you can and should treat them only as a crowd; it comes down to knowing the time' (Nachlaß 1873 KSA 7 29[189]).

Machiavelli truly politicizes Nietzsche, makes him militant, allows him to think of the rule of the *new nobility*, appropriately indirect and disguised, under nihilistic conditions, under conditions of the effective illegitimacy of all foundations and perspectives; allows him to think of the state as a work of art, fully realized under conditions of conflict, and to think through the optimum struggle between Rome and Judea, Judea and Rome.

In Chapter 1, 'Wills to Power, Genealogy: Which Ones are at War?', I will expound the basic itinerary of Nietzsche's political philosophy and the political antagonisms, ideas, tenets and doctrines which inform it, all in the interests of a determination of its political identity or identification. I will show that Nietzsche's critique of morality possesses an inextricable political dimension, that his critique of morality is a critique of politics. I intend to make it evident that this fact finds expression in virtually all key themes, topics and categories of Nietzsche's philosophy such as *décadence* and *ressentiment*. I will establish that Nietzsche reduces morality to politics, that he is profoundly anti-egalitarian, that he is engaged in a war against the European working class, that he supports an antidemocratic *revaluation of all values* which will constitute the power of *order of rank*, an agonistic and *spiritual* politics radically aristocratic and authoritarian in form, and a conception of right as privilege which, in effect, provides incentive for a new aristocratic ruling class or *new nobility*.

In Chapter 2, 'The Radical Liberal Democratic Reading of Nietzsche', I will evaluate the contemporary radical liberal democratic appropriation of Nietzsche. I will provide a generic reading rather than engage all the nuances between the readings which comprise it, disclosing and rendering problematic the key arguments it advances. This chapter will begin with a discussion of the discontinuity which the radical liberal democratic reading posits between Nietzsche's Dionysian philosophy and his radical aristocratic, authoritarian politics. This reading claims that the principal Nietzschean doctrines which it engages possess an aporetic structure that releases them from the restrictions of Nietzschean politics. I will argue that there is no necessary discontinuity between Nietzsche's Dionysian philosophy and his politics, that his philosophical themes of the subject, perspectivism and agonism may be seen to be consistent with his politics of hierarchy and domination. With respect to the Nietzschean subject, I will argue that the radical liberal democratic reading tends to depreciate the theme of strong will in Nietzsche's philosophy. With respect to perspectivism, I will argue that this doctrine is compatible with the Nietzschean economy of exploitation, that not all perspectives are equal, and that we may rethink the doctrine of perspectivism along the lines of political technology. With respect to agonism, I will argue that agonism implies inequality and physical warfare, that it can never, in the Nietzschean sense, model the citizenry as free and equal, and that we may rethink the doctrine of agonism in terms of a regulated factionalism, or controlled violence, although Nietzsche provides little operational detail beyond its suggestion.

In Chapter 3, 'Nietzsche and Aristocratic Liberalism', I will begin to situate Nietzsche historically. In this chapter I will consider Nietzsche's connection to the aristocratic liberal critique of de Tocqueville, Burckhardt and Taine, and the intelligibility of the idea that he is a late-blooming aristocratic liberal. This chapter will provide a selective reading of the salient themes of the aristocratic liberal critique, the state, egalitarianism and individualism. In this chapter I will agree that Nietzsche is complicit with this particular strand of European liberalism. I will argue that Nietzsche assimilates all the vocabulary of the aristocratic liberal critique, that he is oriented towards similar issues around equality, the state and the individual, but that he radicalizes this critique in so far as he is a proponent of centralized rule, an unconditional opponent of democratic equality, and a proponent of an individualism which entails hierarchy and domination.

In the final chapter, 'Nietzsche and Machiavellianism', I will suggest that Nietzsche's radicalization of the aristocratic liberal critique ultimately situates him within the ideological constellation of the neo-Machiavellians, Le Bon, Pareto and Mosca, who were all contemporaries of Nietzsche; that it is with them, and not with the anarchists of his period, as Bergmann claims, that Nietzsche shares deeper ideological premises and commitments. In this chapter I will begin with a broad review of the philosophical parallels between Nietzsche and Machiavelli as background to Nietzsche's Machiavellian discipleship. Subsequently, I will engage, in more specific terms, Nietzsche's adaptation and implementation of Machiavellian *virtù* and immoralism in his moral and political philosophy, concepts which are also present in neo-Machiavellian political theory. *Virtù*, for Nietzsche, means political, legislative capability, overcoming of resistances, freedom from morality and reconciliation with evil, traits which apply to the Nietzschean conception of leadership exemplified by Napoleon Bonaparte.

Immoralism constitutes a thesis regarding the subordination of morality to politics, but also refers to the political technology with which

a moralism?

Nietzschean *virtù* is armed. It becomes the principle of action of the Nietzschean *tractatus politicus*, for the free spirits and new philosophers. I will claim that immoralism is Nietzsche's breakthrough which radicalizes the aristocratic liberal critique, a practical move towards the possibility of new regimes. I will also claim that Nietzschean political theory does not ignore the necessity of principles of legitimacy, as he recommends the use of myth and religion and authors a noble lie in the guise of natural law, will to power and order of rank, and advocates esoteric (or dissimulative) practices with respect to democratic institutions. I will claim that Nietzsche expresses an applied interest in the power religious and political ideals exercise over human beings, in the strategies and tactics employed by priestly-philosophical power-structures, and supports the utilization of practical political techniques to control the constituent power of the democratic masses. I will argue that it is his search for the authoritarian potential within democracy, his similar adaptation and implementation of Machiavellian *virtù* and immoralism, his understanding of political power, and his characterization of the masses, which situate him within the ideological constellation of the neo-Machiavellians. I will conclude with a few remarks distinguishing Nietzschean political doctrine from the anarchist political doctrine of Mikhail Bakunin, whom Nietzsche views as a destroyer of culture.

With respect to situating Nietzsche's political philosophy in relation to the political issues, critiques and movements of his own period, in the interests of establishing his historical intelligibility and political identity or identification, I intend this work to be no more than a prolegomenon. I do not claim that it is the final word on Nietzsche; I do claim, however, that Nietzsche does not resist political codification, that, on the basis of any substantial reading, a reading which breaks the seductive power of the aphorism through rigorous topical organization, he cannot be taken, finally or coherently, as 'the poet laureate of revolutionaries of all sorts'.[15]

1
Wills to Power, Genealogy: Which Ones are at War?

> [Mine] *was an instinct that aligned itself with life and that discovered for itself a fundamentally opposite doctrine and valuation of life – purely artistic and* anti-Christian. . . . *I called it Dionysian.*
>
> (BT P 5)

> *The symbol of this struggle, inscribed in letters legible across all human history, is 'Rome against Judea, Judea against Rome': – there has hitherto been no greater event than* this *struggle, this* question, *this deadly contradiction.*
>
> (GM I 16)

> *Christianity . . . I force a war against it.*
> (WP 200 Nachlaß 1887 KSA 12 10 [191])

Nietzsche's fundamental philosophical problem is the problem of morality, the problem of the origin of our concepts of good and evil, the conditions under which our values have been formed, whom they have conserved and whom suppressed. This fundamental problem is formalized by Nietzsche under the rubric of a critique of moral values, values which have been taken for unconditional and eternal, and a psychology of morals, through which morality is deduced as the 'unconscious disguise of physical needs', as an interpretation of the body. As Nietzsche writes, 'answers to the question about the *value* of existence, may always be considered first of all as the symptoms of certain bodies' (GS P 2). This critique intends 'an actual *history of morality*' (GM P 7), or a genealogy of morals, but is also symptomatology and typology, and is accompanied by the imperative to revalue all values.

But the problem of morality is also a problem of politics in the

Nietzschean corpus such that one is reducible to the other. Nietzsche's critique of morality possesses an indivisible political dimension. This is evident and finds expression in virtually all key themes and categories of Nietzsche's philosophy – such as *décadence, ressentiment, order of rank* and the *revaluation of all values* – as I shall demonstrate in this chapter. In the process of this demonstration I will expound the basic itinerary of Nietzsche's political thought and the political oppositions, ideas, tenets and doctrines which inform and activate it, all in the interests of a determination of its political identity or identification. In this chapter I will seek to establish that Nietzsche reduces morality to politics, that he is profoundly antiegalitarian, viewing the principle of equality as an expression of *ressentiment*; that he is engaged in a war against the European working class, its ascendency through militant labour and justice movements; that he supports an antidemocratic Dionysian, Roman and Hindu-inspired political revaluation, which aims to reestablish order of rank in society, an agonistic and *spiritual* politics radically aristocratic and authoritarian in form, and a conception of right, or sovereignty, as self-designated, or grounded in exception and privilege, which, in effect, provides incentive for a new aristocratic ruling class or *new nobility*.

1. *Ressentiment*

It has been argued, I think correctly, that for Nietzsche all morality is a form of politics or that Nietzsche reduces the moral to the political.[1] This reduction of morality to politics is evident in the fact that Nietzsche defines morality 'as the doctrine of the relations of supremacy' (BGE 19), that is to say, in terms of relations of domination and submission or command and obedience, which may also stand as a basic definition of politics. Tracy Strong expresses it most incisively, perhaps, when he remarks that, for Nietzsche, all morality is a form of politics because, as was demonstrated in *On the Genealogy of Morals*, 'the very existence of moral categories depended on the desire to assert power over another group of people – and under slave morality to *control* and render them predictable'.[2] Because such relations of supremacy, or relations of force, are viewed by Nietzsche to coincide with the very conditions of human life, it can be said that he is the author of a political ontology. This political ontology postulates the will to power as its fundamental principle, and is antidemocratic in its very rationale.

In *On the Genealogy of Morals*, his preliminary study for a revaluation of all values, Nietzsche provides, as an aspect of this reduction, a political explanation of the origin of the antithesis 'good and bad' and of the origin of language. The moral judgment, 'good', he says,

> did *not* originate with those to whom 'goodness' was shown! Rather it was 'the good' themselves . . . the noble, powerful, high-stationed and high-minded, who felt and established themselves and their actions as good . . . in contradistinction to all the low, low-minded, common and plebeian. It was out of this *pathos of distance* (*Pathos der Distanz*) that they first seized the right to create values and to coin names for values. (GM I 2)

Such an explanation is derived from the etymological significance of the designations for 'good' which can be found in the German, Greek, Latin and Gaelic languages Nietzsche samples. These designations reveal etymologically, as Nietzsche discovers, 'the *same conceptual transformation*'. In all demographic cases he examines, the concept of 'noble' or 'aristocratic', in the social and political sense of a domineering, ruling order, is the concept from which the designation 'good' developed. This development 'runs parallel with that other in which "common", "plebeian", "low", or "ruled group" are finally transformed into the concept "bad" ' (GM I 4).

The 'noble' and the 'aristocratic' of the *Ur-Staat* 'designate themselves simply by their superiority in power . . . as "the powerful", "the masters", "the commanders" ', as the supreme, ruling order (GM I 5). Nietzsche summarizes this behaviour through the formulation of a precept which says 'that a concept denoting political superiority always resolves itself into a concept denoting superiority of soul' (GM I 6). He considers this precept, or rule, a general rule of social organization. Nietzsche even conceives 'the origin of language itself as an expression of power on the part of the rulers [who] say "this *is* this and this", [who] seal every thing and event with a sound and . . . take possession of it' (GM I 2).

That all morality is essentially a form of politics for Nietzsche is written into his very conception or definition of values. All social values are enforced quanta of power and are connected to human interests; they are 'the results of certain perspectives of utility designed to maintain and increase human constructs of domination (*Herrschaftsgebilde*)' (WP 12 Nachlaß 1887–88 KSA 13 11[99]). As Nietzsche writes in *Human, All Too Human*, morality is 'preceded by *compulsion*' (H 99) or command, and always involves exploitative relations of domination and submission. Like Machiavelli, Nietzsche claims no inherent moral basis for any form of political legitimacy. Values and doctrines of values are merely the derivations of techniques of power and the exertions of power, as he expresses it in positive historical or genealogical terms.

But Nietzsche's reduction of morality to politics is also evident in his definition of *décadence*, as well as in the fact that the characteristic feature of the Christian morality he criticizes, namely, *ressentiment*, ultimately has its most manifest expression in modern political and social institutions, preeminently in the principle or doctrine of equality (but which accompanies related doctrines of freedom and individualism). Thus Nietzsche views the anarchist, democratic and socialist movements as the successors of the Christian movement, as neo-Christian and, accordingly, the militant European worker or proletariat, as an avatar of Christian 'anarchist agitation in the Empire' (A 58). Any treatment of Nietzsche's critique of morality must address his critique of these institutions and movements or it remains fundamentally deficient or partial, as they are complicit.[3]

Nietzsche is the anti-Christian and the self-avowed destroyer of Christianity who declares war not only on its dogma but, moreover, on its morality which persists in modern, secular political and social institutions. Nietzsche writes, 'I am . . . a world-historical monster – I am, in Greek, and not only in Greek, the *Antichrist*' (EH WGB 2); and Nietzsche refers to Zarathustra as the 'annihilator of morality' (EH WGB 1). The annihilation or negation of morality is essential to Nietzsche's immoralistic economy, as its subordination is essential to Machiavelli's. Nietzsche's immoralism, as he defines it in his autobiographical work, *Ecce Homo*, entails two negations. First, it negates 'a type of man that has so far been considered supreme: the good, the benevolent' man, both Christian and Rousseauian; second, it negates 'a type of morality that has become prevalent and predominant as morality itself – the morality of decadence or . . . *Christian* morality' (EH WD 4).

Though Nietzsche persistently criticizes theological dogma, the ideology and mediations of priestly power, and the religious community of Christianity, his pervasive assessment is that 'the faith in God has collapsed' (GS 358) and, more importantly, that the foundation of the Christian interpretation, its moral world order, is so defectively eroded that it is beyond reparation, that its 'obligatory force must diminish from day to day' (D 453), and that 'we have . . . entered upon the *reverse* course' (GM II 20), which promises the restoration of the '*innocence of becoming*' (TI Errors 8) or the advent of the Dionysian. Nietzsche writes,

> Looking at nature as if it were proof of the . . . governance of a god;
> interpreting history in honor of some divine reason, as a . . . testi-
> mony of a moral world order and ultimate moral purposes . . . as if
> everything were providential . . . designed and ordained for the sake
> of the salvation of the soul – that is *all over* now.   (GS 358)

God is dead, says Nietzsche, but 'we still have to vanquish his shadow,
too' (GS 108), meaning the residual metaphysics, epistemology, morality and politics of the *res publica Christiana*. With respect to politics or
political doctrine, this imperative will basically be directed by Nietzsche
at the legitimacy of classical natural law or natural right theory as found
in Grotius, for example, who fixes a moral law in nature, or in Rousseau,
who considers the sovereignty of the people and the inalienability of
human rights as an expression of natural law, and who is thus seen as
having brought this theory to completion.[4]

Nietzsche's fundamental assertion is that our highest values are *décadence* values. Both individuals and nations have lost, in his vocabulary,
the instincts and conditions 'for growth, for continuance, for accumulation of forces, for *power*: where the will to power [*Wille zur Macht*] is
lacking there is decline'. These values of decline, or nihilistic values,
now 'hold sway under the holiest names' (A 6). In *The Case of Wagner*,
Nietzsche retrospectively writes,

> Nothing has preoccupied me more profoundly than the problem of
> decadence [*décadence*]. . . . Once one has developed a keen eye for the
> symptoms of decline, one understands morality, too, one under-
> stands what is hiding under its most sacred names and value for-
> mulas: impoverished life, the will to the end, the great weariness.
> Morality negates life.   (CW P)

Nietzsche does not mean that *all* morality negates life, for he does
promote and affirm, in what at first glance appears to be post-
Aristotelian virtue theory, certain virtues such as pride, responsibility,
friendship, honesty and courage (not to mention certain kinds of
political institutions and regimes such as the France of Napoleon and
Louis Bonaparte and the *Imperium Romanum*).[5] Rather, Nietzsche comes
to be concerned, primarily, with two forms or types of morality and two
forms of life; two forms which are necessary opposites in the optics of
value: 'ascending' life and 'declining' life. For Nietzsche, every 'individual may be regarded as representing the ascending or descending line
of life' (TI Expeditions 33), may be classified as *higher* or *lower* types.

Thus the beginnings of Nietzsche's typology of morals locates no greater contrast, or real opposition, 'than that between a *master morality* or *noble morality* and the morality of *Christian* value concepts', slave or *ressentiment* morality. These antithetical concepts are initially explored in *Human, All Too Human* and in *Beyond Good and Evil*, and subsequently, and more comprehensively, in *On the Genealogy of Morals*. Master morality (Roman, pagan, classical, Renaissance) represents, according to Nietzsche, 'what has turned out well, of *ascending* life, of the will to power as the principle of life', it *'affirms* as instinctively as Christian morality *negates'*. Rooted in a triumphant Yes to *oneself,* it transfigures, beautifies and makes the world more rational, it 'gives to things out of its own abundance' (CW E).[6]

Christian, or slave morality, conversely, represents a vengeful antipathy to life and disgust with the world through its nihilistic invention of a *beyond* and its condemnations of the passions, the senses and sexuality, but moreover, through its pretence to absolute or universal standards, its monopolization of morality, its claim to be beyond all criticism. Its moral world order represents a 'denaturalizing of natural values' (A 25). As Nietzsche writes, with its imaginary causes, effects, beings, psychology, providence and teleology, 'this entire fictional world has its roots in *hatred* of the natural' (A 15). Christianity, then, is the principal object of Nietzsche's critique, as is its legacy or lineage in the political realm.

In opposition to those who would say that the principal, critical dichotomy in the Nietzschean corpus is aesthetic–unaesthetic, it is important to recognize that Nietzsche's Dionysian philosophy, as he writes in 1886, demotes morality to the 'realm of appearance . . . among "deceptions", as semblance, delusion, error, interpretation, contrivance, art' (BT P 5), that it ultimately subsumes all values under the concept of the aesthetic, or the model of art-making (following the Renaissance notion described by Burckhardt with respect to the state). As Nietzsche's genealogical critique reveals, all values are conditional and evolve out of struggles for supremacy with other values, they are cultural artifacts mediated by contingent, historical structures. Human beings have given themselves their own doctrines of good and evil. Thus Nietzsche can call the Prussian officer corps or the *Imperium Romanum* or the Jesuit order, in spite of their value discrepancy, 'works of art' (WP 796 Nachlaß 1885–86 KSA 12 2[114]). But Nietzsche criticizes Christianity because it refuses to see itself as merely aesthetic, as merely artifice or perspective. This being said, the more relevant critical dichotomy in the Nietzschean corpus is not, in my view, aesthetic–unaesthetic but natural–antinatural. This does not mean that we should abandon the Nietzschean aesthetic deduction, but that we should recognize that the latter dichotomy, natural-antinatural, compels a more constructive critique of Nietzsche which should put into question his recourse to nature as a normative standard and means of legitimation given his declared historical, genealogical method, a manoeuvre I will discuss in Chapter 4. Through his essentially nonaesthetic appeal to nature, which elevates certain societies and their political features over others, Nietzsche naturalizes historical political arrangements or, more precisely, antipolitical arrangements, which appear to maintain a level of controlled conflict or violence or class warfare, as in the Hindu social order he praises.

Christian morality is antinature itself. Christian values are the opposite values of those which would guarantee the health and future of humanity. Thus a crucially important component of Nietzsche's task becomes the 'de-deification' of nature, the naturalization of humanity out of a 'newly discovered, newly redeemed' nature. 'I formulate a principle,' Nietzsche says, all 'naturalism in morality, that is all *healthy* morality, is dominated by an instinct of life' (TI Morality 4) – 'life' being a loaded term. It follows, given the perceived complicity between morality and politics in Nietzsche, that his idea of the naturalization of humanity, of what is healthy and what is unhealthy, also applies to the political realm and social structure, to the doctrines of equality and order of rank, as will become evident below.

It must be said, by inference then, that master or noble morality necessarily represents naturalism in morality and politics. The typical forms of the declining or degenerating instinct, of which master or noble morality is the declared opposite, are not only Christian morality as such, but also the pessimistic philosophy of Arthur Schopenhauer, the philosophies of Plato and Immanuel Kant (sparing Kant's rejection of pity, which Nietzsche views as noble and politically necessary) and all idealism, including political idealism. Schopenhauer is considered by Nietzsche to be an inheritor of the Christian interpretation through his Upanishad-inspired denial of world and will, through his approval of the instincts of pity and self-abnegation. It is principally against Schopenhauer that Nietzsche defines himself as the extreme opposite of a pessimistic philosopher and refers to himself as the first *tragic* philosopher, qualified, invoking the myth of eternal return, as the 'last disciple and initiate' of the 'tempter god' and 'philosopher' *Dionysus* (BGE 295, EH P 2).

As a disciple of the god and philosopher Dionysus, Nietzsche allies himself with the Presocratic philosopher Heraclitus, whose teaching, according to Nietzsche, expresses the principal feature of a Dionysian philosophy: the 'affirmation of passing away *and destroying* . . . of *becoming*, along with a radical repudiation of *being*'; the affirmation of contradiction, opposition, war and eternal contest, or the *agon*. Nietzsche also speculates that Heraclitus may have previously taught the Stoic doctrine of the eternal return, 'of the unconditional and infinitely repeated circular course of all things' (EH BT 3), which Nietzsche himself purports to teach (and not the only one to do so during his time).

Both the doctrine of eternal return and Nietzsche's correlative term, *amor fati* (love of fate), are anti-idealistic formulas for the highest affirmation which claim 'a Yes-saying without reservation, even to suffering, even to guilt, even to everything that is questionable and strange in existence' (EH BT 2). But because these Dionysian formulas also encompass joy in destruction, and because this joy in destruction is an essential component of the conditions for a Dionysian task – 'negating *and destroying* are conditions of saying Yes' – they are selective, not universal in nature.[7] This is because the Christian moral world order, including the egalitarian politics it implies, is finally 'irreconcilable with an ascending, Yes-saying life' (EH WD 4). As a disciple of the hidden god Dionysus, Nietzsche seeks in both morals and politics 'a contrary type that is as little modern as possible – a noble, Yes-saying type' (EH BGE 2).

Nietzsche's critique of Christianity, aside from repudiating articles of Christian dogma such as 'God', 'beyond', 'free will', 'sin', 'true world', 'soul', 'guilt' and 'punishment', and which may be placed under the rubric of a critique of idealism in favour of naturalism or realism, focuses on the problem of *ressentiment*, enlightenment about *ressentiment* and, ultimately, freedom from it. *Ressentiment* represents 'the great rebellion against the dominion of *noble* values' (EH GM). It represents the repression of 'all that represents the *ascending* movement of life, well-constitutedness, power, beauty, self-affirmation on earth' (A 24). It is the 'will to persecute' and 'hatred of those who think differently' (A 21).

In *On the Genealogy of Morals*, Nietzsche locates the origin of the Judeo-Christian slave revolt in morality precisely at that point 'when *ressentiment* itself becomes creative and gives birth to values'. While the noble mode of valuation issues from a triumphant self-affirmation, according to Nietzsche's description, 'slave morality from the outset says No to what is "outside", what is "different", what is "not itself" . . . in order to exist, slave morality always first needs a hostile external world

. . . its action is fundamentally reaction.' As was discussed above, noble or aristocratic morality, on the other hand, 'seeks its opposite only so as to affirm itself more gratefully' (GM I 10). It 'conceives the basic concept "good" in advance' and only subsequently creates the negative concept of 'common' or 'low' in accordance with its political supremacy. The reverse is the case with slave morality which conceives 'evil', in effect, all the fundamental instincts of the noble type, in advance of its own self-image (GM I 11).

Ressentiment finds further expression in what Nietzsche calls the 'ascetic ideal', which is, essentially, simply another name for the Christian moral ideal, for slave morality, but which more deeply encodes its hegemonic designs. This repressive 'mode of valuation stands inscribed in the history of mankind . . . as one of the most . . . enduring of all phenomena'. Again, it represents 'profound disgust' with life, with beauty and physiological well-being and, following the Nietzschean rhetoric, the conservation of ill-constitutedness and degeneration.[8] In the ascetic ideal 'rules a *ressentiment* without equal, that of an insatiable instinct and power-will (*Machtwillens*) that wants to become master over life itself . . . over its most profound, powerful and basic conditions' (GM III 11). This nihilistic power-will may be thought of in terms of an imperialistic *modus operandi* for, as Nietzsche writes in *The Anti-Christ* (or *Anti-Christian*), it constitutes 'the instinctive rejection of every *other* practice, every *other* kind of perspective in the realm of values and practical application' (A 44).[9] Nietzsche will apply this symptomatic, instinctive rejection to egalitarian doctrine, which is the Nietzschean meaning of *ressentiment* I wish to emphasize here.

As I stated above in my demonstration regarding Nietzsche's reduction of morality to politics, Nietzsche's critique of Christianity necessarily involves a critique of political idealism, as he refers to egalitarian ideology, of which liberalism, anarchism, communism, socialism, democracy and the Bismarckian second *Reich* (founded in 1871) are, for Nietzsche, for the most part, a conflated expression. It is the 'sense of justice of the German palate', for instance, 'that finds all causes just and accords all equal rights', that makes the Germans 'idealists' (EH CW 1). Nietzsche equates the Bismarckian *Reich* with 'levelling mediocrity, democracy' (BT 6); 'the "new *Reich*" again founded on the most threadbare and despised ideas: equal rights and universal suffrage' (WP 748 Nachlaß 1887–88 KSA 13 11[235]).

Nietzsche's position must be understood in relation to the aftermath of the 1848 bourgeois liberal revolution which saw the formulation of a German constitution that spelled out fundamental rights and the institution of universal suffrage (1849), which elected the lower chamber of parliament. Although conservative, Bismarck made a number of concessions to both liberal and socialist interests, such as the implementation of health insurance laws. It should be noted that Nietzsche did not criticize Bismarck merely for his power politics or colonial doctrine, but for the concessions he was making to liberal democratic values.

Although Nietzsche will say that '*ressentiment* . . . blooms best today' among the anarchists and anti-Semites (such as Eugen Dühring and Adolf Stöcker) who 'sanctify *revenge* under the name of *justice*' (GM II 11), all modern ideologies, because of the centrality of the egalitarian principle within them, are, according to Nietzsche, ideologies of *ressentiment*, of *décadence*.[10] As he writes, and this quotation encapsulates the primary targets of Nietzsche's political critique, and points again to Nietzsche's reduction of morality to politics, '*décadence*: every time, the anarchy of atoms, disgregation of the will, 'freedom of the individual', to use moral terms – expanded into a political theory, "*equal* rights for all" ' (CW 7).

From a psychological standpoint, as Nietzsche interprets, anarchists, anti-Semites and socialists, that '*declining* strata of society', exhibit the symptoms of *ressentiment* inasmuch as they require and seek someone to blame for their discontent, society, the Jew or the ruling classes.[11] Nietzsche caricatures the *ressentiment* of this '*declining* strata of society', referring to the levelling effects he believes it propagates, saying, 'if I am *canaille* [one of the mob], you must be *canaille* also'. It is this psychology of *ressentiment* which is the catalyst of revolution (TI Expeditions 34), a psychology also explored in *The Origins of Contemporary France* by Nietzsche's correspondent and reader Hippolyte Taine.

Nietzsche sees a 'secret tyranny' in the doctrine of equality. It is *ressentiment* 'against all who are not as we are' (Z Tarantulas). The doctrine constructs a single identity. Anarchists, socialists and democrats are 'at one . . . in their . . . instinctive hostility to every other form of society' (BGE 202). Nietzsche criticizes these 'slave strata' because, among other things, they give themselves 'the appearance of being the only permissible kind of man' (BGE 199), and criticizes their political morality because it reactively resists the possibility that other types of morality or moral activity are possible – 'ought to be possible'. The doctrine of equality of rights, according to Nietzsche, represents a repression of and a 'war on all that is rare, strange, privileged' (BGE 212). It is 'the principle of the decline of the entire social order' (A 62), a proposition which is not intelligible unless the 'social order' to which Nietzsche refers is connected to an actually existing or historical political arrangement, at least in some of its features.

Enlightenment about *ressentiment*, then, also means enlightenment about those 'moral terms expanded into political theory', means enlightenment about 'the fatality that has crept out of Christianity . . . into politics' (A 43), means consciousness of the fact that, ultimately, *ressentiment* has its most 'visible expression' in modern political and social institutions which are, by extension, reactive, imperialistic and repressive. In respect of this visibility, among the symptoms of declining life, Nietzsche will cite 'the advent of democracy, international courts in place of war, equal rights for women, the religion of pity' (GM III 25).

According to Nietzsche's account, two opposing modes of valuation (or *wills* to power), through the atavism of types, have been engaged in an effectively still undecided, merely adjourned, struggle on earth for millennia. 'The symbol of this struggle, inscribed in letters legible across all human history, is 'Rome against Judea, Judea against Rome': – there has hitherto been no greater event than *this* struggle, *this* question, *this* deadly contradiction.' Fundamentally, this symbol stands for the enduring and recurring struggle between natural or aristocratic values – the classical ideal, the noble mode of evaluating things – and antinatural or Christian values. Nietzsche sees the reawakening of aristocratic values, alternately, in the Renaissance, and in 'the last political noblesse in Europe, that of the *French* seventeenth and eighteenth century', and in the person of Napoleon Bonaparte (1769–1821) and the autocratic Bonapartist regime; while he sees the Lutheran Reformation and the French Revolution as *ressentiment* movements. This panhistorical struggle between antinatural and natural values – and this is crucial to note because it reveals the political dimension of this critical dichotomy – is transposed by Nietzsche to the political struggle between the principle of the 'supreme rights of the majority', what Nietzsche calls the 'mendacious slogan of *ressentiment*', and the principle of the 'supreme rights of the few' (GM I 16) – antinatural and natural values respectively, politically determined.

The Christian, Nietzsche writes, 'always lives and struggles for *"equal rights"* ' (A 46). It is through the doctrine of equal rights that Christianity has 'persuaded over to its side everything ill-constituted, rebellious-minded, under-privileged, all the dross and refuse of mankind' (A 41). Thus is the Christian intrinsically encoded by Nietzsche in a social category or class, associated across time, from the *Imperium Romanum* to modern Europe, with 'a collective movement of outcast and refuse elements of every kind' (A 51); 'the lowest classes', the 'disinherited', the 'subjugated' and the 'oppressed' (A 21). Strictly speaking, Nietzsche does not associate slave morality with a particular socioeconomic class (though he connects his typology of master and slave to particular types of political doctrine or ideology), his cultivated person or exemplary human being may be located in all classes, at various levels of education, but it tends to devolve there in his criticism of modern ideologies and in his analysis of the psychology of revolution or in his rejection of the Paris Commune. It is only necessary to follow the migration of the word 'slave' in the Nietzschean corpus. It is a description which Nietzsche applies to the French Revolution, the 'last great slave rebellion' (BGE 46), and to those 'rebellious slave strata' (BGE 225) who espouse democracy, socialism or anarchism. Nietzsche refers to the lower and middle classes as 'the lower kind of spirit and body' (WP 60 Nachlaß 1885 KSA 11 34[43]) and to the doctrine of universal suffrage as the doctrine 'through which the lowest natures prescribe themselves as laws for the higher' (WP 862 Nachlaß 1884 KSA 11 25[211]). And it is the 'lowest classes' who seek their salvation in Christianity (A 21), which is nothing more than *typical socialist doctrine* which teaches that in order to attain happiness it is only necessary to emancipate 'oneself from the institutions . . . of the upper classes' (WP 209 Nachlaß 1887–88 13 11[379]). Christianity 'has forged out of the *ressentiment* of the masses its *chief weapon* against *us*, against everything noble. . . . The aristocratic outlook has been undermined most deeply by the lie of equality of souls . . . the belief in the "prerogative of the majority" ' (A 43). Such are the chains of equivalences Nietzsche constructs between Christianity and political doctrine, between typological and sociological classes, between those who want equality and those who do not.

Nietzsche's principal target is Christian morality and its heritage in political theory (it was Jesuits and Calvinists, for example, who first formulated the right to resist and depose a tyrant), the doctrine of human rights, equality and freedom, and sovereignty of the people which is developed in democratic theory, and the symptomatic atomization and weakness of will which emerge, as Nietzsche interprets it, following Burckhardt and de Tocqueville, in democratic culture. What Nietzsche wishes to reestablish beyond this moral-political structure of *ressentiment*, a concept which, in fact, has a complete political determination for Nietzsche, is a natural order of rank, an elitist or aristocratic system of command and obedience, and finally, an autocratic regime (or will) in the guise of popular rule, which rules through *simulacra libertatis*.

2. Command and obedience

For Nietzsche, an aristocratic social structure, which is built on the relationship of command and obedience, is an essential condition for the enhancement, and 'continual self-overcoming', of the human type. As Nietzsche writes in *Beyond Good and Evil*, every 'enhancement of the type 'man' has so far been the work of an aristocratic society' (*aristokratischen Gesellschaft*) with its 'ingrained difference between strata – when the ruling caste ... looks down upon subjects and instruments and just as constantly practices obedience and command' (BGE 257).

In a general sense, however, Nietzsche, like Aristotle,[12] sees the relationship of command and obedience as essential to the formation of society, as fundamental to social life; he contemplates the original tribal community, which he elucidates in terms of the civil law or contractual relationship between creditor and debtor, and through this analogy, between ancestors and the present generation, the obedience of the latter to the statutes and commands of the former. 'What is essential and inestimable in every morality,' Nietzsche records, 'is that it constitutes a long compulsion ... that there should be *obedience* over a long period of time' (BGE 188). This basic relationship of supremacy, of command (law or compulsion) and obedience, as was indicated above, defines morality itself and makes morality, by definition, political. It is generally descriptive, but Nietzsche clearly prefers a particular structure of command and obedience, clearly expresses his own normative and prescriptive prejudices which may be characterized as radically aristocratic.

All political constitutions imply relations of command and obedience, ruler and ruled. The point is where the power is vested. Of course, and in accordance with Plato's definition, democratic theory postulates the identity of ruler and ruled, or 'no-rule', and Nietzsche, by association, recognizes this when he refers to the formula 'neither master nor servant' as a 'socialist formula' (BGE 202). But Nietzsche sees only relations of domination; there is always a ruling class. A situation of 'no-rule' can never obtain, following the socialist, democratic or anarchistic formula.

Introducing his own political conception, at the basis of his politics, Nietzsche divides 'all living creatures' into either 'obeying creatures' or 'commanding creatures', but his political position is elitist or aristocratic in so far as he assigns the attribute of command to the few or a minority. The relationship of command and obedience he endorses is that appropriate to an aristocratic social structure which implies the indispensability of class differences or, in his terms, of a *pathos of distance*. In this sense, Nietzsche's politics are premodern, looking back to Plato and Aristotle. But they are also modern in so far as he locates sovereign power in the will. All values, Nietzsche says, betray an 'ancient will to power. . . . It was you, wisest men, who put such passengers in this boat and gave them . . . proud names – you and your ruling will' (Z Self-Overcoming). The will, as Nietzsche writes in *The Gay Science*, as the 'affect of command, is the decisive sign of sovereignty and strength' (GS 347). A sovereign and strong will must command, should command because it can. Strength must express itself as strength (GM I 13). As with Thomas Hobbes, Nietzsche conceives of sovereignty as decision and law as command.

Nietzsche also views the act of willing itself in terms of the relationship between command and obedience, on the basis, as it were, of the body defined as 'a social structure composed of many souls' (BGE 19). In this respect, Nietzsche effectively adheres to the classical political conception, following Plato in *The Republic*, that the body resembles a polity or 'commonwealth'. And similarly, Nietzsche redefines the body in terms of an aristocratic political structure and its division of labour.[13] In every act of will or volition, Nietzsche explains, the body contains a ruling thought which is 'essentially the affect of superiority in relation to him who must obey'. This affect of superiority, or command, constitutes the sensation of freedom or strength of will – the sensation of resistances overcome, obedience rendered; for Nietzsche articulates the relationship between command and obedience as generally one of struggle, for growth, supremacy and expansion, and fluctuating power-relations both in the *inner* and *outer* polity. Even in obedience there is a power of resistance, and all commanding must recognize this.

However, what is imperative for Nietzsche, ethico-politically, is 'to test oneself to see that one is destined for independence and command' (BGE 41). Thus Nietzsche is critical of those who need 'to develop unconditional self-confidence on the basis of some ultimate and indisputable commandment', who want to be 'accepted as its servants and instruments (GS 5), who covet 'someone who commands, who commands severely – a god, prince, class, physician, father confessor, dogma, or party conscience'. Yet, at the same time, Nietzsche considers the need for command to be symptomatic, some desire their own repression. The 'instinct of weakness' and 'lack of will' which conserves metaphysical and religious convictions, and which needs Christianity, faith and belief, is the pervasive condition 'in old Europe even today'. Under such conditions, and these conditions are also democratic ones, the instinct of weakness has reached 'the fundamental conviction that [it] *must* be commanded' (GS 347).

This statement translates into an incisive political evaluation, critique and imperative, as can be read in *Beyond Good and Evil*, which demonstrates well the preconceptions and basic terms operating in Nietzsche's political analysis. They concern those in whom the need for obedience is 'innate', and the 'moral hypocrisy of those commanding in Europe today', and the general, further symptomatic condition of the disappearance or replacement of 'independent' or 'sovereign' commanders, of the 'one who commands unconditionally', such as, according to Nietzsche, Napoleon Bonaparte was, his exemplary political master.

Nietzsche's first proposition, basic to elite theory, is that 'as long as there have been human beings' there have been 'a great many people who obeyed compared with the small number of those commanding' ('history is a graveyard of aristocracies', as Pareto says in a well-known phrase), such that nothing has been better cultivated among human beings than obedience, so much so that 'the need for it is now innate in the average man'. Nietzsche's second, critical proposition is that the 'moral hypocrisy of those commanding' is constituted by the fact that they 'pose as the executors of more ancient or higher commands . . . of ancestors, the constitution, of right, the laws . . . of God . . . their people or . . . the commonweal'. Furthermore, the origin of the replacement of 'independent' and 'sovereign' commanders lies in the establishment of representational or 'parliamentary constitutions' (BGE 199). Thus, with these propositions, Nietzsche prepares the ground for a struggle against the governing elites, who have made too many concessions to the people, with the preconception that there will always be those who desire repression. Even 'future Europeans' will be 'poor in will', as Nietzsche anticipates, and still 'in need of a master and commander' (BGE 242). But the force of Nietzsche's struggle is directed primarily against parliamentary and constitutional regimes, since his own philosopher-legislators retain the 'hypocrisy' of 'old Europe' in their Machiavellian tactics as I shall discuss throughout this study.

Nietzschean ideology, rooted in psychological identifications, claims the necessary nonidentity of ruler and ruled, the necessity of command and obedience; anticipates a war with the European ruling classes who are to be replaced with a radical aristocracy, *free spirits* who articulate an authoritarian nomadology and a doctrine of esoteric control in their other war with militant labour and justice movements.

3. Aristocracy, the masses and the European worker

Nietzsche is inspired by certain past, aristocratic social orders, for example, 'of the pattern of Rome or Venice' (TI Expeditions 43) or of the '*French* seventeenth and eighteenth century' (GM I 16); and though his determination of 'aristocratic' or 'noble' values is not, in principle, separate from his reflection upon such social orders, for example, his conception of freedom, his 'new nobility' (a Napoleonic term) is conceived as something 'the like of which no age has yet seen' (GS 377). Nietzsche, of course, enthusiastically embraced the term, 'aristocratic radicalism', which was applied to his philosophy by Brandes.[14]

In keeping with this term, the Nietzschean aristocracy or nobility does not strictly conform to any particular hereditary or existing ruling class or elite, no European royal family. Yet the content of Nietzsche's aristocratic radicalism is derived from historical models which he cites in *The Case of Wagner* as, broadly, Roman, pagan, classical or Renaissance. It is on the basis of these models that the critical opposition or contrast, or the contrary type, is initially conceived and sought by Nietzsche through a genealogy and a typology of morals, with an antimodern moral and political trajectory. These models are representative of a master or noble morality which expresses an antiidealist, anti-Christian, naturalist and realist affirmation of life encapsulated in the term *Dionysian*. Such a morality, in its contemporary incarnation, is actively destructive, it acts to 'excise the degenerating part', but also to prepare the ground, in the activity of the free spirits, for the philosopher-legislators, for the legislation of new values. This implies a strategic rejection of, and resistance to, the despotic and ochlocratic egalitarian ideology which has undermined the aristocratic outlook. As Nietzsche writes in *Thus Spoke Zarathustra*, 'a *new nobility* [is] needed: to oppose all mob-rule and all despotism' (Z Law-Tables 11). This remark should be recognized as a fundamental Nietzschean political imperative central to his political conception.

The philosophical and political objectives of the Nietzschean new nobility are relatively transparent. But Nietzsche does not rest with the statement of the mere philosophical and political profile of this contrary type, which is to say in terms of doctrine; but complements this profile with a character or virtue ethics more Roman or Renaissance-inspired than Greek because of their emphasis on strength and virility, will and passion, rather than on reason or an Aristotelian mean.[15] It should be observed that, for Nietzsche, while morality is in decline, individual virtues are not; and that the 'highest degree of freedom' is compatible with individual virtues (WS 212). In other words, this virtue ethics, which does not entirely do away with rules of conduct, remains a function of his politics, concomitant to a discourse on the organization of resistance and the art of governance. As one commentator aptly remarks, 'Nietzsche's social preferences only subsequently produce an ethical doctrine to suit the foundational bias.'[16] This is because Nietzsche's question, in essence a question of all virtue ethics, 'What is noble? What does the word 'noble' still mean to us today?', is ultimately asked in the interests of the organization of radical aristocratic opposition to 'the beginning rule of the plebs (*Pöbelherrschaft*)' (BGE 287) – a beginning Nietzsche sees in the Paris Commune of 1871, which constituted an attempt to establish a government of the working class – and all that particular, *decadent*, emerging constituent power implies for social and political organization.

The semiotics of the character or virtue ethics Nietzsche develops describes, with certain political resonance, and reminiscent of Machiavelli's discourse on the qualities a prince must possess, a noble type of human agency who, for example, never thinks of degrading its duties into duties for everybody (BGE 272), who is resolute and faithful (BGE 293), who has reverence for itself (BGE 287), who requires enemies, whose actions are not prompted by pity, but by 'excess of power', who 'experiences *itself* as determining values', as '*value-creating*' (BGE 260). Whether the type is dead, contemporary or ulterior, or moreover, one of the phantasms of a multiple subjectivity, it is, none the less, virtually conceived by Nietzsche as a prescription, as something to uncover, as normative.

That Nietzsche's character or virtue ethics is a function of his politics, or secondary to them, can be further adduced in another example of his evolving answer to the question, 'What is noble?' In *Beyond Good and Evil* Nietzsche writes,

> egoism belongs to the nature of a noble soul – I mean that unshakeable faith that to a being such as 'we are' other beings must be subordinate by nature and have to sacrifice themselves. The noble soul accepts this fact of its egoism without any question mark . . . as something that may be founded in the primordial law of things.
>
> (BGE 265)

Such a description serves to motivate and provide agency for Nietzsche's task of the revaluation of all values; or in so far as Christianity, according to Nietzsche, has lowered the value of the individual, has made it 'self-less', already begins to perform such a task. For noble morality stands in an essentially adverse relation to the Christian value of self-lessness or self-abnegation which, in *Ecce Homo*, Nietzsche defines as 'resistance to the natural instincts', namely, the fundamental feature of 'what was hitherto called morality' (EH D 2). But the egoism or indi-vidualism of the noble type can be disconnected neither from a politics ('we are'), nor from a regime (wherein 'other beings must be subordi-nate by nature'). Rather, the traits of nobility must necessarily converse and resonate with the traits of the projected aristocratic regime, which is to say, more concretely, between the figures of the free spirits and the future philosopher-legislators, not only because the type is ideal or atavistic but, more immediately, because Nietzsche's character or virtue ethics amount to testing oneself for independence and command, and not merely for self-command. As with all virtue ethics, the noble type can achieve its most complete expression only in the political or public realm in the form of rule. But in order to accomplish this status, the Nietzschean noble type must abandon, in a Machiavellian register, reliance simply on 'good' character traits. The Nietzschean noble type must also rely on natural instincts, proficiency and even vices, a prin-ciple foreign to virtue theory. Thus Nietzsche's virtue ethics is not a virtue ethics at all, but a *virtù* ethics. His ethics is personified in the figure of the philosopher-legislator, the philosophical lawgiver.

'This present, however, belongs to the mob (*des Pöbels*)' (Z Higher Man 19); and it is 'the kingdom of the mob' (Z Sorcerer), with its guiding utilitarian and democratic principle of the 'happiness of the greatest number', formulated by Jeremy Bentham as the only justifiable goal of legitimate government, which represents the 'greatest danger' to the noble type, and to the advent of the *Übermensch* (Z Higher Man 3); that is Nietzsche's diagnosis and his conviction, and it is often overlooked. Conforming to the absolutist tradition of political philosophy, Niet-zsche objectifies the multitude, makes of them, to borrow a phrase from Negri, the 'object of anguished interrogations',[17] calling them *Pöbel* or *canaille*, or referring to *Pöbelherrschaft*.

The anarchist Peter Kropotkin, for one, in a letter to Max Nettlau, claims that Nietzsche 'did not understand anything about the economic workers' revolt', and that the '*individualismus Nietzscheanum*' can only exist with the condition of the oppression of the masses which, as I just pointed out, is a condition for the advent of the *Übermensch*. Horkheimer notes that Nietzsche, 'this philosopher of the ruling class' (which is not exactly the case), despised the masses.[18] Peter Bergmann comments on Nietzsche's fear of the masses in the wake of the Paris

Commune (1871): the 'Commune was, moreover, a profound shock that seemingly confirmed all his fears of the cultural barbarism of the lower classes'.[19] It is a fear which is present in virtually all of Nietzsche's work, a fear which is transformed into a 'declaration of war'.[20] In *The Case of Wagner*, for example, Nietzsche tendentiously writes that a culture is in decline 'wherever the decision comes to rest with the masses' (CW 11). It is a consequence of such a perspective that Nietzsche opposes the emancipation of women and higher education and voting rights for the European worker. 'Decision' must be ensigned elsewhere.

Nietzsche enacts his declaration of war on the masses, on the egalitarian and majoritarian principle, in his earliest writings. In *The Birth of Tragedy*, Nietzsche designates the 'optimistic spirit', which he interprets as the legacy of Socratic or Alexandrian culture, as 'the germ of destruction in our society'. A typical expression of this 'optimistic spirit' is Bentham's utilitarian formula, 'the belief in the earthly happiness of all' or the 'greatest number'. Nietzsche's concern, only briefly and sententiously expressed here, and thinking, no doubt, of the Paris Commune, is that this belief may change into the demand for its realization, adding that nothing is more 'terrible than a class of barbaric slaves (*barischen Sclavenstand*) who have learned to regard their existence as an injustice, and now prepare to avenge, not only themselves, but all generations' (BT 18). It is this class, the proletariat, who represent the principal danger to the advent of the *Übermensch*. Their desire for 'commune' is a desire for 'the most primitive form of society' (GM I 5).

Nietzsche's own *higher* cultural imperative is crystallized, in opposition to the democratic masses, in his inaugural public lectures, delivered at the University of Basel in 1872, *On the Future of Our Educational Institutions* and in the *Untimely Meditations*.

In *On the Future of Our Educational Institutions*, Nietzsche envisages and anticipates 'serious men, working together in the service of a completely rejuvenated and purified culture' (4); a 'true, aristocratic culture, founded upon a few carefully chosen minds' (92). This rejuvenation, according to Nietzsche, must start with the system of instruction and education in the public schools and universities, and must oppose those deleterious forces of the Bismarckian 'Culture-State' (*Kultur-Staat*) which, in the interests of the universalization of culture, 'would . . . spread learning among the greatest possible number of people', the universal right to higher education which 'would compel education to renounce its highest and most independent claims in order to subordinate itself to the service of the State', to utility and monetary gain. Nietzsche views this development as 'opposed to the eternal purpose of nature as the concentration of education for the few is in harmony with it' (12–13). Only a small number, in principle, can attain 'culture'. Therefore, Nietzsche concludes, the 'education of the masses cannot . . . be our aim' (75), for it would contravene 'the natural hierarchy in the realm of the intellect' (76). Thus, at this early stage, in what constitutes a struggle between 'philosophy' and the 'state', Nietzsche announces his antiegalitarian advocacy of a cultural aristocracy, or cultured minority, with his characteristic appeal to *nature* or the *natural order* (here in terms of *natural* intellectual endowment) and a partial elaboration of the conditions for this minority's existence which becomes a basic theme of his political philosophy; namely, opposition to universal human rights.

In the *Untimely Meditations*, continuing the basic theme of the Basel lectures, sharing the cultural ideals of Ernest Renan, the 'supreme goal of culture' is determined by Nietzsche to be the 'production of the genius' (UM III 6), but moreover, of the 'philosophical genius' (UM III 8), which effectively means, the production of the 'lawgiver' or legislator (UM II 3). 'Humanity,' Nietzsche says, 'must work continually at the production of individual great men'; that should be its primary task (UM III 6); but 'it has been the proper task of all great thinkers to be lawgivers as to the measure, stamp and weight of things' (UM III 3).

Nietzsche says that 'mankind ought to seek out and create the favourable conditions under which . . . great redemptive men can come into existence'. But it is precisely the utilitarian principle of 'the happiness of all or the greatest number' which impedes this noble project. For Nietzsche it is simply a choice between sacrificing your life to 'the rarest and most valuable exemplars', or sacrificing it, wrongly, to the democratic state and to 'the good of the majority' (UM III 6).

In the process of criticizing, in the *Untimely Meditations*, the type of history which is written from 'the standpoint of the *masses*' (say, of the type Michelet wrote), Nietzsche writes that the masses 'deserve notice in three respects only'; namely, 'as faded copies of great men', or 'as a force of resistance to great men', or 'as instruments in the hands of great men' (UM II 9). Nietzsche's political philosophy is fundamentally organized in terms of these 'opposite viewpoints of value' – the 'well-being of the majority and the well-being of the few' (GM II 17), the masses and those he calls the aristocracy or nobility, the supreme rights or prerogatives which belong to each. That is where its problem and its primary tension lie. But its solution is preconceived, so much so that the writing constitutes a form of counteragitation, a rearguard action. For when Nietzsche addresses such issues as the '*impossible class* – factory slaves' (D 206) or the *'labour question'* (TI Expeditions 40), it merely serves as a pretext for an indictment of socialism and of the democratic demand for equality of rights and universal suffrage. Such an indictment is contained in his work from the very beginning and coherently pervades it throughout. It is another seed in the ground of his political philosophy.

Nietzsche, somewhat broadly and only provisionally, rejects industrial culture and capitalism, and their mutual 'glorification of work' (D 173). He criticizes commerce and consumerism where it becomes 'the character of an entire culture, thought through in the minutest . . . detail and imprinted in every will and every faculty' (D 175), and the stock exchange (speculation) and the 'love of accumulated money' (D 204). At times he appears sympathetic towards the working class. In *Human, All Too Human*, he views the condition of the modern European worker as 'worse than slavery' (H 457), and in *The Wanderer and His Shadow* criticizes the exploitation of the worker (WS 286). Sometimes the case is made that Nietzsche is prodemocratic during this, his so-called positivistic, period (1878–82), which has the effect of introducing an *aporia* into his political thinking, an issue I shall address below.[21]

In the 'glorification of work' Nietzsche sees the 'fear of everything individual'. As he writes in *Daybreak*, again appearing sympathetic towards the worker, 'hard industriousness . . . is the best policeman . . . it keeps everyone in bounds and can . . . hinder the development of reason' and the 'desire for independence' (D 173). But Nietzsche concludes, he does not say they should work less or become less industrious and hence more independent, that it is foolish to believe that improvement in working conditions or higher wages could release the 'factory slaves' from their 'impersonal enslavement' – as 'accomplices in the current folly of the nations . . . the folly of wanting above all to produce as much as possible and to become as rich as possible' – could restore their *'inner value'*, for it would not give them any more power over themselves (D 206). Here Nietzsche is rehearsing the old theme of denaturalization through the pursuit of wealth.

Thomas Brobjer writes that Nietzsche was neither ignorant about nor disinterested in political economy, but that his 'relative silence' regarding questions of political economy was a result of his opposition to it, which saw Nietzsche, more precisely, opposing *money* to *spirituality*.[22] This claim is not completely false, but it is misleading and even inaccurate. For the opposition Nietzsche deploys is that between *spirituality* and *wages* to be exact, the demand for higher wages or improvement in working conditions, everything the worker depends upon. Nietzsche does not, ultimately, object to capitalism (if this relation were further explored it would likely be shown that Nietzsche is a supporter of *laissez-faire* capitalism) or to the worker as machine-like or militarized (soldier-worker) but, rather, to worker militancy and socialist agitation.

It is instructive and sobering to compare Nietzsche's discourse on the worker, which does not ultimately assail capitalist production or relations of production, but, rather, worker demands and the Marxist concept of alienation, with that of Friedrich Engels in his book, *The Condition of the Working Class in England*, an empirical study which attempts to faithfully describe the conditions and sufferings of the workers employed in the English factory system, from the poverty of their dwellings to their poor nourishment and physical deformities. It is instructive because, in Nietzsche's account, the *body*, otherwise so prominent in his philosophy (diet, climate, place, etc.), disappears and is replaced by the spirit, by discussion of 'inner value' and worker's 'instincts'.[23] What he does retain of the body in his analysis are those instincts that are ordained by nature, a position which approximates the biologist standpoints of Social Darwinism or fascism, which were inclined to mythicize class conditions and histories.

In *Daybreak*, Nietzsche sees the European worker as having only two alternatives, both of which will keep him in servitude. He can become 'either the slave of the state or the slave of a party of disruption'; the latter alternative meaning, a slave of socialist ideology 'whose design is to enflame . . . with wild hopes' and make 'malicious and conspiratorial'. In the face of these constrictive alternatives, Nietzsche recommends, ostensibly in the interests of the 'individual' and 'self-mastery' and spiritual '*inner value*', that the workers of Europe 'inaugurate . . . an age . . . of free emigration . . . to protest against the machine, against capital' and take their place as colonists 'in new and savage regions of the world'. In their place could be brought in 'numerous *Chinese*' who would bring with them 'Asiatic calm' and 'Asiatic *perseverance*'. This latter thought should leave no doubt as to Nietzsche's actual position regarding the policing 'machine' of 'capital', given that his preeminent desire, in this context, is not for its destabilization *per se*, but rather for 'cleaner air' or the departure (and in favour of a colonization without conviction) of 'that which was at home beginning to degenerate into . . . inclination for crime' (D 206); ostensibly under 'criminal' socialist agitation, the 'party of disruption' and 'conspiracy'.[24] Nietzsche's vocabulary here is complicit with the antisocialist laws introduced in Germany in 1878 and still in effect when Nietzsche wrote these lines.

In *The Gay Science*, Nietzsche blames the 'manufacturers and entre-preneurs of business' for the development of socialism because they have been deficient in exhibiting 'noble manners'. As Nietzsche explains it, such a deficiency communicates the idea 'that it is only accident and luck that have elevated one person above another'. Subsequently, Nietzsche states an idea which, in my estimate, is central to his politi-cal philosophy and which connects Nietzsche to the neo-Machiavellian elite theorists and founders of mass psychology; namely, that 'at bottom the masses are willing to submit to slavery of any kind, if only the higher-ups constantly legitimize themselves as higher, as *born* to command' (GS 40). In other words, the idea of a natural order of rank (*Rangordnung*) should be constantly reinforced because of the psycho-logical nature of the masses, their innate or instinctive need for obedi-ence. For Nietzsche, it is not a question of distributive justice, not a problem of poverty or unsafe workplaces but, rather, of communication, legitimation and control.

In Nietzsche's opinion, the European worker, that avatar of Christian 'anarchist agitation in the Empire' (A 58), will continue to make demands for more, especially now that he has the majority on his side. By the time Nietzsche writes his 'most subversive book', *Twilight of the Idols*, in Turin, all apparent concern for, or interest in, the worker's 'reason', 'independence' or 'self-mastery', which is to say in relation to the 'machine' and 'capital' has completely disappeared. By that time, Nietzsche's concern is for the 'destroyed instincts' of a worker who 'has been made liable for military service . . . [who] has been allowed to form unions and to vote', who has, through disruptive social processes, come to feel his existence, or his class, as 'a state of distress' or '*injustice*'. It is a state of affairs which realizes the worst fears of *The Birth of Tragedy*, of that 'class of barbaric slaves' who are seeking *justice* and *commune*. It is not that Nietzsche opposes military service, unions or voting as such, it is just that 'if one wants slaves, one is a fool if one educates them to be masters' (TI Expeditions 40).

In *The Anti-Christ(ian)*, Nietzsche summarizes, in a formula which may evoke Plato's theory of justice (the idea that each must accommo-date himself to the role that befalls him in the division of labour), his accusation against socialism and his position regarding the European worker: 'To be a public utility, a cog, a function, is a natural vocation'. It is the Socialists who have undermined or perverted 'the worker's instinct . . . his feeling of contentment with his little state of being' (A 57).

One of the tasks of the Nietzschean new nobility is to correct this per-version of the European working class. Nietzsche proposes that the working classes 'learn to feel like soldiers' (soldier-workers), that they receive only an 'honorarium' and not wages. For in his opinion there should be no 'relation between payment and achievement' (WP 763 Nachlaß 1887 KSA 12 9[34]), a remark which reveals that he is no opponent of alienated labour in the Marxian sense. It is clear from Nietzsche's discussion of the European worker what the delimitations and coordinations will be in the command and obedience structure he envisages. His concept of political economy mainly opposes spirituality to wages and the demand for better working conditions; it does not repudiate property rights, exploitation, competition, production, expenditure, surplus value or waste, which are all essential to his 'general economy'.

4. The social contract

Nietzsche subscribes to the Hobbesian notion of the *bellum omnium contra omnes* (UM I 7), that the state of nature is a state of war.[25] But for Nietzsche, as with Baruch Spinoza, the state never really emerges from the state of nature. It attains only a provisional equilibrium since con-flict is at the basis of the social structure.[26] Nietzsche also accepts, with certain modification, the Hobbesian view that society originates out of fear of violent death and insecurity in the interest of self-preservation, although he does not see self-preservation but rather will to power as the primary drive in human beings.

Emerging from Nietzsche's discussion of the social contract are, in fact, two accounts of the origin of society or the state and which con-forms to the Hobbesian delineation of 'commonwealth by institution' and 'commonwealth by acquisition' in *Leviathan*.

As Nietzsche theorizes, a 'community is originally the organization of the weak for the production of an *equilibrium* with powers that threaten it with danger' (WS 22). This equilibrium, as such, is the basis of justice (*Gerechtigkeit*), which Nietzsche defines as 'requital and exchange under the presupposition of an approximately equal power position' (H 92). This presupposition of *approximate* equality is also the basis of civil law and the social contract which constitutes civil society. Of course, Nietzsche conceives of the civil law relationship in the economic terms of the creditor and debtor (contractual) relationship. The 'community', Nietzsche says, 'stands to its members in that same vital basic relation [as] that of the creditor to his debtors'. It provides to its members a sense of fearlessness, peace and security, and protects them from a 'savage and outlaw state' as long as they do not break the contract which has allowed them a share in 'all the benefits and comforts of communal life' (GM II 9).

But the 'outlaw state' always threatens and occasionally breaks through. Thus Nietzsche views the 'rule of law' as an arbitrary and 'temporary means advised by prudence' which only 'continues to exist for so long as the power of those who have concluded [the contract] remains equal'. If one party becomes 'decisively *weaker* than the other then subjection enters in and law *ceases*' (WS 26). It means that any social contract is precarious and cannot be guaranteed, or that power gives the right to break contracts.

The community ('by institution') has been founded, in the interest of security and self-preservation, on the presupposition or postulate of equality. The principle of equality, according to Nietzsche, and contrary to Rousseau, contradicts 'the nature of the individual' and constitutes a form of repression. The nature of the individual is will to power and, accordingly, the more 'the general security is guaranteed, the more do new shoots of the ancient drive to domination assert themselves'. Because Nietzsche views the 'state of nature' as constituted by 'ruthless inequality', as a state of war in which everyone has a right to all things as in Hobbes, the self-assertion of the individual, his will to power, will manifest itself in the 'claim to special dignities and privileges'. Thus does Nietzsche conceive and naturalize the 'division of classes' (WS 31) and praise, *contra* Rousseau and the sovereignty of the general will, the imposition of private will or strong will.

Nietzsche would agree with Aristotle that it 'is always the weaker who go in search of justice and equality',[27] but he would also agree with the Sophist, Thrasymachus, for whom political power is exploitation of one class by another, who says in *The Republic* that right (or justice) is in the interest of the stronger (ruling class) and is grounded in the drive for domination. Nietzsche's conception of natural right most closely approximates Spinoza's, his acknowledged precursor in many other respects.[28] In *Human, All Too Human*, Nietzsche states that '*Rights* originally extend *just as far* as one *appears* valuable, essential . . . unconquerable . . . to the other. In this respect the weaker too possess rights, but more limited ones.' In support of this, Nietzsche quotes Spinoza from the *Tractatus Politicus*: '*each man has as much right as he has power*' (H 93);[29] his natural right is coextensive with his power. Spinoza equates right (*jus*) with power (*potentia*) and supports a might makes right theory of political authority (which includes physical force). Nietzsche considers rights to be 'recognised and guaranteed degrees of power', to be totally dependent on 'momentary' power-relationships. There are no innate, inalienable or indefeasible rights, no fundamental rights of man. In this respect, Nietzsche is opposed to the school of classical Natural Law and Natural Right as it addresses the 'dignity of man', rules of equity and universal principles of moral obligation.[30] In *Daybreak* he writes, 'If power-relationships undergo any material alteration, rights disappear and new ones are created. . . . If our power appears . . . broken, our rights cease to exist . . . if we have grown very much more powerful, the rights of others, as we have previously conceded them, cease to exist for us' (D 112).

That Nietzsche associates power or might with right – and this does not imply that Nietzsche advocates submission to every power, as is clear from his commentary on Hegel in the *Untimely Meditations* (UM II 8) – is further evident in the observation he makes, in *Human, All Too Human*, on the right of the original founder of states (*Staatengründer*) to subjugate the weaker. As Nietzsche concludes, the right of the *Staatengründer* 'is the same as the state now relegates to itself; or rather, there exists no right that can prevent this from happening' (H 99), no law of nature (following Spinoza) which can forbid this power. In *The Greek State*, Nietzsche expresses the idea somewhat more elegantly: 'Power gives the first *right*, and there is no right which at bottom is not presumption, usurpation, violence' (10). While Nietzsche tends to deprecate the use of the 'cruder instruments of force' (GS 358), he, none the less, associates all rights with conquests and necessarily supported by the power of enforcement, a position 'more natural in *politicis*' (WP 120 Nachlaß 1887 KSA 12 10[53]).

In Hobbes (theorist of the absolutist state) and Spinoza (theorist of democracy) there are limitations, the limitations – of natural law, of moral precepts, of civil order and of the dictates of reason. It is Nietzsche who seems to teach the 'natural right of all passions', who affirms the 'highest and strongest drives, when they break out passionately and drive the individual far above . . . the herd' (BGE 201). Because of the will to power, such drives threaten to break out constantly, to discharge themselves. Given this, society is conceived by Nietzsche, as it was by the nineteenth-century conflict theorist Ludwig Gumplowicz (1838–1909), to be an 'unstable equilibrium of forces'.[31]

Like Gumplowicz and other conflict theorists (and like Hegel and Burckhardt), Nietzsche ultimately rejects the idea that the state originated with a social contract (which is not to say that social contracts do not form). The state founds a contract, it is not founded on one. Rather, at the origin of the state was a 'master race . . . organized for war and with the ability to organize' who subjugated a weaker population 'still formless and nomad'. Thus power is the basis of all rights, not a social contract as Rousseau says. Nietzsche provides this account in *On the Genealogy of Morals* in a passage which, in fact, constitutes an encomium for the commander, recalling Machiavelli's prince and his immoralistic egoism. He writes,

> He who can command, he who is by nature 'master', he who is violent in act and bearing – what has he to do with contracts! . . . such natures . . . come like fate . . . their work is an instinctive creation and imposition of forms; they are the most involuntary, unconscious artists there are – wherever they appear something new soon arises, a ruling structure that *lives*, in which parts and functions are delimited and coordinated. . . . They do not know what guilt, responsibility, or consideration are these born organizers; they exemplify that terrible artist's egoism that has the look of bronze and knows itself justified to all eternity. (GM II 17)

In rejecting the social contract, which he finally dismisses as mere 'sentimentalism' (GM II 17), Nietzsche is rejecting abstract or ideal conceptions of freedom, justice and equality; the abstract conception of the person. 'To speak of just or unjust *in itself* is quite senseless.' These exist, Nietzsche says, 'only after the institution of the law'. But the rule of law is unstable and arbitrary, subject to the flux of power-relationships. Thus legal conditions are always merely '*exceptional conditions*'. From the standpoint of life, the standpoint from which Nietzsche claims to speak, legal conditions 'constitute a partial restriction' of its will, 'which is bent upon power, and are subordinate to its total goal . . . as a means of creating *greater* units of power'. The will to power, unlike Spinoza's *conatus*, does not seek self-preservation. Nietzsche's central idea that 'life operates . . . in its basic functions, through injury, assault, exploitation [and] destruction' provides legitimation for the antiegalitarian agonism he espouses. As Rousseau's state of nature is a regulative idea or legal fiction, so Nietzsche's state of nature and doctrine of 'commonwealth by acquisition' are regulative ideas with implications for a conception of law. Its acute opposite, namely, a legal order which would aim to prevent all struggle between power-complexes – as Nietzsche says, 'perhaps after the communistic cliché of Dühring, that every will must consider every other will its equal – would be a principle *hostile to life* . . . an attempt to assassinate the future of man' (GM II 11).

Nietzsche reverses Hobbes and Spinoza and affirms the rule of persons over the law. For Nietzsche, sovereign power is a person. His conception of right as exceptional and self-designated, and which may be constituted through 'arms, trade, commerce or colonization' (WP 728 Nachlaß 1888 KSA 13 14[192]), and of the precarious status of any social contract, provides an incentive for his new nobility, who, like their prototypical free spirits, shall not be bound by any existing laws.

5. Freedom and the free spirits

On the jacket of the 1882 edition of *The Gay Science*, it reads: 'This book marks the conclusion of a series of writings by Friedrich Nietzsche whose common goal it is to erect *a new image and ideal of the free spirit*' (GS p. 30). In *Ecce Homo*, Nietzsche says that by the term 'free spirit' *(freier Geist)*, he 'means a spirit that has become free, that has again taken possession of itself' (EH H 1). Thus the free spirit is an expression of individualism and sovereignty. The figure of the free spirit is important to discuss because it has a more prominent place in the corpus of Nietzsche than does the phantasmal *Übermensch*. The free spirit is the *agent provocateur* of the 'present' who, in the *interregnum*, prepares the ground for a reversal of values and the arrival of a new, radical aristocratic regime. Moreover, Nietzsche identifies himself as a free spirit.

As defined by Nietzsche, the free spirit possesses a number of character traits, virtues and vices, such as self-sufficiency and self-reverence, and the need for masks and cunning. But first and foremost, the free spirit is a sceptic who casts suspicion on all habitual evaluations and perspectives. Such scepticism (antidogmatism) or suspicion is required, as Nietzsche says in *Human, All Too Human*, to weaken the faith and 'belief in ultimate definitive truths' (H 244). Nietzsche continues to connect scepticism to freedom and strength well into *The Anti-Christ(ian)*. There he writes, 'Convictions are prisons. . . . A spirit which wants to do great things, which also wills the means for it, is necessarily a sceptic. Freedom from convictions of any kind, the *capacity* for an unconstrained view, *pertains* to strength' (A 54).

In *Human, All Too Human*, Nietzsche contrasts the free spirit with the 'fettered spirit'. The free spirit is characterized by his liberation from tradition and 'the dominant views of the age', as well as from the expectations of his 'class and profession' (H 225), from all 'states and orderings in society' (H 227). 'As a rule, though, he will none the less have truth on his side, or at least the spirit of inquiry after truth'. Here, in the spirit of the Enlightenment or, perhaps more precisely, in the spirit of Voltairian anticlericalism, Nietzsche says that the free spirit 'demands reasons' while the fettered spirit 'demands faith' (H 225).

For Nietzsche, belief and faith, or the 'need for external regulation' (A 54), command and unconditional truth, is a symptomatic expression of 'selflessness' or weakness, 'a sign of *décadence* [and] of a broken will to live' (A 50). None the less, it cannot be abolished. It is innate in most human beings.

The free spirit is marked by his capacity for continual change and self-overcoming, and his anarchic aversion to dependence on any rule and its prejudice. Nietzsche calls the free spirits 'wanderers' without a final destination (H 638), whose ideal lies in a 'spiritual nomadism' (AOM 211), and 'noble *traitors* to all things that can in any way be betrayed' (H 637). In *The Gay Science*, the free spirit is characterized in terms of a 'power of self-determination' and '*freedom* of the will' (GS 347), what, in *Daybreak*, Nietzsche had favourably conceived as traits of immoralism (D 9). In the 1886 Preface to *Human, All Too Human*, the free spirit is associated with experiment, perspectivism and the reversal of values (H P 3), with self-mastery and discipline (H P 4). Here self-mastery means mastery 'over your virtues' and 'control over your For and Against' (H P 6), while experiment and perspectivism imply, respectively and relatedly, 'access to many and contradictory modes of thought' (H P 4) and the antiteleological 'displacement of horizons', the 'sense of perspective in every value judgment'. The free spirit also incorporates the political idea that 'injustice [is] inseparable from life' (H P 6). Thus the free spirit is both character and doctrine. The free spirit is anti-Christian, a countermovement to the 'un-selfing' effected by Christian morality, as well as a proponent of perspectivist epistemology and ontology, and of antidemocratic politics.

Quoting Ovid's *Amores*, Nietzsche says that the free spirits 'strive for the forbidden' ('*nitimur in vetitum*') (BGE 227). Moreover, the free spirits 'have . . . to *be* something new, to *signify* something new, to *represent* new values' (BGE 253). In *The Anti-Christ(ian)*, Nietzsche writes, 'we free spirits, are already a "revaluation of all values", an *incarnate* declaration of war and victory over all ancient conceptions of "true" and "untrue" ' (A 13). As such, and more specifically, the free spirits make 'war on the "holy lie" even more than on any other lie'. Their decisive first step in this war is the establishment of what, according to Nietzsche, is the 'greatest of all value-antitheses': '*Christian* values – *noble* values'

(A 36–7). Thus the free spirit does not disengage himself from *all* tradition in so far as he situates himself, in allegiance, on one side of this value-antithesis: the pagan.

Nietzsche considers the Holy Roman Emperor Frederick II, probably because of his episodes of defiance against Papal authority,[32] Napoleon and Goethe as free spirits. For Nietzsche, Napoleon and Goethe represent 'a going-*up* to the naturalness of the Renaissance'. This implies the realism, aspiration to totality, freedom and tolerance 'out of strength' that Nietzsche calls *noble* and *Dionysian* (TI Expeditions 49). Nietzsche also refers to the order of Assassins (the eleventh-century Ismaili sect founded by Hasan-ibn-Sabbah, affiliated with Shi'ite Islam, who fought against the Christian crusaders) as 'that order of free spirits *par excellence*'. Their 'watchword' was 'Nothing is true, everything is permitted'. Through this 'watchword', as Nietzsche says approvingly, they abrogated the faith in unconditional and absolute truth (GM III 24).

Nietzsche, furthermore, connects the task and the goal of the free spirits with those he calls the *'good* Europeans' (BGE P). The good Europeans belong to the lineage of scientific atheism, but are primarily representative of Nietzsche's antinationalism and anti-anti-Semitism, and of his Napoleonic ideal of a European political and economic union.

Nietzsche constitutes the individualism and sovereignty of the free spirits in opposition to the Kantian project to derive moral principles from pure reason, against the idea that there is a moral law valid for all. Kant would consider Nietzschean ethics, concerned as it is with contingencies, and the pursuit of happiness and perfection, to be heteronomous in character. Just how heteronomous and contingent it is is evident in *The Gay Science* where Nietzsche writes, 'the determination of what is healthy for your *body* depends on your goal, your horizon, your energies, your impulses, your errors, and above all on the ideals and phantasms of your soul'. Thus 'there are innumerable healths of the body' and each (this would include peoples as well as individuals) must find or devise, according to 'inner necessity' and 'personal choice', his own 'peculiar virtue' and singular value standard. It is antinatural to do otherwise (GS 120, A 11).

In accordance with this, the free spirits reject the idea of universal law, the 'non-arbitrary character of judgments', the idea of a 'universal binding force' (GS 76) and impersonal duty, as expressed in the Kantian categorical imperative and, in general, in the Christian moral domain, in classical natural law. Rather, they stand for experiment and a *'plurality of norms'* and prescriptions against the 'good man', against 'the doctrine of one normal human type', transmitted through liberal democratic universalism, which Nietzsche considers to be 'the greatest danger that has yet confronted humanity' (GS 143). In *Daybreak*, the book which commences his *'campaign against morality'*, Nietzsche writes, 'there is no such thing as a morality with an exclusive monopoly of the moral . . . numerous novel experiments shall be made in ways of life and modes of society'(D 164). This is what Nietzsche, with a motto taken from the Greek poet Pindar, underwrites *'beyond* the old morality' BGE 262); namely, the need or desire *'to become those we are* – human beings who are new, unique, incomparable, who give themselves laws, and create themselves' (GS 335).

But in order *'to become those we are'*, according to Nietzsche, in order for 'the rights . . . the egoism and sovereignty of the individual' (GS 143) to be fully realized, the political doctrine of the equality of all human beings, as well as the doctrine of pity (and of altruism), must be repudiated (GS 120). In this vein, Nietzsche dissociates his conception or *'image'* of the free spirits from the *so-called* free spirits or *'levellers'* who are 'slaves of the democratic taste' and situates them 'at the *other* end from all modern ideology and herd desiderata', inasmuch as they think that suffering and 'everything evil, terrible, tyrannical in man' serves to enhance the human species (BGE 44).

Nietzsche calls the free spirits the 'heralds and precursors' of the 'philosophers of the future'. The philosophers of the future will be free spirits, Nietzsche says, but they will also be 'something more' (BGE 44). They will be *commanders* and *legislators* (BGE 211). In so far as the free spirits are precursors of the philosophers of the future, or the philosopher-legislators, who represent, as in Plato, the coincidence of philosophy and political power, the activity, or resistance, of the free spirits can be said to have political ends. They are necessarily concerned with the fate of the entire social order and favour the establishment of an aristocratic social structure. Such a social structure provides the most favourable conditions for the continual enhancement of the human type. In the sense that the free spirits have to '*signify* something new, to *represent* new values', the philosophers of the future are a projection of what the free spirits must become. Yet the free spirits, these 'firstlings and premature births of the coming century' (GS 342), are still noble, because the 'noble man wants to create new things and a new virtue' (Z Tree on the Mountainside).

Nietzsche writes, 'we feel the tug towards freedom as the strongest drive of our spirit . . . in antithesis to the fettered' (AOM 211). But what is freedom for Nietzsche?

The free spirits are said, paradoxically, to possess an 'excess of "free will" ' (BGE 44), yet, like Spinoza, Nietzsche denies the doctrine of free will, criticizing both its epistemological basis and, in Nietzsche's estimate, its alleged theological purpose. On the one hand, the doctrine of free will is 'incompatible . . . with the idea of a continuous . . . indivisible flowing: it presupposes that *every individual action is isolate and divisible*; it is an atomism in the domain of willing and knowing' (WS 14). It 'amounts to a misuse of cause and effect' and interpreting the subject as *'causa sui'*, for 'ancestors, chance, and society' have a definite impact on our actions and our choices (BGE 21). On the other hand, it is 'the most infamous of all the arts of the theologian for making mankind "accountable" . . . for *making mankind dependent on him'*. The doctrine of free will was invented for the purpose of punishment (TI Errors 7)

In spite of the paradox, it can be said that for Nietzsche, when all is said and done, there is neither free will nor unfree will in itself. They are 'an experience in the social-political domain', where 'the strong man is also the free man'. Thus Nietzsche can say that the doctrine of free will 'is an invention of the *ruling* classes' (WS 9), and that 'in real life it is only a matter of *strong* and *weak* wills' (BGE 21). Furthermore, there is no choice in the matter, the strong are not free to be weak, and vice versa. That the free spirits possess an excess of free will means that they experience the affect of command, the 'decisive sign of sovereignty and strength' (GS 347). In context, Nietzsche is saying that a strong free will does not have the Christian conscience of a weak free will, is not impeded by the feelings of guilt and responsibility Christian culture has introduced. It possesses a higher responsibility, namely, the revaluation of all values, which, in accordance with its nature, it must instinctively enact as an imposition of the will.

In the *Untimely Meditations*, Nietzsche says that 'freedom is . . . a heavy debt which can be discharged only by means of great deeds' or actions (UM III 8). This sense of freedom is preserved and elaborated in *Twilight of the Idols*, as 'the will to self-responsibility', in a passage Nietzsche entitles '*My conception of freedom*'; a conception of freedom he opposes to the liberal democratic conception – because freedom should not simply be given but earned – and connects to the 'aristocratic communities . . . of Rome and Venice'. In the Nietzschean sense, as with Machiavelli, freedom, in respect to both the individual and the nation, may flourish only under agonistic conditions 'where the greatest resistance is constantly being overcome', and is measured 'by the effort it costs to stay *aloft*'. This is why Nietzsche says the free individual is a '*warrior*' (TI Expeditions 38). His freedom is positive freedom. Against the Hobbesian conception, freedom requires external impediments. But freedom, or independence, 'is for the very few' and 'is a privilege of the strong' (BGE 29). Given the value Nietzsche places on freedom and the definition he provides of it, he tends to admire autocratic human beings, both lawgivers and lawbreakers, creators and destroyers.

Nietzsche conceives of the free spirit, as indicated above, in terms not only of the 'untimely' or solitary individual in opposition to the community, but also in terms of an individual who is connected to a community of 'natural allies' (UM IV 4) past, present and future. It is clear, as is evident in many passages throughout his corpus, that he is inspired by the culture of the Renaissance which 'was raised on the shoulders of . . . a hundred men' (UM II 2), and the conceptions of *virtù* and immoralism which emerge from its landscape. Nietzsche extols the noble and 'independent spirituality' which wrecks 'the self-confidence of the community' (BGE 201), and praises the individual who is not afraid to enter into an adverse relationship with the existing social order, but he also speaks of 'we free spirits', which is to say, of a 'community of resistance'.[33] It may be true that Nietzsche has a 'tendency to identify only with imaginary communities', but it is too extreme to state that 'he regularly identifies himself as party to a . . . fictitious collective'.[34] As for the 'imaginary communities', they are futural – 'You solitaries of today, you who have seceded from society, you shall one day be a people' (Z Bestowing Virtue 2) – or he is hopefully seeking them – 'The creator seeks fellow-creators, those who inscribe new values on new tables' (Z Prologue 10), for 'the possibility cannot be excluded that somewhere in Europe there are still *remnants* of stronger generations, of typically untimely human beings' (CW PS). As for the second point, the anti-Christians, antidemocrats, antisocialists and antinationalists of the Europe of Nietzsche's period obviously did not constitute a 'fictitious collective', but rather a political force with various tentacles; and Nietzsche does connect himself, as a 'radical nihilist', to the social critique of Burckhardt and Taine, a connection I shall explore in Chapter 3 on Nietzsche's relation to aristocratic liberalism.[35]

The mission of the free spirits is to prepare a reversal of values. Nietzsche describes them as transgressive and expedient, but they do have political ideals. They represent both resistance and recodification in terms of laws, contracts and institutions, a revaluation which intends to constitute the power of order of rank, and not mere aristocratic democracy or meritocracy in opposition to levelling mediocrity.

6. Order of rank

Nietzsche says that the problem of the free spirits is the problem of order of rank (H P 6) or hierarchy. In one sense of the term, order of rank simply refers to an anthropological or ethnographic observation of the fact of differences and ranking of differences in standards, in values, in moralities, in human types (states of the soul, impulses and actions) between cultures, peoples and individuals. As Nietzsche writes, the 'difference among men becomes manifest . . . in their difference between their tablets of good – in . . . that they consider different goods worth striving for' (BGE 194). Values and orders of rank among values are defined by Nietzsche as the 'expressions of the needs of a community', relative to whatever benefits it, the conditions for its preservation (GS 16). This discourse on the differences between moralities or value systems may operate in support of a philosophy of general decolonization against the hegemony of Christian democratic humanization, the ascetic ideal's rejection and suppression of other practices and perspectives, as was commented upon in the above section on *Ressentiment*.

In the more pervasive sense of the term, however, order of rank is a reflection of Nietzsche's own stronger ideological priorities. In this sense, the problem of order of rank, which is also 'the future task of the philosophers', is precisely the determination of the *order of rank among our values* (GM I 17). Such a determination judges whether our values are signs of 'degeneration' or signs of 'plenitude, force, and will of life' (GM P 3). Given that Nietzsche considers our highest values to be decadent and nihilistic values, his determination of the order of rank among values constitutes an ideological recoding and revaluation, or inversion, which places noble values and the power and right of *high spirituality* on top. *High spirituality* is the 'right to philosophy' itself, 'the readiness for great responsibilities', the 'art of command' for which one is born or predestined (BGE 213) or, at least, for which one claims one is born. It is indifferent to those who say, 'what is fair for one is fair for the other', a proposition Nietzsche associates with John Stuart Mill (WP 926 Nachlaß 1887–88 KSA 13 11[127]). It considers 'detrimental' the 'demand of one morality for all' (BGE 228). Its glances are 'glances that dominate and look down, feeling separated from the crowd and its duties and virtues' (BGE 213).

But Nietzsche goes somewhat beyond this task of the determination of an order of rank among values and turns the idea of order of rank itself into antisocialist and antidemocratic ideology, wherein it becomes the 'mission' of 'high spirituality . . . to maintain the *order of rank* in the world', according to the Nietzschean codes of strength and health, in opposition to those who fight for equality and equal rights or for the 'general welfare' (BGE 228). In this sense, order of rank refers to a politics of caste and class division. It comes to mean 'ingrained difference between strata', a mythicizing of class structure, and *pathos of distance*, a necessary feature of the esoteric, radical aristocratic regime. Its political intonation is evident where Nietzsche equates the socialist conception of society with the 'lowest in the order of rank' (WP 51 Nachlaß 1888 KSA 13 14[6]).

For Nietzsche, the order of rank serves the 'will of life' or, more exactly, as Nietzsche writes in *The Anti-Christ(ian)*, 'formulates the supreme law of life itself'. In other words, the '*order of castes*, the supreme, the dominating law, is only the sanctioning of a *natural order* . . . over which . . . no "modern idea" has any power' (A 57). Thus Nietzsche naturalizes order of rank, aristocracy and his preferred structure of command and obedience in a way that complements his description of the egoism, or self-affirmation, of the noble type – its 'faith that . . . other beings must be subordinate by nature' – which finds itself reflected in the 'primordial law of things' (BGE 265). These passages point clearly to Nietzsche's appeal to *nature* or *life* as a normative standard, or noble lie, wherein the binary opposition is nature–modernity or natural–antinatural. It is a reversal of classical natural law theory where democracy is situated closer to the state of nature, as in Rousseau, and a position similar to those expressed by the conservative political forces of his generation, for example, Henrich von Treitschke.[36]

7. The reverence for institutions[37]

As was stated above, Nietzsche admires and affirms certain kinds of institutions and political regimes, such as the aristocratic commonwealth of the ancient Greek *polis* and the *Imperium Romanum*. How 'wretched', Nietzsche writes, 'we modern men appear when compared with the Greeks and Romans' (UM III 1). Greek and Roman societies were societies that respected the 'law of life', and for Nietzsche, are models for emulation to 'help create the future' (AOM 99).

Nietzsche, writing in *The Greek State*, considers the Greeks as the 'political men in themselves'. He defines their 'political passion', in opposition to the liberal optimistic view rooted in 'the doctrines of French Rationalism and the French Revolution', in terms of the unconditional subjection of all interests to the natural 'State-instinct', by which he means, the artistic and passionate maintenance of a state of war, the 'bloody jealousy of city against city, of party against party . . . the incessant renewal of . . . Trojan scenes of struggle'. Thus Nietzsche affirms here, without utilizing the term, the Greek *agon*, or the agonistic situation of competition and perpetual conflict between individuals and power-complexes (also articulated by the conservative political forces of his generation).[38]

Nietzsche writes this essay, in fact, as a *'Paean* on war' against the 'dissemination of liberal optimism' and the ascendency of the 'money-tendency'. Liberalism's rational use of the state, according to Nietzsche, aims essentially to obstruct political separatisms and factionalism, or 'through the establishment of large *equipoised* State-bodies [aims] to make . . . war itself the greatest improbability'. In this early essay, for this reason, Nietzsche discerns 'dangerous atrophies of the political sphere'; which is to say, atrophies caused by the *'fear of war'*, which he sees embodied in the pervasive doctrines of equal rights, universal suffrage and the fundamental rights of man.

Nietzsche continues his affirmation of the *agon* in *Homer's Contest*. In this essay, which discusses the Greek ethical concept of *Eris* (strife), the destructive 'action of war to the knife' and the 'war of extermination' is represented, reading Hesiod, as the incitement of an 'evil *Eris*', while the 'action of contest' (*agon*) is represented as the incitement of a 'good *Eris*' (55).

Here the 'peculiar institution' of the Greek *polis*, the *agon*, the 'Hellenic contest-conception', is elucidated through the concept of 'ostracism'. In order to maintain the perpetual 'contest of forces' the best, or 'all-excelling individual', had to be ostracized so as not to subvert the agonistic 'eternal life-basis of the Hellenic State'. This was true in the *gymnasium* or the *palaestra*, as well as in the city. Thus ostracism was also applied to 'contesting politicians and party-leaders' where they threatened to subvert the *agon* between cities and political parties. The institutions of the *agon* and ostracism structured Greek political life. As Nietzsche writes, 'the aim of the agonistic education was the welfare . . . of the civic society. Every Athenian . . . was to cultivate his Ego in contest'. But the nature of the *agon* is such that 'it abominates autocracy, and fears its dangers; it desires as a *preventive* against the genius – a second genius . . . *several* geniuses which incite one another to action' (58).

The agonistic conception, as 'good *Eris*', does not exclude war but 'wars of extermination'. The 'noblest Greek states' degenerated and perished, according to Nietzsche's assessment, through acts of *hubris*; when they had 'destroyed the independence of [their] allies and avenged with severity the rebellions of [their] subjected foes'; when they had relinquished 'the noblest Hellenic fundamental thought, the contest'. Then the world conqueror Alexander ('the Great') appeared and invented, as Nietzsche says critically, 'the cosmopolitan Hellene' (61–2). It is likely that Nietzsche is thinking here of Alexander's ideal of *homonoia*, which is a predecessor of the Stoic *cosmopolis*.

In Nietzsche's posthumously published *Philosophy in the Tragic Age of the Greeks*, he connects the idea of the *agon* to the philosophy of Heraclitus and the Dionysian principle. Nietzsche affirms the Heraclitean notion that 'strife embodies the everlasting sovereignty of strict justice'. Accordingly, as Nietzsche writes in *The Birth of Tragedy*, Heraclitus compares 'the world-building force to a playing child that . . . builds sand hills only to overthrow them again'. This eternal contest and strife of opposites, and the finitude of all regimes, constitutes 'the Dionysian basic ground of the world' (BT 24–5). Heraclitus, Nietzsche says, converts Hesiod's 'good *Eris*' into a 'cosmic principle'. His principle of strife is, in effect, 'the contest-idea of the Greek individual and the Greek state, taken from the gymnasium . . . from the contest between political parties and . . . cities . . . transformed into universal application so that now the wheels of the cosmos turn on it' (PTG 5 55).

Thus it can be said that in Nietzsche's text the political sense of the Dionysian is agonism, and agonism is an ideal in Nietzsche's own conception of sociopolitical organization, and combined with anti-egalitarianism, the proper meaning of Nietzschean *justice*. As is clear in *The Greek State*, and the idea is maintained throughout the Nietzschean corpus, agonism implies inequality, class struggle and class war, the 'spiritualization of enmity' or the value of having enemies both in the individual and geopolitical sense. The idea of the *agon* informs Nietzsche's own conception of freedom as its condition, and his positive evaluation of it makes more comprehensible his praise of the aristocratic morality which seeks its opposite so as to affirm itself more gratefully. But Nietzsche ultimately desires a regulated factionalism, a controlled conflict, the maintenance of enemies and enemy states, but with mastery over them.

It may be the case that Nietzsche, as Chytry says, 'shifted his loyalties from *polis* to *imperium*'.[39] Whatever the case may be, Nietzsche embraces the *Imperium Romanum*, principally between *Beyond Good and Evil* and *The Anti-Christ(ian)*, for reasons essentially opposite to those for which he embraces the Greek *polis*. It is probably more accurate to say that Nietzsche continued to embrace aspects of both societies, but that he ultimately found Roman society superior. As Nietzsche says, both regimes reflect the 'law of life' and 'nature', both are 'realistic' and 'fact-oriented', and both embody 'aristocratic' values. 'Greeks! Romans! nobility of instinct, of taste, methodical investigation, genius for organization and government, the faith in the *will* to a future for mankind, the great Yes to all things' (A 59). But 'the Romans were the strong and noble, and nobody stronger and nobler has yet existed on earth' (GM I 16).

Chytry is right, and the transition in loyalties occurs where Nietzsche affirms, as he does in a more pronounced way in his post-Zarathustran writings, the institution of agonism, but without the institution of ostracism in a way that favours autocracy. There are particular currents in Roman history and society which Nietzsche approves. He praises the Roman emperor Julius Caesar, who was hostile to republican government, for his 'bolder and private morality' (GS 23). But the tenets of his political philosophy are in contrast to the Roman natural law tradition (Cicero, Marcus Aurelius, Ulpian) and its precursor, the Stoic ideal of *cosmopolis* or the universal city.

The *Imperium Romanum* expresses, for Nietzsche, 'extreme secularization' (BT 21) and an 'education for tolerance' (BGE 46), but moreover, Nietzsche, like Machiavelli, admires the *Imperium Romanum* – 'this most admirable of all works of art in the grand style' – because its 'structure was calculated to *prove* itself by millennia', because it was constructed '*sub specie aeterni*'. The *Imperium Romanum* was 'the most grandiose form of organization . . . which has hitherto been achieved'. It possessed 'duration' and promised 'life' and 'future'. It is significant to note, in this context in *The Anti-Christ(ian)*, that Nietzsche refers to the 'purpose' to 'eternalize a grand organization of society' as the 'supreme condition for the *prosperity* of life' (A 58) and thus appears to contravene his affirmation of the Dionysian (Heraclitean) principle of radical flux. Such a reference begs the question as to what extent Nietzsche truly is the philosopher of anarchic power and unqualified antistatism, as he is frequently taken to be. I will revisit this issue in subsequent chapters.

In any case, Nietzsche is clearly not anti-institutional, even though he says, against the socialists, in the interest of a 'general economy of life', that 'vice, disease, prostitution, distress' cannot be eliminated by means of institutions (WP 40 Nachlaß 1888 KSA 13 14[75]). It would be 'condemning life' to believe that such problems can be disposed of. In fact, when Nietzsche says that '*All of us are no longer material for a society*' (GS 356), he is not criticizing all possible social institutions, rather, he is criticizing modern, 'liberal instincts' which are, in his opinion, incapable of constructing durable institutions, which are oriented towards living 'for today' and thus, 'irresponsibly', with a skewed conception of freedom which considers authority anathema. As Nietzsche writes,

> For institutions to exist there must be the kind of will . . . which is anti-liberal to the point of malice: the will to tradition, to authority, to centuries-long responsibility, to *solidarity* between succeeding generations backwards and forewards *in infinitum*.

This type of will was present, according to Nietzsche, in the *Imperium Romanum* and in nineteenth-century Russia, whose power Nietzsche viewed in contradistinction to 'European petty-state politics', and which he referred to as 'the only power today' which has 'durability' and 'promise' in it (TI Expeditions 39).[40]

That Nietzsche is not anti-institutional is also intimated when he writes in *Ecce Homo*, that 'Someday institutions will be needed in which men live and teach as I conceive of living and teaching' (EH WGB 1). This is stated because Nietzsche reads his own work as recodification in process in terms of laws, contracts and institutions. These institutions, according to the logic of Nietzschean agonism, will act contrary to the principle of equality, will maintain an order of rank and the class divisions it implies. Resistance will lie at its basis, but regulation will emanate from its apex.

8. The revaluation of all values: *Die große Politik*

Nietzsche says that the free spirits already represent a revaluation of all values, an expression he introduces in *Beyond Good and Evil* and which, in *The Anti-Christ(ian)*, he qualifies as 'an *incarnate* declaration of war and victory over all ancient conceptions of "true" and "untrue" ' (A 13). It is, however, much more specific in focus. The revaluation of all values comprises both a genealogical critique (an inquiry into the foundations of morality) and a reversal or inversion of Christian decadent and nihilistic values, which looks 'toward *healthier* concepts and values' (EH WW 1) and 'new orders of life' (BGE 248). It is conceived as a destructive and a reconstructive and revisionist task.

Regarding this 'decisive task', Nietzsche writes in a letter to Paul Deussen from 1888, 'Hereafter, much that was free will *not* be free any more; the realm of tolerance is reduced. . . . To be a Christian . . . will be hereafter *improper*.'[41] He expresses essentially the same thought in *Ecce Homo*: 'The uncovering of Christian morality breaks the history of mankind in two. One lives before him, or one lives after him' (EH WD 8).

Nietzsche describes Judeo-Christianity, which marks 'the beginning of the slave rebellion in morals' (BGE 195), as a 'revaluation of all values of antiquity' (BGE 46). Here 'revaluation' signifies the total inversion (motivated by revenge or *ressentiment*) of aristocratic or noble values, Roman or pagan values. It is a process which involves an inversion in language which oversees the fusion, for example, of 'sensual' with 'evil' or 'poor' with 'holy'. Within its culture the word 'world' is used 'as an opprobrium' (BGE 195).

> It was the Jews who... dared to invert the aristocratic value-equation ... saying 'the wretched alone are the good; the poor, impotent, lowly alone are the good; the suffering, deprived, sick, ugly alone are pious, alone are blessed by God ... and you the powerful and noble, are on the contrary the evil, the cruel ... the godless to all eternity; and you shall be in all eternity the unblessed, accursed, and damned'.
>
> (GM I 7)

Nietzsche's revaluation in turn constitutes a re-reversal or re-inversion in so far as it seeks 'out everything strange and questionable in existence, everything so far placed under a ban by morality' (EH P 3), which is to say, Christian morality. It selectively affirms and expresses confidence in 'all that has hitherto been forbidden, despised, and damned' (EH D 1), guided by Ovid's motto, the motto of the free spirits, '*nitimur in vetitum*' (EH P 3). Thus, in so far as the 'forbidden' should be known, the predominant trajectory of Nietzsche's revaluation of all values is not so much the creation or legislation of new values – though this is demanded and deemed necessary also – but the revival of devalued, '*healthier*' values. He shares the view of Machiavelli that the morality of antiquity was superior and seeks to imitate it. That this was Nietzsche's intention is given clear expression in a notebook entry from 1888 where he writes, 'I sought in history the beginning of the construction of reverse ideals (the concepts "pagan", "classical", "noble" newly discovered and expounded –)' (WP 1041 Nachlaß 1888 KSA 13 16[32]). One could add here 'Renaissance', as it was in the Epilogue to the *Case of Wagner*, for the Renaissance represents a revaluation of Christian values, the 'reawakening of the ... noble mode of evaluating all things' (GM I 16). More specifically, in terms of what these '*healthier*' values might be, Nietzsche writes in *Thus Spoke Zarathustra*, '*Sensual pleasure, lust for power, selfishness* ... these three I weigh well' (Z Three Evil Things), as opposed to the traits of the 'good man': modesty, temperance and industriousness.

Nietzsche says that the '*first* example' of his revaluation of all values is the reversal of the universal, imperative 'ought' at the basis of every religion and morality. In effect, this means that the initial gesture of Nietzsche's revaluation of all values is the affirmation of a character ethics, which claims that a well-constituted human being must perform certain actions 'instinctively' (TI Errors 2), and counsels the 'devising of one's *own* virtue', one's own 'right' and 'philosophy' (GS 289). For Nietzsche, it is 'naivety . . . to say "man *ought* to be thus and thus!" Reality shows us an enchanting wealth of types.' This wealth of types refers to those that have been suppressed or excluded by Christianity and are, in principle, recuperated by Nietzsche's immoralistic economy – which is also an economy of *virtù* – which 'needs and knows how to use all that which . . . the priest rejects' (TI Morality 6).

Nietzsche's general project of a genealogy of morals, which is preliminary to a revaluation of all values, demands that various kinds of morality be examined and compared from different ages and peoples: 'all their reason and all their evaluations and perspectives on things have to be brought into the light' (GS 7); 'a vast realm of subtle feelings of value and differences of value . . . all to prepare a *typology* of morals'. This is necessary because Christian morality has come to be accepted as given, and the 'real problems of morality . . . emerge only when we compare *many* moralities' (BGE 186). Thus the revaluation of all values is predicated on the perspectivistic recognition of the general validity of other systems of value, other practices, guided by the precept that 'there is no such thing as a morality with an exclusive monopoly of the moral'(D 164); that there are different goods worth striving for. This is one sense of the meaning of Nietzschean *justice*, which, as was said above, may support general decolonization against the hegemony of Christian democratic humanization. As Nietzsche writes in *The Gay Science*, 'what is needful is a new *justice*. . . . The moral earth, too, has its antipodes. The antipodes, too, have the right to exist' (GS 289).

However, even though Nietzsche's immoralism may celebrate a wealth of types, the typology he ultimately produces is not pluralistic but dualistic: there is master (or noble) morality and slave morality. Genealogical critique discloses the master morality which has been suppressed or devalued by slave morality in spite of various atavistic recurrences in history, various returns of the repressed. Master morality is a naturalistic character, or *virtù* ethics, which places emphasis on the whole human being, is free from *ressentiment* and conveys an aristocratic political dispensation, while slave morality has its foundation in an antinatural or transcendental lie and despises the body, and conveys a democratic or egalitarian political dispensation. These are, essentially, the only clearly defined perspectives Nietzsche presents, and they are reversed and recoded according to a new order of rank. 'Now I . . . have the know-how to reverse perspectives: the first reason why a "revaluation of all values" is perhaps also possible for me alone' (EH WW 1). This statement regarding possession of the 'know-how' (or technique) to reverse perspectives implies that the *virtù* (or capacity) at the basis of the Nietzschean reversal is armed with political technology (*immoralism*).

Nietzsche says that the revaluation of all values is his 'formula for an act of supreme self-examination on the part of humanity' (EH WD 1) and that it is a 'world-historical' task. As executor of this task, Nietzsche defines himself as a 'destiny' and a '*world-governing* spirit', which means 'one who first *creates* truth' (EH Z 6), who legislates and prescribes for culture and humanity in general and globally (EH TI 2). It is a system of global surveillance. Yet Nietzsche does not conceive of this task as a work of solitude, for he anticipates that 'great noon' during which the 'most elect consecrate themselves for the greatest of all tasks' (EH BT 4), just as he identifies historical agents and agents of the present who shall directly or indirectly assist him.

The revaluation of all values presupposes that humanity is not 'governed divinely' and that its highest and 'holiest value concepts' are decadent (EH D 2). The construction of reverse ideals begins with newly expounding classical and pagan ideals. Such a hermeneutic process involves recovery and emulation of these ideals and not their mere restoration, as there can be no turning back, as Nietzsche says against the conservatives (TI Expeditions 43).[42] But why does Nietzsche complement his concept of the revaluation of all values with the concept of 'great' or 'grand politics' (*die große Politik*)?[43] Whatever the precise answer, it indicates that Nietzsche conceives of the project of the revaluation of all values in terms of total, global revolution – which concerns 'all power structures of the old society' – and that the revaluation of all values possesses a definite political dimension, but which presupposes a changed concept of politics, wherein the 'concept of politics will have merged with a war of spirits (*Geisterkrieg*)' (EH WD 1). A concept of politics is crucial to the revaluation of all values, which is why Nietzsche's philosopher-legislators represent the coincidence of philosophy and political power, the incarnate desire to be lawgivers, as in Plato.

It should be said that although Nietzsche embraces the term *die große Politik*, he opposes Bismarck's *große Politik*, in the sense of the imperialist and 'blood and iron' (*Machtpolitik*) policies of the Bismarckian *Reich*, that 'monster of empire and power, they call "great" ' (BGE 241). However, in *Twilight of the Idols*, Nietzsche affirms another sense of *die große Politik*, which he associates with the *Reich* and with '*grand* life' – and which he could have associated with Machiavelli – which 'consists in . . . grasping the value of having enemies', of preserving opposition, war and contradiction (TI Morality 3); in other words, in terms of his agonistic ideal.[44] Peter Bergmann writes that Nietzsche 'embraced the concept of *große Politik* precisely at the moment when Germany was suddenly creating her colonial empire' (1884–85).[45] In fact, during roughly the same period, in *Beyond Good and Evil* (1886), Nietzsche observes that the 'time for petty politics is over: the very next century will bring the fight for the dominion of the earth (*die Erd-Herrschaft*) – the *compulsion* to large-scale (*großen*) politics' (BGE 208). But even as early as *Human, All Too Human*, Nietzsche speaks of the 'good Europeans' whose 'great task' will be, imperially, 'the direction and supervision of the total culture of the earth' (WS 87).

Whatever we may conclude from this, *die große Politik* is a term that supplements the revaluation of all values as a '*declaration of war*' and indicates that the revaluation of all values is also a politics. In other words, the revaluation of all decadent values must also revalue all decadent political values. But it is also antipolitics, because it does not foresee the end of violence. To assert that humanity is not 'governed divinely' has self-evident consequences for what Nietzsche calls political 'idealism' – for the classical ideas of natural right and natural law. Furthermore, for Nietzsche, real human flourishing requires a fundamental and total transformation in the social structure, an alternative form of political organization, which is why Nietzsche so extensively criticizes democracy and socialism, and all other modern ideologies which, according to his reading, have their origin in Christianity. Although the general tenor of his thinking is that social transformation should be gradual and not necessarily destroy all existing social and political institutions (rather, infiltrate them) contrary to the anarchist doctrine of Bakunin, as Nietzsche reads this doctrine in, what he considered to be, the catastrophic event of the Paris Commune.

Die große Politik is conceived as a war of spirits and a war of cunning, an 'ideological warfare',[46] which allies itself with a 'truth' opposed to the 'lies of millennia' and which envisages the repercussions of this war in terms of major sociopolitical convulsions. That is how it is conceived in *Ecce Homo* where Nietzsche writes, 'It is only beginning with me that the earth knows great politics' (EH WD 1).

9. Political organization and resistance:
The 'new party of life'

In the Nietzschean corpus the primary tension is between Christian morality and the *noble* mode of evaluation, between *ressentiment* morality and the opposing ideals generated by the revaluation of all values; the opposite doctrine and valuation which claims to speak from the standpoint of life and for the 'most fundamental presuppositions of life' (GM III 28). Christian morality, as stated above, encompasses in this corpus all modern ideologies including anarchism, liberalism, democracy and socialism. Thus Nietzsche's critique of morality is also necessarily a critique of politics. These are all decadent descendants of the Christian movement whose political theory is broadly summarized by Nietzsche as 'anarchy of atoms', 'disgregation of the will', 'freedom of the individual' and 'equal rights for all' (CW 7). The principle of equality, which is singled out more than the others, has undermined the noble or aristocratic outlook and represents 'the decline of the entire social order' (A 62).

As was pointed out, Nietzsche clearly favours governmental regimes or institutions aristocratic or oligarchic in nature which reinforce class distinctions, order of rank, hierarchy or a *pathos of distance*. An aristocratic social structure (or culture) is more natural and is an essential condition for the enhancement of the human type and for the production and conscious breeding (*Züchtung*) of the *Übermensch*, Nietzsche's principal goal.[47] Keith Ansell-Pearson writes that Nietzsche is 'seeking to retrieve an ancient understanding of the political'.[48] This may encompass the Greek *agon*, as Ansell-Pearson recognizes, but it also encompasses the idea of the indispensability of class differences and of slavery and noncitizenry. What Nietzsche makes clear about his understanding with respect to ancient constitutions is that they 'knew of no constitutional representation of the people in *praxi*' (BT 7). In the *Gay Science*, Nietzsche writes, 'we think about the necessity for new orders, also for a new slavery – for every strengthening and enhancement of the human type also involves a new kind of enslavement' (GS 377). Slavery is 'a condition of every higher culture, every enhancement of culture' (BGE 239). It is a position basically maintained since the writing of *The Greek State*, where it is proposed that the 'proper aim of the State' is the 'Olympian existence and . . . procreation . . . of the genius – compared with which all other things are only tools, expedients and factors towards realisation' (17).

With the death of God, the free spirits are exhilarated (GS 342), not least because now 'mankind can do with itself whatever it wishes' (AOM 179), because the future is now 'dependent on a human will' (BGE 203). Society is thus viewed as an experiment, but an experiment in command and obedience, which seeks the 'commander' and not a social contract. A *'new nobility'* is required 'to oppose all mob-rule' (Z Law-Tables 25, 11). In *Daybreak*, Nietzsche had already anticipated an experimental 'counter-force' to the Christian moral monopoly. There he writes,

> At the present time . . . those who do not regard themselves as being bound by existing laws and customs are making the first attempts to organize themselves and therewith to create for themselves a *right*. . . . One ought to find this on the whole *fair and right*, even though it may make the coming century a dangerous one and put everybody under the necessity of carrying a gun: by this fact alone it constitutes a counter-force which is a constant reminder that there is no such thing as a morality with an exclusive monopoly of the moral . . . numerous novel experiments shall be made in ways of life and modes of society. (D 164)

What Nietzsche wishes to see is the organization of a new aristocracy, or nobility, by which he means 'an elite humanity and higher caste' (WP 752 Nachlaß 1884 KSA 11 26[282]). A new caste that will rule Europe (*regierenden Kaste*), that will participate in the transition or *'compulsion* to large-scale politics' which ultimately brings 'the fight for the dominion of the earth' (BGE 208). 'Herd-animal ideals', Nietzsche notes, '[a]gainst them I defend aristocracy' (WP 936 Nachlaß 1887–88 KSA 13 11[140]) – 'For, my brothers: the best shall rule, the best *wants* to rule' (Z Law-Tables 21).

Nietzsche believes that every enhancement and self-overcoming (*Selbstüberwindung*) of the human type has been, and will continue to be, accomplished by an aristocratic society. Nietzsche describes the features of such a society in terms of order of rank, differences in value between man and man, ingrained difference between strata, *pathos of distance* and the need for slavery. Furthermore, every 'healthy aristocracy' views itself as the '*meaning* and highest justification' of the state and not as its function. Consequently, it 'accepts with a good conscience the sacrifice of untold human beings who, *for its sake*, must be reduced and lowered to incomplete human beings, to slaves, to instruments' (BGE 258).

Like Plato, and in contrast to Hegel, Nietzsche conceives of his philosopher-legislators as ruling above the state, treating it and its rulers as their instrument. The state should not be an end but the foundation for a noble type of culture and humanity. Society 'must *not* exist for society's sake but only as the foundation . . . on which a choice type of being is able to raise itself . . . to a higher state of *being*' (BGE 258). The expression 'for society's sake' means 'for the general welfare', and the general welfare can be no ideal. This means that the masses, or the 'people', should not be negotiated with for power, which is what contemporary elites and rulers do, and why Nietzsche repudiates them.

Nietzsche's aristocratic or noble type, for their complete realization, presupposes that other beings must be subordinate by nature. The noble type is anti-Christian and antimodern, characterized by strength of will and high spirituality, who experience themselves as creating values, or more precisely, as possessing the right to do so, since 'it is the characteristic *right of masters* to create values' (BGE 261). In the present, in the guise of the noble free spirits, they are engaged in an ideological war and a war of cunning, and support a reversal of values in which, generally, premodern, classical values take precedence. Their ultimate objective is to resist and subvert egalitarianism and undermine the democratic social contract, or at least control it.

It has been argued that during the period 1878–82, between *Human, All Too Human* and *Daybreak*, Nietzsche is pro-democratic because he thinks that it is 'the political form of the modern world which is able to offer the best protection of culture', and that he 'envisages social and moral change taking place through a process of liberal recommendation'.[49] Such an argument has the effect of introducing an *aporia* into Nietzsche's aristocratic political thinking. However, the preponderant evidence demonstrates that he had expedient reasons for provisionally adopting a pro-democratic stance, and reasons whose preconceptions reveal that he was neither liberal nor democrat.

Typical of Nietzsche's thought during this period is praise for the criticism of unconditional authority and for the liberation of the individual. These positive forces Nietzsche sees in modern culture (in the Enlightenment) but owe their existence to the Italian Renaissance (H 237), where they were more strongly manifested. Typical also during this period is the rejection of socialism and of the idea of the violent 'revolutionary overthrow of society' (H 454).

In the theory of revolution, Nietzsche sees operative a perilous delusion of 'political and social fantasists' who believe, following Rousseau, that there is a repressed 'goodness of human nature', who resentfully blame 'the institutions of culture in the form of society, state and education' for this repression, and who believe that with the subversion of 'all social orders' this 'goodness' will reemerge. But every revolution, Nietzsche says, releases 'savage energies' and 'excesses' (H 463), no doubt reflecting on the Jacobin Terror, and this idea of '*sudden recovery*' makes all 'political invalids' of the present '*impatient and dangerous*' (D 534). Thus what needs to be called back is '*Voltaire's* moderate nature . . . *the spirit of the Enlightenment and of progressive evolution*' (H 463), the gradual transformation of 'customs and institutions' (WS 221) which is a certain precondition for any profound transformation in the social order; new evaluations need time to install new instincts.

During this period, Nietzsche criticizes socialism for its rejection of property rights which, in Nietzsche's view, 'rests upon a defective knowledge of man' (WS 285); but moreover, because the socialist, utopian ideal of the 'perfect state', were it to be attained, would result in the dissolution of the individual (H 454) in so far as the individual would be reduced to a 'useful *organ of the community*' (H 473), to a 'useful member and instrument of the whole' (D 132). The principal danger of socialism is that it 'desires an abundance of state power', that it desires to be the inheritor of 'the Caesarian despotic state', but 'requires a more complete subservience of the citizen to the absolute state than has ever existed before' (H 473). In contrast, 'modern democracy is the historical form of the *decay of the state*' (H 472).

In *Human, All Too Human*, Nietzsche defines democratic government as 'the instrument of the popular will, not as an Above in relation to a Below but merely as a function of the sole sovereign power, the people'. Nietzsche does not say that democracy is the political form which provides the best protection of culture, rather, he says that with the rise of democracy, because previously 'the interests of tutelary government and the interests of religion' were codetermined (namely, under monarchy or the *ancien régime*), as religion declines and becomes a private concern, reverence and devotion to the state declines also; 'the state . . . loses its ancient Isis veil . . . the sovereignty of the people serves . . . to banish the last remnant of magic'. Thus a certain kind of political culture dies out and another replaces it; one that liberates not the individual, as Nietzsche stresses, but the 'private person'. This is the purpose of the democratic state. It generates, ultimately, 'distrust of all government' and produces a private person who acts only for his or her own advantage, who is prudent and self-interested; each living for the moment, reluctant to undertake projects which require 'decades or centuries' to mature; obedient 'for the moment to the force which backs up the law', then setting at once 'to work to subvert it with a new force, the creation of a new majority'.

This death or *'decay of the state'* does not imply that there will be no one to conduct the affairs of the state. In fact, Nietzsche foresees, under a democratic order, the affairs of the state gradually absorbed by 'private companies' or corporations. As opposed to it protecting culture, what Nietzsche does say is that the 'prospect presented by this certain decay is . . . not in every respect an unhappy one', but adds, in his characteristic antirevolutionary mode, that we should 'preserve the existence of the state for some time yet and . . . repulse the destructive experiments of the precipitate' (H 472). It is not an unhappy prospect because it represents, in opposition to socialism's watchword *'as much state as possible'*, a tendency towards *'as little state as possible'* and can reveal, through contrast, the dangers of extreme 'accumulations of state power' (H 473). Therefore, it is more accurate to say, as Lukács does, that during this period Nietzsche supports democracy only as a 'counterpoise' to socialism.[50]

Democracy and socialism possess different traits, for Nietzsche, but they are the same in so far as both erode tradition and destroy the individual in the Nietzschean sense, and thus neither can be seen ultimately to protect the culture Nietzsche promotes. Democracy may be preferable because it does not encourage the same degree of subservience to the state encouraged by socialism, but this does not imply that Nietzsche envisages social change taking place through a process of liberal recommendation (excluding his gradualism or his respect for property rights). For Nietzsche's idea of the individual and his idea of freedom, even at this time, is different from those ideas endorsed by liberalism, as is evident, for example, in Nietzsche's assertion that the 'nationalists' – and the national unification of Germany was, essentially, a liberal idea – disdain 'self-evolved individuals unwilling to let themselves be enlisted in the ranks for the production of a mass effect' (H 480). In other words, for Nietzsche, the liberal individual is neither self-evolved nor free. Also, Nietzsche is an enemy of the bourgeois liberal revolution of 1848, which promoted the installation of a constitutional and parliamentary regime.

Nietzsche believes that socialism – 'the doctrine that the aquisition of property ought to be abolished' (WS 292) – can hope to exist only for short periods of time, in Nietzsche's words, 'only through the exercise of extreme terrorism' (H 473), because it is a doctrine essentially alien to the human being and human desire.[51] The spread of democracy or 'the domination by the democratic principle', on the other hand,

Nietzsche believes to be inevitable, 'for *all* parties are nowadays obliged to flatter the "people" and to bestow on it . . . liberties of every kind through which it will in the end become omnipotent' (WS 292); a tendency which compels Nietzsche, as he does more aggressively in *Thus Spoke Zarathustra*, to excoriate his contemporary elites and rulers.[52]

Although Nietzsche sees the spread of democratization as inevitable, it cannot plausibly be maintained that Nietzsche is pro-democratic during the period 1878–82. It can be said that his judgments are pronounced somewhat more cautiously during this period than in subsequent works, but he is obviously antimajoritarian and antiegalitarian, viewing the demand for equality of rights not as an expression of 'justice but of greed' (H 451). Furthermore, he opposes party politics, and his conception of right, directed as it is against the fundamental rights of man, and his stance against sympathy and pity, against 'individual empathy and social feeling' (the foundation of democratic social justice), which he sees as contributing to the weakening of the individual, is developed in acute opposition to the principles of the French Revolution (D 132). No doubt during this period Nietzsche criticizes, primarily, socialist systems, but in the process he is undermining democratic principles.

In contrast to party politics and 'the now dominant belief in numbers', Nietzsche advocates the formation or election, through a highly selective process, of a 'lawgiving body' made up of 'experts and men of knowledge'; a technocracy, as existed in the Bonapartist regimes. In such a lawgiving body the vote would be left to the lawgivers themselves, 'so that in the strictest sense the law would proceed out of the understanding of those who understand best', or an *aristocracy*, as opposed to proceeding from the vote of parties who are, as Nietzsche writes, 'ill-informed and incapable of judgement' (AOM 318).

In *Human, All Too Human*, in the context of his general diatribe against the 'evil eye' of nationalism and socialism, Nietzsche encourages his ideal readers to 'Live as higher men and perform perpetually the deeds of higher culture' (H 480). Nietzsche says that in the 'spheres of higher culture there will always have to be a sovereign authority (*Herrschaft*)'. Here, anticipating his aristocratic philosopher-legislators at the summit of his ideal social order, he defines this 'sovereign authority' as a *spiritual* oligarchy, referring to its members as '*oligarchs of the spirit*'. The oligarchs of the spirit are 'spatially' and 'politically' divided; nevertheless, 'they constitute a close-knit society whose members *know* and *recognize* one another', united by their 'spiritual superiority'. They comprise an agonistic community wherein each has need of the other, but wherein each remains 'free' and in 'his *own* place' for which he has fought and conquered. Their principal struggle is against 'ochlocracy' and any attempt made 'to erect a tyranny with the aid of the masses'; they 'would rather perish than submit' (H 261).

It may also appear that Nietzsche is pro-democratic during this period since he places significant value on independence and, in *The Wanderer and His Shadow*, says that democracy 'wants to create . . . as much *independence* as possible'. But here Nietzsche is 'speaking of democracy as of something yet to come'; and this future democracy, as conceived by Nietzsche, will need 'to deprive of the right to vote both those who possess no property and the genuinely rich'; and will need to obstruct the organization of political parties. For the extreme poor (those without property) the rich and political parties are the 'three great enemies of independence' (WS 293). Nietzsche will continue to criticize these agents as his work develops, but, more forcefully and less ironically. If his is a democratic model or ideal of governance during this period, then it is clearly exclusive, a democracy for some and not for others.

Between 1883 and 1888, his final, productive year, Nietzsche, more than once, concedes victory to the democratic principle. It now poisons 'the entire body of mankind' (GM I 9) and has taken hold of its 'entire destiny' (Z Higher Man 3). The 'people (*das Volk*) have won – or "the slaves" (*die Sklaven*) or "the mob" (*der Pöbel*). . . . The "redemption" of the human race (from "the masters", that is) is going forward' (GM I 9). In this period, Nietzsche tends to conflate democracy, socialism, anarchism and liberalism, viewing them all as decadent expressions of *ressentiment*, as inherited from Christianity, Rousseau and the French Revolution. All share the same levelling ideals of equal rights and social justice, expressing 'sympathy with all that suffers'. They are at one in their repudiation of 'master' and 'servant', or order of rank, in their 'resistance to every special claim . . . right and privilege . . . in their faith in the community as the *saviour*' (BGE 202).

Nietzsche will continue to say that democracy is 'the declining form of the power to organize' and 'the *decaying form* of the state' – he counts the German *Reich* as one of its 'imperfect manifestations' (TI Expeditions 39) – but he will add, following the aristocratic liberal critique, that it is also 'a form of the decay . . . of man, making him mediocre and lowering his value'. Thus, in *Beyond Good and Evil*, Nietzsche expresses hope for the advent of new philosophers and commanders who will 'provide the stimuli for opposite valuations' and force 'the will of millennia upon *new* tracks'. These commanders will possess the discipline and responsibility to perform the task of a revaluation of all values which, as it is delineated there, will put an end to the 'gruesome dominion of nonsense and accident that has so far been called "history" – [and] the nonsense of the "greatest number" [which] is merely its ultimate form'. This passage should leave no doubt that the revaluation of all values has a political dimension, as it fully reveals that the revaluation of all values represents a counterrevolutionary counterattack against the 'animalization of man into the dwarf animal of equal rights and claims' (BGE 203).

In his notebooks from this period, Nietzsche suggests that socialism is more violent than democracy, and as such 'delays . . . the total mollification of the democratic herd animal' (WP 125 Nachlaß 1885 KSA 11 37[11]). Democracy conversely represents 'weariness' and '*weakness*' (WP 762 Nachlaß 1885 KSA 11 34[164]). If Nietzsche prefers democracy here, as he does ultimately, it can be said that it is for provisional, strategic purpose. In *Beyond Good and Evil*, Nietzsche says that the democratization of Europe involuntarily produces conditions which will lead not only to 'the levelling and mediocritization of man', but to 'extremely employable' workers, 'who will be poor in will' – 'a type that is prepared for *slavery* in the subtlest sense'. Nietzsche, somewhat vaguely, characterizes these conditions in terms of continual change and transience, whereby some new work is initiated 'with every generation, almost with every decade'. But these same conditions will also produce, because of the nature of democratic education, 'exceptional human beings of the most dangerous and attractive quality', a '*strong* human being' – who Nietzsche defines in terms of the 'democratic' features of 'absence of prejudice' and 'manifoldness of practice, art and mask' – '*tyrants*' in every sense of the word, 'including the most spiritual'. Their arrival will coincide with another feature of such general conditions, namely, the *need* of these workers, poor in will, for 'a master and commander' (BGE 242). Perhaps what Nietzsche means to crystallize here he says more bluntly in his notebooks: 'for the present we support the religions and moralities of the herd instinct: for these prepare a type of man that must one day fall into our hands, that must desire our hands. . . . We probably support the development . . . of democratic institutions: they enhance weakness of will' (WP 132 Nachlaß 1885 KSA 11 35[9]).

In retrospect, it appears that Nietzsche is quite consistent even between the longer period of 1878–88. He opportunistically supports democracy as a 'counterpoise' to socialism because socialism, in his view, readily resorts to violence and terror and delays the weakening of the will that democracy inevitably brings. Even though socialism may

force the European to retain spirit, it is the weakness of will, characteristic of democracy, that will produce the conditions for the commanders Nietzsche envisages.

Nietzsche's logic can be summarized this way: democracy, or democratic culture, produces ambiguous identities and encourages multiple
social roles. A strong will (*virtù*) can expediently utilize, or govern with,
the face of ambiguous identities (immoralism as dissimulation) even
though he really has one. He can govern through increasing deterri-
torialization of self-image, playing off one identity against another in a
controlled *agon*. An excellent historical example is Napoleon Bonaparte,
who ruled in the guise of popular will and through constant warfare.
In the above quoted passage from *Beyond Good and Evil*, Nietzsche is
identifying opportunity and recommending esotericism (*Arcana rei
publicae*).

Nietzsche does not overtly advocate the use of force, coercion or violence as an agent of social change (excluding his early essay, *The Greek
State*), as is clear, for example, from his commentary against violent
social revolution. He does not associate an 'ascending' will to power
with physical might or violence. An 'ascending' will to power is not a
principle of naked power politics or brute domination. Rather, violence
is an expression of a 'declining' will to power. The 'state in which we
hurt others . . . is a sign that we are still lacking power' (GS 13). Still,
what are we to make of his comment, in *On the Genealogy of Morals* (GM
III 25), against international courts replacing war, which he also considers a symptom of declining power? On the one hand, Nietzsche
wishes to overcome the 'master race' of the 'blond beast' – their
deficiency of cunning and cleverness – yet, on the other, he continues
to make more covert or undeveloped assertions (which enables a
metaphoric reading) in favour of war. I will explore this issue further in
Chapter 2 in the section on agonism and the radical liberal democratic
reading of Nietzsche.

Let us assume that when Nietzsche says that 'one can confer rights
only out of the possession of *power*' (D 437) he does not ultimately mean
physical power, but spiritual power and strength of soul. Let us also take
him at his word that he is for a *Geisterkrieg* or an ideological or cultural
war, a war between values, not a war of force. Still, we would have to
acknowledge the connection in meaning between the terms 'spiritual'
and 'ideological'. The concern of the *Geisterkrieg* are values. All
'spiritual forces' are value-perspectives and values are 'quanta of power'.
Second, we would have to acknowledge that the term 'spiritual' in
the Nietzschean corpus does not necessarily mean nonrepressive. The

Jews, for example, when they revalued Roman values, were engaged in 'an act of the *most spiritual revenge'* (GM I 7); and all 'spiritual forces', Nietzsche says, 'exercise beside their liberating effect also a repressive one' (H 262).[53]

Thus, although Nietzsche does not clearly advocate domination through overt coercion or violence, I think it can be argued that he does not renounce domination through spiritual control. This corresponds to his general interest in more comprehensive forms of domination and to his doctrine that there is no absolute person, as the fundamental rights of man proclaim, but only, to adapt a phrase from *The Greek State*, wholly determined beings serving unconscious purposes (17). Nietzsche's interest in control is evident in his discussion of the ancient Hindu *Laws of Manu*, in which he sees operative 'power through the lie', a system of oppression born of the same 'cold-blooded' reflection found in Plato's *Republic* (WP 142 Nachlaß 1888 KSA 13 15[45]).[54]

Before I discuss Nietzsche's appropriation of these laws, it should be said that, for Nietzsche, the *weak* are in power because the ancient aristocrats did not have 'real knowledge' of the 'lower orders'. They misunderstood the sphere they despised. They were more naive, less clever than the slave type who were inclined to secrecy and covert action (GM I 10). The priestly type of this class possessed a superior psychology and superior artifice. They knew better, for example, how to exploit the *'sense of guilt'* (GM III 20). They were more cunning. As Nietzsche writes, the 'priest . . . will not be spared war with the beasts of prey, a war of cunning (of the "spirit") rather than one of force . . . to fight it he will . . . need to evolve a virtually new type of preying animal out of himself' (GM III 15). This passage applies to Nietzsche himself, who does not entirely reject the ascetic ideal, and who believes that in the 'rekindling' of the war of types the noble must become more cunning.

In the Hindu *Laws of Manu*, Nietzsche finds an approximation of his ideal of political organization, namely, an aristocratic social structure or political regime based on a hierarchical order of rank or order of castes, where rights and duties are not shared, ruled by the 'most spiritual human beings', the noble class, who are beyond good and evil. It is the nearest Nietzsche approaches to providing a template for the aristocratic society he wants. In his notebooks, Nietzsche refers to the law-book of Manu as 'an *affirmative* Aryan religion, the product of the *ruling* class' (WP 145 Nachlaß 1888 KSA 13 14[195]). In *The Anti-Christ(ian)*, he asserts that the law-book has 'a real philosophy behind it. . . . noble values everywhere, a feeling of perfection, an affirmation of life' (A 56–7).

In *Twilight of the Idols*, Nietzsche correctly reproduces the four castes, and the one *outcaste*, presented in the law-book: a priestly caste (the *Brahmins*); a warrior caste (the *ksatriya*); a merchant and agricultural class (the *vaisya*); and the class of workers (the *sudras*). Those excluded from the caste system who, according to one edict, will have for clothing only rags from corpses, are the *untouchables* or the *Chandala*. Nietzsche argues that this political organization 'needed to be *dreadful*' in its struggle with these 'non-bred' human beings, who were the 'great majority'. But he criticizes it, not because it practised political exclusion as such, but because the basis of this exclusion was racist.[55] We learn from the law-book, Nietzsche writes, that the idea of 'pure blood' is a harmful idea (TI 'Improvers' 3–4). It is the point at which the system of Manu deviates from nature and tends towards degenerative artificiality, towards the corrupt idea of the hereditary transmission of rule.

But Nietzsche adds that we also learn in exactly which people the hatred for '*Aryan* humanity' is best embodied, namely, the Christian. Christianity constitutes a reaction against the Aryan morality of privilege, 'the victory of Chandala values, the evangel preached to the poor and lowly, the collective rebellion of everything downtrodden' (TI 'Improvers' 4). What is notable here is Nietzsche's appropriation of the Indian-Aryan term *Chandala*, as code for 'Christian'. It will also be invoked for socialist and anarchist.

Nietzsche recognizes that the law-book of Manu is founded on a 'holy lie' or supernatural justifications (WP 142 Nachlaß 1888 KSA 13 15[45]), but he is not critical of this fact as such, for ultimately, as he writes, 'the point is to what *end* a lie is told' (clearly he is making certain concessions here with respect to his critique of antinaturalism and the free-spirited war on the 'holy lie' and pious fraud), '[that] "holy" ends are lacking in Christianity is *my* objection to its means' (A 56). The code of laws of Manu generally serve the ends of life and are thus good, while the doctrines of Christianity do not – because they proceed from weakness, envy and *ressentiment* – and are thus bad.

In *The Anti-Christ(ian)*, Nietzsche offers his ideal of social and political organization which approximates the system depicted in the *Laws of Manu* but, in fact, is a Platonic modification of it, which is to say, Plato's elitist authoritarianism without the morality and the metaphysics.[56]

Every higher culture, Nietzsche says, is a 'pyramid' which consists of, if it is healthy, three types of human being, 'each of which possesses its own hygiene, its own realm of work, its own sort of mastery and feeling of perfection' and its own morality. Criticizing the *Laws of Manu* and their predisposition towards perverse artificiality, Nietzsche writes that it is nature '*not* Manu' which distinguishes these types, which he identifies as the 'spiritual', the 'muscular and temperamental', and the 'mediocre'.

At the apex of the pyramid are the 'most spiritual human beings', '*the very few*'. They are the most enlightened, 'cheerful' and 'amiable', a minority severe towards themselves, who 'find their happiness where others would find their destruction', they 'play with vices' which would 'overwhelm others'; for them, an arduous task and responsibility is a 'privilege'. 'They rule not because they want to but because they *are*.' This 'perfect caste', with their affirmative instincts, view the world as 'perfect'; and 'everything *beneath* us', they say, the *pathos of distance* between human types, 'the Chandala themselves pertain to this perfection'. Second in rank are the 'guardians of the law' who maintain 'order and security'; 'noble warriors' (among whom Nietzsche includes the 'king', suggesting an affirmation of monarchy) who are 'executives' of the perfect caste, alleviating 'them of everything *coarse* in the work of ruling'. Like the Brahmins, Nietzsche's perfect caste constitutes a minority who are beyond good and evil, advise the 'king' and rule the state or society indirectly or by proxy (cf. BGE 61). Third and last in rank are the great majority, the 'mediocre'. Their activity encompasses all '*professional* activity', including 'crafts, trade, agriculture, *science*, the greater part of art'. Every high and exceptional culture, according to Nietzsche, must stand on the broad foundation of a 'soundly consolidated mediocrity'. In fact, it is conditional on it. Thus Nietzsche has no objection to the mediocre *per se*. They too have privileges, which are determined by the nature of their being, their 'natural instincts', and proper to their function as 'intelligent machines', whatever their specialization. 'To be a public utility, a cog, a function, is a natural vocation. . . . For the mediocre it is happiness to be mediocre.' What Nietzsche does object to, abandoning, momentarily, his ideology of the 'perfect world', is the 'Socialist rabble and Chandala apostles' who make the mediocre, the worker or proletariat, envious and resentful, who 'undermine' or pervert his natural instincts, 'his feeling of contentment with his little state of being'.

The division of these three types, Nietzsche writes, 'is necessary for the preservation of society, for making possible higher and higher types'. Furthermore, and more radically stated, the order of castes and order of rank 'formulates the supreme law of life', sanctioning a '*natural order*'. This conception is resolutely affirmed against modernity and 'modern ideas' (or modern ideas of *natural order*), but it is fundamentally aimed at the doctrine of equality of rights. For, in Nietzsche's opinion, injustice 'never lies in unequal rights', but rather 'in the claim to *"equal"* rights' (A 57).

George Stack claims that Nietzsche, in spite of his ratification of an aristocratic social structure, did not conceive of his perfect caste as exercising oppressive, exploitive power, suppressing 'the development of diverse individuals'.[57] Nietzsche, of course, did not conceive of the social order he endorsed as maintained through overt force or violence (although warfare is part of its practical administration); rather, ideally, he wants each individual member to interiorize his place, police himself, according to his natural instincts in a kind of pre-established harmony; and he certainly wants the most enlightened human beings to handle the mediocre most gently and moderately (A 57). What Nietzsche wants is that the law be made unconscious. This is one reason why he is so fascinated by the law-book of Manu, for it contains the 'rationale' for achieving the 'automatism of instinct', for making a 'way of life recognized as correct'. In fact, Nietzsche states that the principal difference between the *Laws of Manu* and, for example, the Old or New Testaments (which are also founded on 'holy lies') 'is the means by which the *noble* orders, the philosophers and the warriors, keep the mob under control' (A 56). In effect, Nietzsche is reproducing in his preferred regime a structural feature of the despotic socialist state he had so reviled in *Daybreak*, namely, the reduction of the individual to a useful instrument of the whole. And this is further supported by Nietzsche's assertions in *The Gay Science*, and elsewhere, regarding the necessity of slavery (GS 377). Consequently, the political organization Nietzsche endorses is predicated on political exclusion and structural violence, or nonrecognition.

It can be said that, like the elite theorists and the aristocratic liberals, Nietzsche is committed to the fluidity of individuals but not classes; and he is opposed to any universal support structure, anything *gratis*, the social welfare state. Thus, in so far as Nietzsche dismisses universal voting rights and rights to higher education, is he not potentially discouraging, contrary to what Stack says, the development of diverse individuals? What Nietzsche wishes to see maintained is a *pathos of distance*, whereby the 'higher' are not degraded 'to the status of an instrument of the lower'(or a state governed by the 'lower') whereby their respective activities or tasks remain 'eternally separate' (GM III 14). Nevertheless, 'higher' and 'lower', as well as 'healthy' and 'sick', 'strong' and 'weak' are, in the Nietzschean corpus, preconceived political codes. Each has encrypted within them their own concepts of 'goodness' and 'justice'. The will to power of the 'sick' and the 'weak', for instance,

Nietzsche associates with 'aggressive collective action' and 'herd organization' (GM III 18); with the 'conspiracy' against the 'well-constituted' and the monopolization of virtue: 'these weak . . . people . . . "we alone are the good and just", they say'; and it is they 'who spell disaster for the strong' (GM III 14).

In *Human, All Too Human*, Nietzsche had declared that a caste system is a prerequisite for a high culture (H 439). He conceives of his perfect caste as forming an agonistic oligarchy or aristocracy which, because the strong and born masters are 'disquieted by organization', 'constantly trembles with the tension each member feels in maintaining control over his lust [for tyranny]' (GM III 18). This form of aristocratic individualism is its generator, which does not alter the social structure *per se*, but enables the circulation of elites.

In the immediate, Nietzsche anticipates an affirmative 'new party of life' who, as he writes in *Ecce Homo*, would 'attempt to raise humanity higher' and resuscitate a Dionysian 'excess of life'. Here a necessary precondition is not sustained conflict between power-complexes, but 'the relentless destruction of everything . . . degenerating' (EH BT 4), the dominion over the earth and the annihilation of universal suffrage (WP 862 Nachlaß 1884 KSA 11 25[211]). The resuscitation of excess means, for example *contra*, the kinds of social institutions proposed by socialism, a return to a 'general economy of life' (an expenditure which would not result in the welfare of all), a return wholly in accord with Nietzsche's rejection of pity. This general economy says, in principle, that society must necessarily produce 'refuse and waste materials', 'failures and deformities' (WP 40 Nachlaß 1888 KSA 13 14[75]), in the interest of growth, in the interest of having and wanting more, that is the 'doctrine preached by life itself' (WP 125 Nachlaß 1885 KSA 11 37[11]). It considers, in principle, hatred, evil and lust to rule as essential and fundamental conditions. It promises a return to a 'multiplicity of types' – 'the chasm between man and man, class and class' (*'die Kluft zwischen Mensch und Mensch, Stand und Stand, die Vielheit der Typen'*) (TI Expeditions 37).

In this chapter I supported the view that Nietzsche reduces morality to politics, but more specifically, that there is a necessary complicity between his critique of morality and his critique of egalitarian politics, that they are intrinsically linked through Nietzsche's concepts of *décadence* and *ressentiment*. I demonstrated that, aside from Nietzsche's direct engagement with political categories such as the social contract, there is a definite political dimension to virtually all key themes and categories of his philosophy, such as order of rank and the revaluation of all values, most of which will be revisited in subsequent chapters. After all, he does qualify his revaluation of all values as *die große Politik*. And he also provides an endorsement of the type of political regime he prefers, aristocratic and authoritarian in form, Platonic in its structure, Machiavellian in its precepts, reproducing its plan in 1888. My view is that Nietzsche has a political philosophy, but also that his philosophy is a political ontology (not *un*political but *anti*political).

I also demonstrated that Nietzsche is engaged in class warfare, and that this position is deeply entrenched and encoded in his corpus. He is consistently antiegalitarian, as is clear from his doctrine of right, and even from his concept of political economy. He is an enemy of 1789, 1848 and 1871. To base his position in events, his aversion for the Paris Commune should not be minimized, nor his appreciation for the Bonapartist reactions of 1799 and 1852.

In addition, I addressed two key questions which need to be explored further, as they are relevant to Nietzsche's general antidemocratic position and his doctrine of agonism: the question of Nietzsche's pro-democratic position during the period 1878–82; and the question of Nietzsche's position on violence, or physical warfare, which I will again address in subsequent chapters. In the process, I disclosed the basic oppositions, mediations and allegiances, the tenets and doctrines – *natural* and *antinatural* – which govern his political thinking as a prolegomenon to its political definition, which the remainder of this study will develop.

2

The Radical Liberal Democratic
Reading of Nietzsche

*Now a comic fact, which is coming more and more to my notice – I
have an 'influence', very subterranean to be sure, I enjoy a strange
and almost mysterious respect among all radical parties (Socialists,
Nihilists, anti-Semites, Orthodox Christians, Wagnerians).*
Letter to Franz Overbeck, 1887

A dominant reading formation in contemporary Nietzsche studies and
political theory is the radical democratic reading of Nietzsche. Since this
reading locates not only democratic (egalitarian), but primarily liberal
(individualistic, pluralistic) and libertarian conceptual resources in the
Nietzschean corpus, it is more explicit to refer to it as a radical liberal
democratic reading. The radical, or anticlassical liberal, aspect of
its approach is constituted in the fact that it elicits from Nietzsche's
philosophy of the subject (as decentred, infinite process and self-
overcoming) a libertarian challenge to any politics of identity (ethnic
or cultural), which often harden into forms of *ressentiment*, and from
Nietzsche's philosophy of perspectivism (antidogmatism, contingency
and the imperative to multiply perspectives) and agonism (the maintenance of tension and conflict, antagonism and competing views in the
public space) a challenge to any form of totalitarianism. For the radical
liberal democratic reader, Nietzschean agonism is grounded in the
attunement to the differences of others and thus in respect and empathy
(or tolerance) and in accordance with a democratic ethos.

In this chapter I will elucidate and evaluate the contemporary radical
liberal democratic reading of Nietzsche.[1] My intention is to provide a
generalized, synthetic account of this reading – a generic reading –
rather than engage all the nuances between the readings which comprise it, to disclose the key arguments in its treatments of the themes

of Nietzsche's philosophy upon which it concentrates and to render them problematic. This reading is rhetorically complex and perhaps impossible to refute absolutely, if only because its reductions are so elusive.

I will begin with a discussion of the discontinuity which the radical liberal democratic reading posits between Nietzsche's Dionysian philosophy and his aristocratic politics. This reading claims that the principal Nietzschean doctrines which it engages possess an aporetic structure that releases them from the restrictions of Nietzschean politics. I will argue that there is no necessary discontinuity between Nietzsche's Dionysian philosophy and his aristocratic, authoritarian politics; that his treatment of the themes of the subject, perspectivism and agonism can be seen to be consistent with his politics of hierarchy and domination.

With respect to the Nietzschean subject, I will argue that the radical liberal democratic reading tends to depreciate the theme of strong will in Nietzsche's philosophy; with respect to perspectivism, I will argue that it is compatible with the Nietzschean economy of exploitation, that not all perspectives are equal and that we may rethink the doctrine of perspectivism along the lines of political technology; with respect to agonism, I will argue that agonism implies inequality, that it can never, in the Nietzschean sense, model the citizenry as free and equal, that it does not imply empathy for those in positions of social subordination, and that Nietzsche conceives the doctrine of agonism in terms of a regulated factionalism, a controlled violence over a government of mixed physiologies and moralities, although he provides little operational detail beyond its suggestion.

1. The thesis of a discontinuity between Nietzsche's philosophy and his politics

Nietzsche was denazified by Walter Kaufmann in 1950 'to suit the purposes of American imperialism', according to Lukács.[2] But Kaufmann went beyond the mere denazification of Nietzsche and performed a general depoliticization of his thought. This has been severely criticized and effectively retracted in recent years with the appearance of many books on Nietzsche and politics. (These, however, express no consensus on whether Nietzsche's politics represent a unified political position.) Kaufmann exercised a considerable influence on Nietzsche studies and there are still a few scholars today who continue to say that Nietzsche was apolitical or that his work is without political implications.[3]

At the core of Kaufmann's reading was the offensive reduction of Nietzsche's concept of will to power to 'an apolitical principle of personal, existential self-overcoming and self-transcendence'.[4] Kaufmann's view was that Nietzsche 'was not primarily a social or political philosopher'. Rather, Nietzsche's basic theme was 'the antipolitical individual who seeks self-perfection far from the modern world'.[5]

But Karl Jaspers may be seen, in his work from 1935, to have performed the initial and effectively more profound operation to insulate Nietzsche from any attempt at precise political identification, and particularly from the proposition that his work legitimates an authoritarian or fascist politics, when he characterizes Nietzsche's production as a 'self-dissembling writing, groundless thought, and an infinitely self-completing dialectic that brings all apodictic statements into question through the consideration of new possibilities'.[6] Bataille drew on this principle in defending Nietzsche from fascist appropriation in 1937, explaining that the 'very movement of Nietzsche's thought implies a destruction of the different possible foundations of current political positions';[7] and Deleuze took it up again in his essay 'Pensée nomade'[8] (although Deleuze does not depoliticize Nietzsche, but ultimately sees him as an anarchist and antistatist). In so far as contradiction could be viewed as the organizing principle of Nietzsche's thought, this thought could provide neither justification nor sanction for any political order. Rather, it would evade all attempts at political codification.

In claiming its aporetic structure, Deleuze says that it is Nietzsche's *method that makes Nietzsche's text into something not to be characterized in itself as "fascist", "bourgeois", or "revolutionary", but to be regarded as an exterior field where fascist, bourgeois, and revolutionary forces meet head on'.*[9] Yet Mussolini says essentially the same about fascism and the eclecticism of its ideology: 'Fascism uses in its construction whatever elements in the Liberal, Social or Democratic doctrines [that] still have a living value . . . it rejects . . . the conception that there can be any doctrine of unquestioned efficacy for all times and all peoples.'[10] And, perhaps more to the point, in his essay entitled 'Relativism and Fascism', he writes, 'fascists can be aristocrats and democrats, revolutionaries and reactionaries, proletarians and anti-proletarians, pacifists and anti-pacifists'.[11] These references to Mussolini are not gratuitous. Scholars of fascism routinely point to the spectral-syncretic or eclectic features of fascist political philosophy. This is to suggest only that the Deleuzian reading may be overlooking the possible adherence on Nietzsche's part to what is, ultimately, a Machiavellian principle, as it is so regarded by Nietzsche in *Human, All Too Human*, that the form of government is of only minimal importance, that the 'great goal of politics should be *permanence*' or durability (H 224). Serious consideration of this point on method should insinuate that Nietzsche may be tactical (dissimulative or esoteric), rather than merely contradictory. There is evidence for this view in the fact that Nietzsche supports democracy, for example (very moderately and expediently as he does between 1878 and 1880), only in so far as it represents a counterpoise to socialism (and anarchism) and, in later writings, only in so far as it encourages weakness of will. I will discuss this further in Chapter 4. Nietzsche writes of his 'delight in masks and the good conscience in using any kind of mask' (GS 77). Such 'good conscience' informs the techniques and tactics of governance of the 'philosopher as *we* understand him, we free spirits' who, as Nietzsche writes in *Beyond Good and Evil*, 'will make use of religions' and 'whatever political and economic states are at hand' to advance his 'project of cultivation and education' (BGE 61).

The reading of Jaspers, and those others I have cited as conduits of his view, constitutes the background to the contemporary radical liberal democratic reading of Nietzsche. This reading does not say, like Kaufmann, that Nietzsche is antipolitical, nor does it say, like Deleuze, although it makes use of the argument for *aporia*, that Nietzsche resists political codification. Rather, it says that Nietzsche may be read, because of the aporetic structure of his text, and in spite of his overt opposition to liberal democratic principles, as consonant with liberal democratic pluralism, and even issues imperatives to read him as such.[12]

The earliest interpretation of this kind can be found in Henry Kariel's essay 'Nietzsche's Preface to Constitutionalism', which views Nietzsche's philosophy as espousing a form of radical individualism which 'gives sanction to no social order – no human community, no social class, no political regime'. But because Nietzsche's philosophy attributes, according to Kariel, 'absolute sanctity to the individual person' (a proposition at the basis of liberalism and liberal democracy), because it preserves the integrity, potential and irreducibility of the individual person, and because it regards life as an interminable process of creation and destruction, in accordance with Nietzsche's Dionysian conception, Kariel concludes that 'reflection makes clear that the only kind of political machinery appropriate to Nietzsche's basic outlook is that associated with liberal constitutionalism'.[13] Such an interpretation clearly exceeds the Deleuzian one, which only implicitly imposes a political code (anarchist and anti-statist) on Nietzsche and is important to the radical liberal democratic reading for its emphasis on process. Yet even though it articulates Nietzsche's dormant compatibility with liberal democratic theory, unlike Kariel, the radical liberal democratic reading of Nietzsche recognizes that his philosophy does not attribute absolute sanctity to the individual person in so far as Nietzsche supports the institution of slavery, natural division of labour and order of rank. Although it does say, once construed as *power for* rather than *power over*, Nietzsche's concept of will to power 'should lead to a high evaluation of social and political organizations that maximize individual power'.[14] Like Kariel, this reading does focus on and stress Nietzsche's Dionysian philosophy of perpetual overcoming and finitude, of contradiction, resistance and ontological anarchy (antifoundationalism) which it sees expressed through Nietzsche's antidogmatic, perspectivist epistemology, his agonistic politics and his suspicion of unconditional authority; and it sees this Dionysian philosophy as amenable to a duly radicalized liberal democratic form or process of government or liberal democratic ethos; a philosophy that points towards an affirmation of individualism, pluralism, difference and 'otherness' (without 'deviance', without *ressentiment*).

The liberal democracy of this reading can be described as radical and post-Nietzschean primarily in so far as it embraces Nietzsche's 'radical reconceptualization of the subject'[15] (who resists all totalizing identity formations or structures). This reconceptualization theorizes the subject as decentred, 'multiple' and situated, undermining the atomistic and ahistorical conception of the subject, the conception of the subject as disembodied and immortal, characteristic of Christian metaphysics, Cartesian and Kantian epistemology and classical (even Rawlsian) liberalism. This reading embraces the perspective of Nietzsche's genealogical critique where the subject is seen as entirely contingent, 'produced under particular historical conditions to express the practical interests of a specific community',[16] or even resist them should they become oppressive or abusive.

This reading acknowledges that, given Nietzsche's critique of equality and freedom, 'attempts to harmonize Nietzsche with certain features of liberal theory is precarious';[17] or it expresses concern that, in appropriating Nietzsche 'in support of a modified democratic perspective',[18] Nietzsche's text may be reduced to 'a bloody mess'.[19] None the less, it proceeds to 'cut out central elements' in Nietzsche's 'message',[20] with the claim – and this is designed to give the impression that the integrity of the text is being preserved – that, ultimately, any *aporia* or discontinuity in Nietzsche's philosophy is Nietzsche's own, regardless of whether he was aware of it or not. Thus Lawrence Hatab can say that Nietzsche 'should have preferred democracy to any other political arrangement – and this in the spirit of his own thinking'.[21]

But since an essential aim of this project is to free, as Mark Warren says, 'Nietzsche's philosophy from its political straitjacket',[22] versus the idea that Nietzsche's philosophy is impregnated by his politics, the discontinuity is posited between Nietzsche's philosophy (his critique of metaphysics, his theory of truth, or his ethics) and his radical aristocratic politics of hierarchy and domination. More specifically, this means excluding those aspects or uncritical assumptions, such as natural division of labour and order of rank, characteristic of Nietzsche's 'political vision' which are 'premodern' and 'distinctly fascist'.[23] And this further entails reading Nietzsche's will to power not as a Hobbesian will to dominate, but as a principle of differentiation or sublimated *self-overcoming*. Once read this way, the will to power 'cannot be restricted to modes of physical, social or political control'.[24] Thus Warren, for example, interprets the will to power as a process of reflexive self-constitution (self-overcoming), as *power for* rather than *power over*, where the value is placed on the maximization of individual power without exploitive or oppressive consequences. But it also means locating a contradiction within Nietzsche's text whereby Nietzsche's pluralistic conception of truth, or perspectivist epistemology, 'rules out potential totalitarianism'.[25] Thus Nietzsche is seen to contradict his concept of the will to power, as a ground or *principium* which justifies political domination and exploitation, through his critique of metaphysics.[26]

William Connolly, in his adaptation of Nietzsche to a radicalized liberal democratic ethos which he calls 'agono-pluralism',[27] implicitly posits this discontinuity between Nietzsche's philosophy and his politics when he locates two alternative 'ethics' in Nietzsche. One 'counsels humanity to complete its project of assuming mastery over the world, accepting the implication that many human beings will have to be subjugated'; the other 'counsels us to come to terms with difference'. Connolly embraces the Foucauldian (and Deleuzian) reading of Nietzsche's concept of the will to power as an anarchic principle of differentiation (and resistance). This ultimately means reading the will to power (or 'life') as a 'set of fugitive energies and possibilities that exceed any particular identity'.[28] This 'excess of life over identity', writes Connolly in *The Augustinian Imperative*, 'provides the fugitive source from which one comes to appreciate . . . the an-archy of being'.[29] Thus Connolly is able to treat Nietzsche's philosophy 'as a problematic which . . . contains a diverse set of ethical and political possibilities'.[30]

But there are exclusions here as well. *With* Nietzsche, these ethical and political possibilities must exclude transcendental and teleological theories, must oppose *ressentiment* (as fundamentalism) and normalization, and must affirm contingency, finitude, contest and aversion to totalization (resistance to closure). 'One seeks to remain tied to Nietzsche's sceptical contestation of transcendental and teleological philosophies, indebted to his genealogies, touched by his reverence for life and the earth.'[31] *Against* Nietzsche, the aristocratic distinction between the few (the cultured minority) and the many (the masses or the multitude) must be relinquished as it is not politically viable, and the *Übermensch* democratized, construed as a 'set of dispositions that may compete for presence in any self'.[32]

In claiming a discontinuity between Nietzsche's philosophy and his politics, which enables it to choose 'the philosophical Nietzsche while excluding his politics',[33] the radical liberal democratic reading ultimately privileges Nietzsche's concept of the will to power as a principle of self-overcoming described as a principle of differentiation and resistance to totalization. The philosophical Nietzsche is read as a radical pluralist, for whom the Dionysian and the tragic means 'multiple and pluralist affirmation'[34] (in accordance with Nietzsche's pluralistic conception of truth or perspectivism), as well as the affirmation of finitude.

Ansell-Pearson writes that Nietzsche's Dionysian thinking 'undermines the foundations on which his conception of political order is constructed'.[35] This continues to be the principal line of argument in Nietzsche studies to clear him of any strictly authoritarian or fascist affiliation. A similar strategy is employed in Heidegger studies, for the same purpose, where it is stated that Heidegger is an ontological anarchist whose hypothesis of withering principial representations, once translated into the political realm, is 'subversive' in so far as it implies the introduction of 'radical fluidity into social institutions'.[36] Unfortunately, because it is detrimental to historical understanding, it is never asked, in view of the intrinsic incompatibility which is claimed here, how it is that a fascist philosopher, a philosopher of National Socialism like Alfred Bäumler, could exalt the idea that 'Nietzsche's 'values' . . . cannot be petrified into dogma';[37] or the idea that Nietzsche's politics repudiates a stable world of norms and values.[38] Or how it is that Oswald Spengler, or other conservative revolutionaries, could favour an authoritarian polity without a commitment to 'eternal values and absolute truths'.[39]

That Nietzsche's philosophy entails an interminable process of creation and destruction, a force of resistance in every social formation (the right to resist), and the pluralistic and provisional nature of truth, does nothing to undermine the foundations of Nietzsche's political philosophy: will to power, nature (later expressed in the vocabulary of 'natural right' and 'natural law' although not in their classical senses) and order of rank.

With respect to Nietzsche's affirmation of finitude as 'the law of life' (GM III 27) – the 'affirmation of passing away *and destroying . . .* of *becoming*, along with a radical repudiation of *being'* – this argument neglects to acknowledge the Apollonian principle inherent in the Dionysian, the fact that stabilizations can and do occur; that, in spite of this Dionysian universe, certain formations of domination have been 'allowed to flourish' (GM III 23); and that Nietzsche does not disavow longevity with respect to select political orders, such as the *Imperium Romanum* or the Tsarist empire, and criticizes liberal democratic institutions for their lack of durability and power to organize (TI Expeditions 39). In other words, the desire for durable institutions (for Apollo), or the desire to eternalize, need not offend the Dionysian philosophy of finitude or continual flux.[40]

Furthermore, Nietzsche's idea of the Dionysian, in a more immediate sense, is not 'perpetual improvisation' (GS 295). It is, rather, the 'desire for *destruction*, change, and becoming', but towards a future goal (which involves social and political organization). Nietzsche is careful to distinguish his sense of the Dionysian from that other (anarchist) sense of the Dionysian which is symptomatic of 'the hatred of the ill-constituted, disinherited, and underprivileged, who destroy, *must* destroy, because what exists, indeed all existence . . . outrages and provokes them' (GS 370). And Nietzsche does anticipate, in *Thus Spoke Zarathustra*, the coming of a finite regime or empire, namely, the 'thousand-year empire of Zarathustra'.[41]

With respect to difference and pluralism, Nietzsche is committed to hierarchical distributions of power, to a vision of a *pathos of distance* between classes and types, to an order of rank. This means that Nietzschean plurality is organized according to an aristocratic structure of command and obedience, which he sees as the fundamental structure of social life. Nietzschean genealogy and comparative morality promise, in theory, a return of the repressed against Christian and neo-Christian hegemony, a release of a plurality of forces – so the Nietzschean philosophy does have its moment of decolonization. But the *'problem of the legislator'*, as conceived by Nietzsche, implies that the 'forces that have been unleashed must be harnessed again' (WP 69 n. 39 Nachlaß 1886 KSA 12 2[100]), as they are, prospectively, in dual typology and order of rank, but also in a critique of laws, contracts and institutions. Thus Nietzsche's philosophy tends towards recodification. For Nietzsche, pluralism ultimately means that each rank of society, according to his radical aristocratic ideal, should possess a 'fundamentally different valuation for their own actions', that the leaders, the independent and the *herd* (the masses or the multitude) should each be governed by fundamentally different moralities, with the former (the sovereign) possessing the right to exceptional actions (WP 287 Nachlaß 1886–87 KSA 12 7[6], WP 921 Nachlaß 1887–88 KSA 13 11[146]) and exceptional laws. However, this alters nothing with respect to the order of governance Nietzsche desires, nor with respect to the fact that 'the herd animal [is] . . . incapable of leading itself', that it requires a 'shepherd' or a commander (WP 282 Nachlaß 1888 KSA 10 23[4], BGE 242), a prominent theme in the Nietzschean corpus.

Nietzsche says that 'life' (or will to power) is that '*which must overcome itself again and again*', that it is 'struggle and becoming and goal and conflict of goals' which does not merely aim at self-preservation. Everything it creates it must eventually oppose or resist (Z Self-Overcoming). That is a 'law of life' (GM III 27). But Nietzsche also says that 'every enhancement of the type "man" has so far been the work of an aristocratic society', which maintains the 'ingrained difference between strata' (BGE 257), social hierarchy, order of rank or plurality in relations of command and obedience. The idea of enhancement implies that the process of overcoming (creation and destruction) can or may be controlled (this idea is behind the plan for the breeding of the *Übermensch*). It is a question of willing or breeding a 'more valuable' type which has so far, historically, appeared only by accident (A 3). For example, in order for life to '*overcome itself again and again*', there 'should be more war and inequality' (Z Tarantulas); these basic social conditions should be cultivated and encouraged. The creation of these social conditions are thought by Nietzsche in terms of real conditions and material transformations. The Nietzschean revolution would involve, for example, the demobilization of militant labour and the annihilation of equal rights and universal suffrage.

The radical liberal democratic reading of Nietzsche claims that his doctrine of will to power may be read as *power for*, without the logic of domination, without authoritarian or fascist legitimation. The radical liberal democratic readers say, essentially, what Randolph Bourne said in 1917: that will to power 'may be transcended . . . into harmless and creative forms of power'.[42] Yet, in *On the Genealogy of Morals*, Nietzsche opposes his 'theory that in all events a *will to power* is operating' to the 'democratic idiosyncrasy which opposes everything that dominates and wants to dominate'; that 'modern *misarchism*' (hatred of rule or government) which has permeated the 'sciences' and 'taken charge of all physiology and theory of life' (GM II 12).[43] If this reading is to be, effectively, no more than merely the use of the proper name *Nietzsche* for legitimation or *spectacular* purposes, if in excising central elements of Nietzsche's thought it cannot avoid a disfiguring reduction of the text, respecting the design of its own concerns, then it must demonstrate that all the Nietzschean doctrines it treats inherently possess an aporetic structure that releases them from Nietzschean politics. This is why this reading forces a discontinuity between Nietzsche's 'philosophy' and his 'politics' and why it is not sufficient for a critique of this reading merely to point out that Nietzsche was antidemocratic. Radical liberal democratic readers generally acknowledge this fact. Rather, it must be demonstrated that Nietzsche's philosophy of the subject, perspectivism and agonism is entirely compatible with Nietzsche's radical aristocratic and authoritarian politics. This can be accomplished in two ways: through an immanent reading and the accumulation of textual evidence and through locating these Nietzschean doctrines in antiliberal democratic political philosophies.

2. The subject

The Nietzschean subject is not something that 'remains constant in the midst of all flux'; it is not an *aeterna veritas*, neither an unchanging essence nor an enduring substance, nor identical with itself (H 18). It is advanced as contingent, dependent on historical and cultural conditions. As such, it is opposed to the Cartesian and Kantian conceptions of the subject (as *res cogitans* and *pure reason*) inherited from Christian metaphysics, to the 'ego as cause' which presupposes a rational disengagement from the body and from tradition, and to the 'timeless knowing subject' which demands 'that we should think of an eye that is completely unthinkable' (GM III 12). As Nietzsche writes, 'Christianity has taught best . . . the soul atomism . . . the belief which regards the soul as something indestructible, eternal, indivisible, as a monad, as an *atomon*' (BGE 12). This is also the conception of the subject which informs classical liberalism. Nietzsche criticizes this conception in *On the Genealogy of Morals*, and this is where his epistemology connects to his politics, the Rousseauian subject of social contract theory, the belief in the 'neutral, independent' subject which 'makes possible to the majority . . . the weak and oppressed of every kind, the . . . self-deception that interprets weakness as freedom' (GM I 13). Nietzsche's refinement of the soul-hypothesis essentially consists of reconceptualizing the soul (*Seele*) as 'mortal soul', as 'subjective multiplicity' and as a 'social structure of the drives and affects' (BGE 12). Nietzsche calls it '*My hypothesis*: The subject as multiplicity'.[44] This hypothesis implies a depreciation of the idea of consciousness, or the intellect, as that which 'constitutes the *kernel* of man; what is abiding, eternal, ultimate, and most original in him . . . [as] the "unity of the organism" ' (GS 11). In Nietzsche's epiphenomenal view, 'consciousness *is* a surface' (EH WC 9) and the intellect is merely an instrument of rival drives and instincts. Thus Nietzsche criticizes Socrates who made 'a tyrant of *reason*' and rationality over the instincts and the unconscious (TI Socrates10) and the Greek philosophers who posited 'the conscious state as more valuable' (WP 439 Nachlaß 1888 KSA 13, 14 [131]).

Nietzsche thus reconceptualizes the subject in a way that not only gives primacy to historical and cultural conditions, but also to the unconscious, the body and physiological processes. For 'the greatest part of our spirit's activity remains unconscious and unfelt' (GS 333). The unity of consciousness is only the 'semblance of unity', a supposition or fiction (GS 370). No person can know the elusive and complex 'totality of *drives* which constitute his being' (D 119) or 'the essential nature of an action' (D 116). Nietzsche says 'a thought comes when "it" wishes' (BGE 17), and thus it remains possible that we may be 'merely incarnation, merely mouthpiece, merely a medium of overpowering forces' (EH Z 3).

The post-Nietzschean liberal democratic reading affirms the contingency and decentring and decentralizing effect of Nietzsche's multiple subject. It privileges, in general, the idea that the Nietzschean subject is 'an arena for an irresolvable contest of differing drives, each seeking mastery',[45] and is thus excessive and evasive of any fixed identity which the radical democratic readers consider a danger to democracy. This description may essentially be confirmed by the aphorism in *Beyond Good and Evil* which says, 'the basic drives . . . every single one of them would like only too well to represent *itself* as the ultimate purpose of existence and the legitimate *master* of all other drives. For every drive wants to be master' (BGE 6). In effect, any drive or constellation of drives may consolidate itself as the ego, may use the intellect as an instrument, though as it may be conceded, not indefinitely.

The radical liberal democratic description of the Nietzschean subject is not incorrect or inaccurate *per se*, but with its emphasis on process, becoming, contingency, irresolvability and evasion of fixed identity (individual or collective), it tends to ignore or depreciate both the theme of strong and weak wills in Nietzsche's philosophy and the Lamarckian-inspired theme of inherited traits or acquired characteristics (typology). This tendency in this reading system is primarily what I wish to address here.

Warren is an exception to this tendency in so far as he reads the will to power in terms of a general desire to experience the self as an autonomous, self-determining 'agent unity' (he does not say 'will' as Nietzsche does). In other words, Warren reads will to power as *power for* rather than *power over*, which should 'enable the positive freedom of individuals' and 'should lead to a high evaluation of social and political organizations that maximize individual power'. None the less, since Nietzsche was not aware of the real implications of his philosophy, as Warren says, this finds no expression in his politics, where domination is construed as an ontological necessity – and descriptive of political domination over others – and sovereign individuality the attribute solely of a cultured minority.[46]

Nietzsche does not value a subjectivity lost in the mercurial stream of becoming, but a unified and strong personality, a 'totality' such as the free-spirited Goethe was (TI Expeditions 49). True strength is bounded by a horizon. The modern type, Nietzsche says, 'suffers from a weakened personality' (UM II 5). What is imperative for him is strength of will, discipline, self-control and self-mastery, the 'genius' of *Daybreak* who represents 'the imposition of order and choice upon the influx of tasks and impressions' (D 548), traits or attributes of the noble type or, in Machiavellian terms, of the *virtù* that tames *fortuna*.

The will, according to Nietzsche, is not simple, not a faculty, but 'a complex of sensation and thinking'. But it is 'above all an affect, and specifically the *affect* of command' (BGE 19). To will is to command. A strong will resolves and coordinates the multiplicity of rival drives, affects and instincts 'under a single predominant impulse', while a weak will is left with a disaggregation and deprivation of any 'systematic order' (WP 46 Nachlaß 1888 KSA 13 14[219]). Nietzsche is philosophically interested in the ordering and organization of this chaotic perspective-multiplicity because he wishes to see overcome the paralysis and sickness of the will, because he is against – and the radical liberal democratic reading generally ignores this – the weak 'will that no longer commands, no longer is capable of commanding' (BGE 209).

In *The Case of Wagner*, Nietzsche defines *décadence*, in part, as the 'disgregation of the will' (CW 7). It constitutes one of the principal targets of his political critique, as I pointed out in Chapter 1. The radical liberal democratic reading of Nietzsche ignores and deprecates the extent to which Nietzsche wishes to liberate the will from this disaggregation, to make subservient, or obedient, inner capacities to a dominant task or goal. As with the Stoics and theologians whom Nietzsche criticizes in *The Gay Science* (GS 326), this reading tends to silence Nietzsche's decisive, liberated will, his antiliberal, antidemocratic will which wishes to seize the right to determine new values, to restore to the earth the goal of the Antichrist and antinihilist (GM II 24) and force 'the will of millennia upon new tracks' (BGE 203).[47] Likewise, it tends to ignore or deprecate the extent to which Nietzsche views democratic institutions as enhancing weakness of will, how they represent the declining form of the power to organize, how the democratization of Europe, according to Nietzsche's prognostics, will lead to a type 'poor in will' and 'prepared for *slavery*', and in need of a commander (BGE 242). Nietzsche assesses a human being according to the 'quantum of power and abundance of his will' (WP 382 Nachlaß 1887 KSA 12 10[118]). And his sovereign individual, rich in will and command, is cognizant of how his 'mastery over himself . . . gives him mastery over . . . all more short-willed and unreliable creatures' (GM II 12). Thus Nietzsche's philosophy of the subject, while it is concerned with the maximization of individual power, does not envisage this maximization of power as consonant with a liberal democratic polity, but rather with a radical aristocratic one (subordination is an effect of its power). Second, the *power for* this maximization implies, as indicated by the awareness of Nietzsche's sovereign individual, also clearly implies *power over*.

The radical liberal democratic reading also neglects to interrogate the importance of the doctrine of inherited traits and atavism for Nietzsche. This may be because this doctrine compromises the perspective of Nietzsche's genealogical critique, as interpreted by the liberal democratic reading, that the subject expresses the particular historical conditions and practical interests of a specific community. For this doctrine implies that the Nietzschean subject may also be the product of a delayed effect and express historical conditions which are not fully contemporaneous with it. In this vein, in the process of criticizing the 'theory of milieu' in *Twilight of the Idols*, Nietzsche says that great human beings are 'necessary' while the epoch in which they appear is 'accidental' (TI Expeditions 44). Nietzsche's doctrine, like the doctrine of cellular memory, is that we carry within our bodies 'the curriculum of earlier mankind' (H 12). In *Beyond Good and Evil* Nietzsche writes, 'It is simply not possible that a human being should not have the qualities and preferences of his parents and ancestors in his body, what-ever appearances may suggest to the contrary' (BGE 262). The individ-ual 'constitutes the entire *single* line "man" up to and including himself' (TI Expeditions 33). Every individual represents the whole evolutionary trajectory, which does not just begin at birth, and characteristics acquired in earlier stages may 'suddenly emerge . . . perhaps after cen-turies' (GS 9). The subject is thus conceptualized by Nietzsche as the potential for a return of the repressed. But it seems to occur only in rare or great human beings, as suggested by the fact that Nietzsche calls 'rare human beings . . . suddenly emerging late ghosts of past cultures and their powers' (GS 10), and says that every great human being 'exerts a retroactive force' through which 'a thousand secrets of the past crawl out of their hiding places' (GS 34). (Following Taine, Nietzsche sees Napoleon, for example, as a late representative of the Renaissance.) In this sense, an individual is born, or predestined, for the art of command (BGE 213). But Nietzsche's doctrine is far from developed. Sometimes there is a return of the repressed (typological palingenesis) in the 'untimely' human being, sometimes the content can be retrieved as if through psychoanalysis. It is not my intention to make a major point of this doctrine against the radical liberal democratic reading, but it deserves mention in so far as it applies to Nietzsche's reconceptualiza-tion of the subject and is actively deployed in the doctrine of types in his genealogical critique of modernity.

As an example of the way it is used in this critique, Nietzsche says that all of us carry within us 'the heritage of multiple origins', opposite 'drives and value standards that fight each other' (BGE 200); 'all of us have unconsciously . . . in our bodies values, words, formulas, morali-ties of *opposite* descent' (CW E). But it is especially in a democratic age, where classes and races increasingly interact and intermingle (affirmed in Nietzsche's concept of the *good European*) that human beings feel more acutely this war within their bodies, which amounts to increased access to different forms and ways of life. Yet the modern subject, as Nietzsche sees it, wants this war within itself to come to an end; this defines its weakness. It desires a secure resting-place and happiness, with the 'taste and tongue for everything', a desire Nietzsche calls *'ignoble'*. Of course, this pronouncement is no more than a thinly veiled critique of liberal tolerance and of the bourgeois *'last man'* who is interested only in his own comfort and self-preservation. The strong will, conversely, will confront this multiplicity with self-mastery and self-control, with the distillation of a 'definite Yes and No' typical of noble culture (BGE 200). Nietzsche gives expression to this in *The Anti-Christ(ian)*: 'formula of our happiness: a Yes, a No, a straight line, a goal' (A 1). Nietzsche extols the 'synthetic man', as opposed to the 'multifarious man' (WP 883 Nachlaß 1887 KSA 12 9[119]) who is more autonomous precisely because his affects and passions are under control, dominated and capable of being pressed into service for a single goal (WP 881 Nachlaß 1887 KSA 12 10[111]). This defines his 'greatness of character' (WP 928 Nachlaß 1887 KSA 13 11[353]). The modern subject is that 'multifarious man' who represents *'innocence* among opposites' and a *'contradiction of values'*. He 'says Yes and No in the same breath' (CW E). He no longer knows 'independence of decisions', his will is paralysed (BGE 208). He is physiologically *'false'* (CW E).

Nietzsche ultimately reduces the multiplicity within the subject to 'moralities of *opposite* descent'. These are master and slave moralities, active and reactive, the terms of Nietzsche's dual typology. While the modern subject remains weak and contradictory, a strong will, or *higher nature*, recognizes itself as 'a genuine battleground of these opposed values' (GM I 16) and innate psychologies which have grown together, and recognizes that it is imperative that 'a resolute incision' be performed *within itself* in order to isolate or separate them (CW E). This would constitute an act of supreme self-examination. Thus a strong will is resolved and coordinated under the 'ruling thought' of the task and goal of the revaluation of all values, or the coming of the *Übermensch*, for this is what this analytic self-examination and resolute incision prepares. In this sense, the strong will is the free spirit who establishes the principal value-antithesis between Christian, neo-Christian and noble, selecting and affirming the latter, the pagan values.

The radical liberal democratic reading, in ignoring the theme of strong will in the Nietzschean corpus, is led to ignore or exclude the theme of the new philosophers and commanders who will 'provide the stimuli for opposite valuations' (BGE 242), as well as the strong will in its most grandiose projection in that corpus, where it is *'one will'* in the form of a new ruling caste who preside over a new European political and economic union (BGE 208), an imperial idea of Napoleonic inspiration.

The radical liberal democratic reading defines the Nietzschean subject in a way that overemphasizes its irresolvability and depreciates its liberation. It reads the Nietzschean subject as a democratic subject, as an 'arena for an irresolvable contest of differing drives'. It is not an inaccurate description *per se*. The reading does reproduce something essential about the Nietzschean subject, but Nietzsche is somewhat more exacting in his description.

For Nietzsche, as with Plato, the body and psyche resembles a polity or, more specifically, an aristocratic political structure. It is described in terms of a multiplicity of drives in relations of command and obedience, as a 'struggle between cells', slavery and division of labour (WP 660 Nachlaß 1885–86 KSA 12 2[76]). Nietzsche does not ask how this multiplicity of drives should be organized or ordered politically. Rather, he merely asserts that it is ordered in terms of the joint rule of an 'aristocracy of equals', where a prevailing 'subject-unity' acts as 'regents' ruling a community organized according to order of rank (WP 492 Nachlaß 1885 KSA 11 40[42]). Thus the body (the internal *agon*) is represented by Nietzsche as a *tableau vivant* of the form of political organization he affirms. To be sure, it is a dynamic model. It reproduces conflict and fluctuating power, and the renewal or circulation of elites, the sovereign authority which trembles with tension, but it also reproduces an enduring and prevailing will, a will Nietzsche opposes to the wills of 'countless incomplete fragmentary men' (WP 997 Nachlaß 1884 KSA 11 27[16]), which possesses a *higher* duty and a *higher* responsibility.[48]

3. Perspectivism

The Nietzschean doctrine of perspectivism is the linchpin of the radical liberal democratic reading. For, according to this reading, it is through this doctrine that the 'most aristocratic of modern thinkers deconstructs himself repeatedly into the most democratic'.[49] What this doctrine claims, in terms of a theory of truth, is that all truth-claims are interpretations connected to specific human interests and practices. They neither correspond to nor can be grounded in any transcendent world or objective essences. It has as its consequences antifoundationalism, anti-dogmatism and a suspicion of unconditional authority.

For the radical liberal democratic reading, this antifoundational, perspectivist theory of truth can be converted into a political theory consonant with liberal democratic pluralism, a democratic ethos respectful of difference and 'otherness'. Thus it is viewed as consonant with liberal tolerance, even though Nietzsche rejects this (TI Expeditions 25) and the principle of the 'equal right to claim political authority'.[50] What it means in terms of both the *inner* and *outer* polity is that there can be no privileged perspective, no privileged self or political regime. Perspectivism represents or implies the refusal to grant sovereignty to any one perspective over another,[51] it undermines all hierarchies, including the very aristocratic and authoritarian regime Nietzsche endorses. It represents or implies 'a sensitivity to all types of life' and the 'openness to engage other viewpoints', without closure[52] and in the interests of a 'practice of perpetual self-transformation',[53] whether Nietzsche was aware of it or not.[54]

Nietzschean perspectivism, from an epistemological standpoint, constitutes a critique of the Cartesian *res cogitans* and Kantian *pure reason*, and of the idea of disinterested knowledge. As a methodological corrective to the latter idea, Nietzschean genealogy inquires after the particular active and interpreting forces which comprise any particular perspective, its will to power. It also implies a pluralistic conception of truth as is evident in the following excerpt from *On the Genealogy of Morals*: 'There is *only* a perspective seeing, *only* a perspective "knowing"; and the *more* affects we allow to speak about one thing, the *more* eyes, different eyes, we can use to observe one thing the more complete will our "concept" of this thing, our "objectivity" be' (GM III 12). This excerpt has been read by Alan Schrift, for example, to coincide with democratic optics[55] (the capacity to see from multiple subject positions and an ethics of empathy for those in positions of social subordination derived from the attunement to differences perspectivism basically implies).[56]

Each of our drives, our needs, our values, interprets; each has its own perspective which it would like to impose on the others as a norm. Each expresses a will to power. From an ontological standpoint, Nietzschean perspectivism categorically refers to the horizon, form of life or power-complex each specific body finds itself situated within. In keeping with the conflict theory he espouses, Nietzsche writes, 'every specific body strives to become master over all space and to extend its force . . . and to thrust back all that resists its extension. But it continually encounters similar efforts on the part of other bodies' (WP 636 Nachlaß 1888 KSA 13 14[186]). Where resistance is overcome – and this defines Nietzsche's concept of freedom – new perspectives develop and new horizons and agonistic conflicts open up. Genealogical critique reveals that all values evolve out of struggles for supremacy with other values. However, this does not mean, as the radical liberal democrat tends to see it, that there is no domination and only a perpetual struggle for domination, for the Dionysian universe does allow for the consolidation and will to durability of power-complexes and institutions.

The radical liberal democratic reading does not do absolute violence to Nietzsche's text in so far as Nietzsche's hypothesis of the will to power and his doctrine of perspectivism do imply the rejection of rational foundations and absolute standards. With respect to the former, what lies at the *origin* are human interests in conflict with other human interests, all of which merely seek to grow and expand. With respect to the latter, Nietzsche finds exemplary, for example, the morality of Greek and Roman antiquity because it stood opposed to the unconditional trust in authority. An authority, according to Nietzsche, must not be unwilling 'to let itself become the object of criticism' (D P 3). The conditional nature of its right to exist must be felt continually. In this respect, Nietzsche criticizes Christianity because, with its antinatural appeal to a transcendental origin, it refuses to see itself as merely *perspective*, and thus effectively places itself beyond any criticism. Nietzsche affirms the scepticism and suspicion of the free spirits, their *an-archic* repudiation of 'ultimate truth' (H 244), their necessary 'access to many and contradictory modes of thought' (H P 4), their call for a '*plurality of norms*' against one normal human type (GS 143), and expresses an 'aversion to reposing once and for all in any one total view of the world' (WP 470 Nachlaß 1885–86 KSA 12 2[155]).

But the key question is whether or not this epistemology and ontology of perspectivism and the suspicion it implies – the pluralistic conception of truth and the posited normativity of a continual *agon* between power-complexes – contradicts an authoritarian politics of hierarchy and domination. The radical liberal democratic reading says it does. It sees in the doctrine of perspectivism a major *aporia* and discontinuity within Nietzsche's thought which may be converted into a political theory consonant with liberal democratic pluralism.

As was stated above, Nietzsche opposes his hypothesis of the will to power to the democratic and modern *misarchism* (hatred of rule or government) which has expropriated all theory of life (GM II 12). That is the rationale which devolves into total war. As such, Nietzsche theorizes domination as an ontological necessity, as necessary to life. This means that all perspectives are grounded in the will to power, which Nietzsche calls the 'fundamental instinct of life' (GS 349) and the '*primordial fact* of all history' (BGE 259). It is a theory which not only describes, but justifies, political domination and exploitation. We know from Nietzsche that self-command means command over others, that the egoism of a noble soul communicates with the conviction that 'other beings must be subordinate by nature' (BGE 265). From the outset, then, *perspective* and *power* in the Nietzschean corpus are imbricated. Since 'life itself is *will to power*' (BGE 13) it must follow that all perspectives aim at 'the *expansion of power*'; their struggle, or *agon*, with other perspectives 'always revolves around superiority, around growth and expansion' (GS 349). But the self-overcoming of certain perspectives does not leave others untouched or unaffected, since life also operates as 'essentially ... overpowering of what is alien and weaker; suppression ... imposition of one's own forms, incorporation ... exploitation' (BGE 259). Will to power names each perspective, but it also describes the relational and agonistic plurality of perspectives (perspectivism) which form the 'continuous sign-chain of ever new interpretations and adaptations', describes the successive 'processes of subduing' and 'counteractions' (GM II 12), closure and resistance to closure.[57] Every perspective represents the attempt to master as well as the resistance to the attempt to master on the part of other perspectives. Thus every *power for* implies *power over*.

It is thus clear that Nietzsche conceives perspectivism (via the design of each perspective) as connected to domination and the will to dominate, and thus within the purview of his own radical aristocratic politics. When the post-Nietzschean liberal democratic reading recognizes this, as it sometimes does, then it emphasizes the process of the struggle for domination within the general, endless Dionysian process of creation and destruction. Then it argues that the authoritarian political regime Nietzsche endorses is undermined by his own ontology – by the 'groundless energies' of the will to power, by death and the emergence of new possibilities.[58] (In the Nietzschean sense, however, this would also mean new forms of domination.) But, as mentioned above, the new order Nietzsche anticipates is fully compatible with an affirmation of finitude and contingency. And ontological anarchy is fully compatible with the philosophers of the future, who are called '*attempters* [*Versucher*]' (BGE 42). The free spirits, the prototypical commanders, represent the counteraction, while the philosophers of the future represent the attempt to subdue and the project of mastery and recodification. They view their political activity as an experiment, but one in command and obedience.

I want now to address two propositions expressed in the radical liberal democratic reading by Hatab, and which are germane to the general discussion. The first is that because Nietzsche rejects universal law and refuses to posit an absolute source of authority, because the free spirits reject an ultimate truth and Nietzsche opposes convictions or dogmatism, he may be seen to contradict the authoritarian regime he endorses because 'Authoritarian regimes have never described themselves ... as arbitrary, but rather as securing some truth or virtue.'[59] Of course, the same can be said for democratic regimes, as can be confirmed by a cursory reading of the *Declaration of Independence* or *The Declaration of the Rights of Man*. But if we consider the authoritarian and totalitarian regimes of the twentieth century – the fascist regimes, for example – these were never grounded in a notion of universal law or *consensus iuris*; they never viewed their own source of authority as eternal or permanent.[60] Rather, like Nietzsche in *On the Genealogy of Morals*, they viewed legal conditions as 'exceptional conditions' (GM II 11), they did not view their law as 'absolutely just' but as 'subjective justice based upon the communal interest' or the interest of the state.[61] Thus Hatab's inference is problematic, and Nietzsche may still be considered consistently authoritarian even though he does not claim a guaranteed source of authority or, like Spengler, even though he does not promote eternal values and absolute truths.[62]

Hatab also claims that the creation of culture in the Nietzschean sense is 'ungrounded and open'.[63] Such a claim is inconsistent with Nietzsche's rejection of the Bismarckian *Kultur-Staat*, found in his reflections on education in *On the Future of Our Educational Institutions* (and, later, in *Twilight of the Idols*) which may be viewed as the starting-point or ground of Nietzsche's culture-creation. From the standpoint of an imagined Nietzschean social and political policy, Nietzsche's rejection of the *Kultur-Staat*, and his opposition to other policies implemented under the Bismarckian *Reich* (basically, liberal democratic concessions), would imply the delegitimization or nonrecognition of the validity of certain perspectives or social interests such as the democratization of education or the granting of voting rights to the German worker (universal suffrage).[64] The coming to power of the philosopher-legislators would mean a reversal in the political culture (concretely, the reversal of liberal democratic victories) and imply political exclusion and social control (although, ideally interiorized as *reverence for* or *belief in* the myth of the exemplary human type; its system grounded in a *law of nature*). It would undermine the very openness Hatab attributes to Nietzsche. To begin to understand the political basis of Nietzsche's cultural agenda and his project of cultural renewal it is imperative to situate him in the context of his period, for example, in relation to the *Kulturkampf* (1872–79), which was a campaign to reduce the power of the Roman Catholic Church over education and to ratify the rights of the state over religion in general (Nietzsche's own *'campaign against morality'*, which commences with *Daybreak*, can be viewed as its posthumous accomplice), or to the Jewish or labour question, or to the antisocialist laws (enacted in 1878 after the attempted assassination of William I) banning the Marxist SPD.[65] (Nietzsche can be seen as a collaborator of these laws in *Human, All Too Human*.)

Even though the counteractive free spirits reject ultimate truth, they still inquire after truth; and even though they are antidogmatic, they form their own dogma, the dogma of nature (a concept of 'natural right' and 'natural law'), will to power, order of rank, freedom for the few and the need of the masses or the multitude for a commander. When they oppose 'any ultimate wisdom, ultimate goodness' or 'ultimate power' (GS 285), it is to violate the 'central law of all morality: the hostility against the impulse to have an ideal or a virtue of one's *own*' (GS 143). This means, precisely, that they do not treat all perspectives equally, respective of their right to claim political authority; it means that some perspectives are sovereign over others.

In *The Gay Science*, Nietzsche ostensibly supports a *'plurality of norms'* (GS 143). Yet as his position develops, he conceives plurality or difference in the refined terms of order of rank, in hierarchical relations of command and obedience, dividing society into those who command and those who obey, promoting a *pathos of distance* between classes and types. Each class would be governed by fundamentally different moralities, with fundamentally different rights. Nietzsche posits plurality *against* equality. The human type Nietzsche considers *normal* is the human type who is considered *equal*. Committed to hierarchical distributions of power for his own project of enhancement, he ultimately reduces the plurality of forces to 'two basic types' and 'one basic difference' (BGE 260),[66] and moves towards a moral monopoly as to what is preferable, even, at times, expressing *ressentiment* towards Christianity.

Simply because Nietzsche acknowledges the existence of many moralities does not, of course, make him a moral pluralist.[67] Recall his letter to Deussen of 1888, where he states that with the revaluation of all values 'the realm of tolerance' is reduced.[68] There should be caution in reading Nietzsche's 'multiple and pluralist affirmation'. Again, the revaluation of all values, as opposed to the ascetic ideal, is predicated on the perspectivistic recognition of the general validity of other systems of value and openness to different practices and forms of society, but ultimately it accomplishes a mere reversal and reduction to a dual typology.

Nietzsche says that the counteractive free spirits have 'access to many and contradictory modes of thought' (H P 4). In the same vein, he says that the 'seekers after knowledge' have the capacity to employ a diversity of perspectives and interpretations (GM III 12). This rare capacity is considered a precondition to undertaking the revaluation of all values, and a necessary preparation to '*the problem of order of rank*' (H P 7), which is the quintessential problem of the free spirits. This conforms to what I said in the preceding section about the autonomous strong will. It is constituted by the rare capacity for self-mastery which involves the control of multiple passions and affects, a 'control over your For and Against . . . in accordance with your higher goal' (H P 6). This suggests that seeing with '*more* eyes, different eyes' and 'objectivity' is solely the ability or capacity of the higher, more spiritual type, of the free spirits, 'genuine philosophers' and commanders who have an 'unconstrained view', and not of the majority (the masses or the multitude) who have need of 'external regulation' (A 54). What Nietzsche affirms here is not democracy, but a perspectival art of governance (such as is found in Machiavelli's *The Prince*) the employment of a political technology which makes use of whatever perspectives are at hand to advance its radical aristocratic project. We may mark its steady conversion from those 'genuine philosophers' who are '*able* to see with many different eyes and consciences', which is a precondition for the creation of values (BGE 211), to the elaboration of a political technique which arms itself with the capacity (*virtù*) to employ diverse perspectives and interpretations, with a willingness to use (*immoralism*) whatever economic, religious and political states are current, guided by the strategic concept that new values will have to 'appear in association with the prevailing moral laws, in the guise of their terms and forms', and that in order for this to happen 'many transitional means of deception', or intelligent dissimulation, will have to be devised (WP 957 Nachlaß 1885 KSA 11 37[8]), all in the pursuit of social control, and more far-reaching social and political goals.

Self-mastery is such that it must remain sovereign over its 'For and Against', which implies that these need not be considered absolute or unconditional. The free spirits are not dependent on any rule or prejudice. They do not develop unconditional self-confidence in any commandments. Perspectives may be revised as circumstances call for it. Nietzsche is not opposed to having convictions *per se*; rather, he views convictions as a *means*, which is testimony to the inherently tactical (esoteric) or spectral-syncretic nature of his political thinking. (I discuss this further in Chapter 4.)

Perhaps the strongest point the radical liberal democratic reading makes for an *aporia* in Nietzsche's aristocratic, authoritarian politics concerns his suspicion of authority, the fact that he encourages criticism and opposes unconditional authority. Yet this may be seen to be compatible with his spiritual oligarchy or aristocracy in so far as it is conceived in terms of a joint rule of an aristocracy of equals who each hold the drive for tyranny in the others in critical check, and which periodically requires regeneration, similar to Pareto's 'circulation of elites', and in conformity with the intrasocial antagonisms Nietzsche's radical aristocratic polity is envisaged to maintain.[69]

This spiritual oligarchy or aristocracy is comprised of many noblemen 'and noblemen of many kinds', a plurality which is a precondition of the existence of nobility – 'that there are gods but no God'. They regard each other with a certain antagonism, but they are united in their opposition to ochlocracy, which is how they regard government by the people. Nietzsche's *'new nobility'* are conceived as many, but also constitute 'one will' in the interests of a social experiment in command and obedience, in express opposition to the idea of a democratic social contract (Z Law-Tables 11, 25). This is the point to which the 'numerous novel experiments' of *Daybreak* evolve (D 164).

Nietzsche's expression of an aversion to one total view of the world in a notebook entry from 1884 is essentially equivalent to his affirmation of perspectivism, which encourages an *agon* between power-complexes, and which in turn implies the instability of all horizons and resistance to closure because of the ontology of perpetual overcoming and the possibility of *'infinite interpretations'* (GS 374), among which are Nietzsche's own. But this ontology also implies potential construction and consolidation (hegemonic articulation) and its logic should not undermine Nietzsche's impetus to fight for his own place, to work to establish the political regime he prefers, nor his advocacy or *attempting* of a new project of social mastery, nor the experiment in command and obedience which aims to undermine or subvert the democratic social contract, its legal framework, and the 'weakness' at its basis.

4. Agonism

The radical liberal democratic reading tends to privilege the motifs of resistance and destruction in the Nietzschean corpus, and not the motifs of reconstruction or recodification, neither the revaluation of all values, nor the goals Nietzsche wishes to see accomplished. This is what Nietzschean agonism means to the radical liberal democratic reading: that it subverts Nietzsche's project of social mastery because it implies and affirms a principle of resistance in every social formation.

Agonism is a feature of Nietzsche's perspectivist ontology, which views perspectives or interpretations, individuals or collectives, states or power-complexes, in relations of perpetual conflict. Every such entity, in so far as it is will to power, strives to dominate but encounters resistance by other such entities. For Nietzsche, agonism is both an ontological generalization, a normative value and a socio-political ideal.

The radical liberal democratic reading sees in Nietzschean agonism an ontology of resistance and a politics of continual overcoming. It believes that this ontology, and Nietzsche's reverence for agonistic institutions, contradicts the motifs of domination in Nietzsche's political philosophy.[70] According to this reading, agonism represents enmity towards every form of order and organization, all totalization and closure. It inherently contests all claims to universality and hegemony.[71] Nietzschean agonism may be suitable to a democratic ethos because it represents respect for, and affirmation of, one's opponents, and because it implicity recognizes the contingency of all perspectives. Unlike fundamentalisms and the *ressentiment* of the ascetic ideal, it does not seek to eliminate them. It implies the 'virtue of toleration'[72] because it postulates the interdependence of all opposing forces such that 'each party comes to appreciate the extent to which its self-definition is bound up with the other'.[73] Thus it is seen to 'undermine Nietzsche's political authoritarianism'.[74]

This is how William Connolly, for example, reads Nietzsche's theme of the 'spiritualization of enmity' in *Twilight of the Idols* (TI Morality 3). In this respective aphorism, Connolly sees operative an 'agono-pluralistic ethic',[75] which is to say, an agono-*perspectivistic* ethic which denies absolute truth and theoretically prohibits the absolute rule of any one perspective. Because of this theoretical prohibition, David Owen, for example, believes that Nietzschean political agonism essentially 'models an understanding of citizens as free and equal'[76] in spite of Nietzsche's unequivocal rejection of the liberal democratic interpretation of these terms.

Bonnie Honig, for her part, reads Nietzschean agonism primarily through Nietzsche's essay, *Homer's Contest* (1871–72), which elucidates the Greek institution of the *agon* through the concept of 'ostracism'. As Nietzsche explains in this early essay, in order to maintain the perpetual contest of forces among, for example, politicians and party leaders, anyone who attempted to subvert the agonistic basis of the Greek state, who threatened to subvert the perpetual *agon* between cities and political parties, was ostracized. In this essay, Nietzsche stakes a claim for '*several* geniuses' over autocratic domination. Thus, in this context, Honig is correct to remark that, for Nietzsche, 'the ancient Greek practice of ostracism provides an institutional expression of [his] commitment to contest over closure by protecting the agon from domination by any one ... individual or hegemon'.[77] There is, however, a broken line between Nietzsche's agonistic conception in *Homer's Contest*, which is conceived with the institution of ostracism, and his agonistic conception in his later works, which is conceived without it. The difference being that in *Homer's Contest* he thinks of competition and contestation in a way that does not favour the development of autocracy, mediated by the institution of ostracism, while in his later works, he thinks of competition and contestation with domination and the lust to dominate, in a way that favours the development of autocracy and the manipulations which must accompany it. In the later Nietzsche, a commitment to the *agon* does not mean a commitment to freedom from dominance for all social actors, as Honig claims when she argues that Nietzsche's conception of law, articulated in *On the Genealogy of Morals*, is fully consistent with his conception of agonism as expressed in *Homer's Contest*. Nietzschean law, according to Honig, is conceived as 'stabilizing an ordered site of contest without dominating it'.[78]

Nietzschean agonism does generally affirm the value of resistance in every social formation, but, more specifically, affirms the value of overcoming resistance as a measure of power and freedom. Freedom, in the Nietzschean sense, can flourish only under agonistic conditions 'where the greatest resistance is constantly being overcome', and is measured 'by the effort it costs to stay *aloft*' (TI Expeditions 38). But freedom, as Nietzsche conceives it, 'is for the very few' (BGE 29); it does not belong to all as a right. The full benefit of freedom, in the Nietzschean sense, where freedom is the privilege of the few and not considered an inalienable right, can be appreciated only under agonistic conditions where order of rank, war and inequality prevail.

The Nietzschean individual requires opponents for a sense of its own self-identity, a difference comprehended entirely as opposition. Noble or aristocratic morality 'seeks its opposite only so as to affirm itself more gratefully' (GM I 10). The precondition of strength and growth for Nietzsche is an '*aggressive* pathos' which meets objects of resistance. Strong natures require the opposition of a worthy enemy, enemies 'that are our *equals*' (EH WW 7), which is to say, those who can resist those 'strong natures' with equal force, an equation that lays down the legitimacy of any potential overcoming.

Nietzsche's idea of the 'spiritualization of *enmity*' means precisely 'grasping the value of having enemies'. He sees this idea in contradistinction to the behaviour of the Christian Church which has always sought to destroy its enemies. Preserving opposition, war and contradiction is necessary for the 'immoralists and anti-Christians', who see that it is to their 'advantage that the Church exist'. They do not aim to destroy the Christian ideal but only to end, or overcome, its tyranny. For 'the continuance of the Christian ideal is one of the most desirable things there are'. The immoralists require that their enemies 'retain their strength', but at the same time they want 'to become *master over them*' (WP 361 Nachlaß 1887 KSA 12 10[117]), perhaps to make them an instrument of governance or for the purpose of external regulation, and which indicates that Nietzsche did not dismiss the use of the pious fraud (following Machiavelli, and thinking perhaps of Napoleon's *Concordat* of 1801 with the Church). But Nietzsche also sees the idea of the 'spiritualization of enmity' in the politics of his day, grasped by virtually all political parties, where the 'more spiritual' means the 'more prudent'. It is an idea he associates with *die große Politik*, the *Bismarckian Reich*, and with '*grand* life'. The general precept expressed by Nietzsche is that 'one remains *young* only on condition the soul . . . does not long for peace', for '*grand* life' is renounced 'when one renounces war' (TI Morality 3).

Agonism for Nietzsche is a sociopolitical ideal, but contrary to what Honig says in referring to Nietzschean law, it does imply domination (to dominate the site means to stabilize the antagonisms) and does not contravene Nietzsche's project of social mastery. Nietzschean law is unimpeded natural right (in the Hobbesian sense), at most limited by 'precepts of health' and 'voluntary discipline'. It should be understood that when Nietzsche presents his idea of the *agon*, it is most often formulated in opposition to a political site where the principle of equality prevails, in opposition to those specifically egalitarian legal orders 'which would aim to prevent all struggle between power-complexes' (GM II 11). Thus Nietzsche can say that there should be more war and inequality and reject the universal fraternity of the French Revolution, its anticipated future 'realm of justice and concord' (GS 377). Clearly, Nietzschean agonism does not model the citizenry as free and equal. Its conceptual basis entails the formation of an antagonistic hierarchical class organization.

What Nietzsche has in mind, rather, is controlled conflict and controlled enhancement (or breeding through education) against the decadent 'anarchy of atoms' of modernity (CW 7). His ideal is to stay aloft against the resistance (or force) of the Christian ideal and its neo-Christian secular manifestations. In effect, Nietzsche wants the institution of agonism without the institution of ostracism which would protect against authoritarianism. His interest is in social control and external regulation. Thus is domination inscribed – in the form of a regulated factionalism or controlled violence – in the Nietzschean *agon*, as duration and points of stabilization (laws, treaties, contracts, institutions) may be as well.

As was mentioned above, enhancement and continual overcoming require 'the ingrained difference between strata'. Self-command requires command over others. Nietzsche is of the opinion that the human type has 'grown most vigorously' under dangerous conditions, under 'prolonged pressure and constraint' where there is 'forcefulness' and 'slavery', for 'everything evil, terrible, tyrannical in man . . . serves the enhancement of the species' (BGE 44). And he wishes to see such conditions maintained and even cultivated. To claim that Nietzschean agonism models the citizenry as free and equal when he supports slavery and the necessity of 'masters and servants' is obviously untenable.

Nietzschean agonism is thought *along with* will to power, which says, in an anti-Marxist register, that life operates on the basis of exploitation, and *with* order of rank, which says that an order of rank is an order of power which presupposes 'war and danger' (WP 856 Nachlaß 1885–86 KSA 12 2[131]). It justifies natural class divisions against those who fight for equal rights (BGE 219). It does not imply a 'democratic contest of speeches', as Hatab claims,[79] as if the doctrine were a template for the electoral process, because Nietzsche rejects 'Parliamentarianism' (GS 174), but implies political exclusion and structural violence, just as the revaluation of all values reduces the realm of tolerance.

Nietzsche does not overtly advocate the use of force or violence as an agent of social transformation (other than in his early essays of 1871–72), and even condemns it, as is clear from his gradualist commentary against violent social revolution or insurrection in *Human, All Too Human*. Although in *Human, All Too Human* we also read that war is '*indispensable*' as a 'means to culture', and that it does refer to 'acts of wickedness' (H 477). But, overtly, Nietzsche views violence as an expression of a 'declining' will to power. As he writes in *The Gay Science*, the 'state in which we hurt others . . . is a sign that we are still lacking power' (GS 13). This is consistent with his rejection of the *Machtpolitik* ('blood and iron') policies of the Bismarckian *Reich* and with his concept of a 'war of spirits' (*Geisterkrieg*). To be sure, the revaluation of all values is a war 'without powder and smoke' (EH H 1), an ideological war. Yet Nietzsche continually makes more covert comments (which might enable a 'spiritual' or metaphorical reading) in favour of war, and some overtly in favour of military culture. For example, in *Human, All Too Human*, he suggests 'that life should retain its violent character and savage forces and energies . . . be called up again and again' (H 235); and in *The Gay Science*, he suggests that one ought to 'resist any ultimate peace', that one ought to 'will the eternal recurrence of war and peace' (GS 285). Still, what is to be made of Nietzsche's disparagement in 1887 of the advent of international courts in place of war (GM III 25)? In this context can the term 'war' be sensibly construed as metaphorical or spiritual? And what can Nietzsche mean when he says, advancing geopolitical doctrine, that he wishes to see 'an increase in the menace of Russia', such that Europe would 'resolve to become menacing too' as a prelude to the formation of 'a new caste that would rule Europe', which would ultimately promise the termination of 'Its many splinter states' and 'democratic splinter wills' (BGE 208)? The radical liberal democratic reading of Nietzsche never submits that Nietzschean agonism, the perpetual struggle between power-complexes, may imply physical killing or militarism, but it should at least admit the presence of a strong ambiguity in this regard in the Nietzschean corpus. Nietzsche does say that noble institutions forbid themselves 'the use of all the cruder instruments of force' (GS 358), but he also says that he is '*glad* about the military development of Europe' and, given the soldiers Borgia and Napoleon, sets his account of *virtù* in military institutions (WP 127 Nachlaß 1884 KSA 11 26[417]); elsewhere he expresses himself in favour of 'universal military service' (WP 126 Nachlaß 1887 KSA 12 9[165]).

In his early essays of 1871–72, the agonistic conception Nietzsche endorses does not exclude physical warfare, but wars of extermination (*bellum internecinum*). In *The Greek State*, which is written as a '*Paean* to war' in opposition to the tendency of liberalism to impede political factionalism and to make 'war itself the greatest improbability', the prevention of war – represented through the developing doctrines of equal rights, universal suffrage and the 'rights of man' – is interpreted by Nietzsche as an atrophy of the political sphere. This position is fully consistent with Nietzsche's critique of liberal institutions in *Twilight of the Idols* (1888) as deleterious to freedom. This is because liberal institutions suppress war and, for Nietzsche, 'war is a training in freedom'. In the passage in question, 'war' is opposed to the happiness and 'well-being dreamed of by shopkeepers . . . and other democrats'. The state of war is the state of freedom – danger, resistance, the effort to 'stay *aloft*' – and, metaphorical or sublimated readings aside, it does imply, that 'one has become more indifferent . . . even to life. That one is ready to sacrifice men to one's cause, oneself not excepted' (TI Expeditions 38).

Nietzsche approvingly cites fragment 53 of Heraclitus, '*War is the father of all good things*' (GS 92). Here it should be said, against the tenor of the radical liberal democratic interpretation, that Nietzschean agonism is basically compatible (taking into account the vacillations I referred to above) with the commitment to perpetual war or permanent confrontation characteristic of fascist ideology, as well as with its critique of the liberal (and Kantian) conception of the political as a site without conflict (beyond mere debating adversaries). In accordance with fascist ideology, Nietzsche reduces the social body to the Hobbesian *bellum omnium contra omnes*, transposes the Hobbesian state of nature into the concept of the political, and in this sense violates classical natural law. For Nietzsche, the state never really emerges from the state of nature, it attains only a provisional equilibrium, since conflict is at the basis of the social order (cf. *The Greek State*). The Nietzschean conception of agonism is formulated in terms of hostile confrontation and subordination and, as such, is closer to the agonistic conception articulated by Carl Schmitt.[80] In fact, as with fascist ideology, when Nietzsche disparages international courts in *On the Genealogy of Morals*, and as additional evidence indicates, he does so against the Kantian notion of perpetual peace among states (the end of all hostilities) and for the universalization of conflict. 'Life is a consequence of war,' he says, 'society itself a means to war' (WP 53 Nachlaß 1888 KSA 13 14[40]). The radical liberal democratic reading should demonstrate how Nietzschean agonism is more like democratic agonism (which affirms the normative value of competition, tension and conflict) and less like fascist agonism (which also affirms the normative value of competition, tension and conflict).

There is an indication in Nietzsche's final work that his reverence for agonistic institutions is notably diminished and turns to *ressentiment*. It appears now that he wishes to eliminate his opponents. Nietzsche has to recognize every other self, class, type or race as radically singular values in order for his 'war' to occur. In other words, individuals, classes, types, do not, according to Nietzsche, belong to 'humanity' in the democratic sense; they are not 'equal', but differentiated according to an order of rank. Nietzschean agonism presupposes a politics of identity. This means that the anti-Christian identity cannot be other than it is. This is because Christianity and all neo-Christian politics are finally 'irreconcilable with an ascending, Yes-saying life' (EH WD 4). In this sense, Nietzschean agonism moves towards Fundamentalism. In *Ecce Homo*, Nietzsche wants to destroy utterly the other when the demand (in the name of *physiology*) is made to excise the degenerating part. No longer does he advocate the sustained conflict between power-complexes, but 'the relentless destruction of everything . . . degenerating' (EH BT 4), for the 'physiologist . . . denies all solidarity with what degenerates' (EH D 2). The radical liberal democratic reading recognizes this tendency, but believes the alleged *aporia* may negate it.

5. Pity

The radical liberal democratic reading of Nietzsche does not address the question of the status of pity in the Nietzschean corpus. But Nietzsche's political rejection of the decadent religion and morality of pity, which represents an attack on the foundations of political democracy and socialism, is inextricably linked to his Dionysian philosophy of suffering, and demonstrates well the seamless continuity between his philosophy and his politics.

Nietzsche places significant value on suffering. It is a requirement of creativity (Z Blissful Islands). He calls Zarathustra the 'advocate of suffering' (Z Convalescent) and condemns those who would wish to abolish it (BGE 44). It is the 'discipline of suffering' that has produced all enhancements in culture (BGE 225). It virtually determines order of rank. It 'makes noble' (BGE 270).

Nietzsche identifies pity as a 'residuum' of Christianity. Of those in the pro-pity tradition, he criticizes Schopenhauer and John Stuart Mill. He also identifies the teaching of pity (and altruism) with the French Revolution (whose principles he rejects). Since that time, he writes, 'every socialist system' has based itself on the 'common ground' of this teaching of 'individual empathy and social feeling' (D 132). In this respect, Nietzsche criticizes 'pity with social "distress" with "society" and its sick and unfortunate members, with those addicted to vice and maimed from the start' as expressed by those 'rebellious slave strata who long for dominion, calling it "freedom" ' (BGE 225).

It is these 'slave strata' – anarchists, socialists and democrats – who view suffering and tragedy as an argument against life (GM II 7, EH WD 2). In doing so, they refuse to recognize the fundamental, Dionysian, tragic constitution of reality. Against these 'slaves of the democratic taste', who seek to establish a life of 'security, lack of danger' and 'comfort' through the doctrines of equal rights and 'sympathy for all that suffers' (BGE 44), who seek to 'defend life's disinherited' (A 7, 2), Nietzsche opposes a 'general economy of life', which would necessarily produce 'refuse and waste materials' (WP 40 Nachlaß 1888 KSA 13 14[75]), which would have the 'strength to *excrete*' (WP 50 Nachlaß 1888 KSA 13 16[53]). Such an economy would encourage suffering, sacrifice and selection. Of suffering Nietzsche writes, 'It really seems that we would rather have it higher and worse than ever. Well-being as you understand it – that is no goal, that seems to us an *end*' (BGE 225). In the vocabulary of this oppositional dynamic, Nietzsche enters into a *rapprochement* with Social Darwinism, although for Nietzsche, it should be remembered, those in power are not necessarily the *stronger*. Nietzsche would reject the Social Darwinist idea of inherent progress or increasing and higher levels of adaptation to society precisely where this progress would imply, as it did for Herbert Spencer, increasing cooperation, altruism and recognition of basic rights to liberty.[81] However, like the Social Darwinists who, for example, were opposed to providing welfare to the poor, Nietzsche presents exploitation, oppression and inequality as 'laws of nature',[82] profoundly committed to the Hobbesian *bellum*, which he early on associated with Darwin.

Nietzsche counts the *'overcoming* of pity . . . among the noble virtues' (EH WW 4). Politically, the rejection of pity means the rejection of Christian and democratic social justice ('communal feeling', 'love of one's neighbour'). Overcoming pity means cultivating social conditions of class conflict and inequality against the general welfare and universal security; that is the meaning of Dionysian excess translated into the sociopolitical realm.

Radical liberal democratic readers are not wrong to see in Nietzsche's critique of the ascetic ideal an attunement to the differences of other traditions, other cultures or 'tablets of good'. However, they are wrong in believing that this attunement to the other in Nietzsche is based on empathy, as Nietzsche rejects empathy as a negative social development from the French Revolution. It is difficult to view Nietzsche as an activist for those who suffer from unjust or inequitable distributions of power, goods and privileges, for those in positions of social subordination, particularly in so far as he regards the democratic demand for justice (the demand for equality), denouncing anarchist and Marxist positions against exploitation, as the reason for the 'decline of the entire social order' (A 62). Rather, his attunement to the differences of others is based on an oppositional politics of identity (typology). There are certain cultures or traditions, or aspects of certain cultures or traditions (pagan, classical, Roman, Renaissance), even oppressive ones, he simply respects and adulates. In general terms, Nietzsche articulates a philosophy of decolonization against Christian democratic hegemony which threatens to homogenize existing cultures or, as he expresses it, detach them from the conditions under which they have originated (BGE 242). If, as the radical liberal democratic readers say, Nietzsche were opposed to a politics of identity, the distinction he makes between 'peoples' and 'states' in *Thus Spoke Zarathustra* would not be intelligible (Z New Idol). In respect of this distinction, what Nietzsche's decentring of the subject implies is a renunciation of the universality of human values and an emphasis on historic (organic) communities. I think it is Fanon who is more consistently Nietzschean when he invokes Nietzsche in the context of anticolonial resistance.[83] But Nietzsche's search is for something typologically specific: '*remnants* of stronger generations, of typically untimely human beings' (CW SP).

In this chapter it has been my intention to render problematic the contemporary radical liberal democratic reading and appropriation of Nietzsche by demonstrating that there is no necessary discontinuity between his antifoundational philosophy and his aristocratic, authoritarian politics; that the Nietzschean subject and the Nietzschean themes of perspectivism and agonism, and the concomitant affirmation of plurality, resistance and finitude, may be seen to be consistent with his politics of hierarchy and domination. In my view, the contemporary radical liberal democratic reading of Nietzsche cannot effectively demonstrate the aporetic structure it claims resides in Nietzsche's thought, which is to say without exclusions (keeping in mind their concern about mutilating Nietzsche's text), and thus the attempt of this reading to appropriate Nietzsche for a radicalized liberal democratic political theory is profoundly compromised. Connolly, for example, sees 'agonistic reciprocity' in Nietzsche's call for *many* who are noble,[84] but fails to point out that for Nietzsche 'a *new nobility* [is] needed to oppose all mob-rule' (Z Law-Tables 11), which, for Nietzsche, means all anarchist, communist, socialist and democratic movements.

Without revisiting all the points made in this essay, it is clear that Nietzschean plurality is a plurality in hierarchical relations of command and obedience. Furthermore, although Nietzsche may affirm a force of resistance in every social formation, he also affirms durability, following Machiavelli, and points of stabilization, and specifically against liberal 'instincts' and liberal institutions.[85] In addition, perspectivism and agonism can hardly translate into equal respect and tolerance. Finally, like Aristotle and Machiavelli, Nietzsche would say that all regimes are corrupted by time; however, it is simplistic to claim that this principle of finitude or self-overcoming should undermine Nietzsche's authoritarian preferences.[86]

One of the flaws of the radical liberal democratic reading (perhaps with the exception of Warren) is that it does not seriously engage Nietzsche's relation to the Right in Europe from the French Revolution onwards, their similar rejection of abstraction, of systems and universalism, and their aspiration to the particular (historic and organic), nor does it appreciate the intellectual variants within fascism and protofascism, which leads it to caricature their political philosophies and to think it can easily perform liberal democratic conversions when the Nietzschean subject (anti-Christian, pan-European identity, typological palingenesis) and Nietzsche's doctrines of agonism (perpetual war) and perspectivism (spectral-syncretism or eclecticism) are entirely compatible with generic fascism. For the radical liberal democrat it is all so uncomplicated: 'the fascist is committed to the elimination of the very differences that make one's agonal partners possible',[87] which does not apply to Carl Schmitt's agonistic conception of 'friend and foe', nor to the agonistic conception of the authoritarian-anarch, Ernst Jünger,[88] and when a scholar of fascist political philosophy writes, 'fascist ultra-nationalism does not . . . necessarily involve . . . hatred directed against any particular group perceived as culturally or genetically different . . . does not necessarily lead to a call for other races to be persecuted *per se*'.[89]

It is obviously important to acknowledge intellectual variants within the political philosophy of fascism.[90] These variants exhibit a certain fluidity with respect to notions of nation or state (as in Gentile)[91] or race (as in Evola). All things considered, it cannot be maintained, as the radical democrat maintains, that 'Fascist agonism is tied to rigid identity categories'.[92] In Evola's work, *Pagan Imperialism*, the 'race' conception possesses a rhizomatic structure: Egyptian-Chaldaic, Etruscan, Hellenic, Persian, Syrian, Roman, Mithraic.[93]

The realization that Nietzschean 'identity' or 'strong will' is not substantial or enduring, or does not have a metaphysical foundation, does not negate its activity; nor does its finitude – the acknowledgement of temporal limitations as in Polybius – negate its shaping power or its will to power, its proposal for political organization. Nietzschean 'identity' requires cultural conditions only. It mobilizes according to certain principles and certain myths. The subject-position is anti-Christian and, positively, pan-European. It produces divisions and equivalences. 'Christianity . . . I force a war against it' (WP 200 Nachlaß 1887–88 KSA 12 10[191]). Its 'identity', or 'will', is constituted by a 'task' (*Aufgabe*) and as a symbolic unity (eternal return, typological palingenesis). 'The symbol of this struggle, inscribed in letters legible across all human history, is "Rome against Judea, Judea against Rome": – there has hitherto been no greater event than *this* struggle, *this* question, *this* deadly contradiction' (GM I 16). It performs an incision within political space to prevent a concentration of power in Christianity. And we are familiar with the kind of lineage of alliance Nietzsche draws from the Renaissance to Napoleon.

In the radical liberal democratic reading, the emphasis on the 'constantly changing play of forces that is continually becoming-*other*'[94] is really a piece of sophistry, especially inasmuch as it is not accompanied by any sense of historical demarcation, any analysis of time. Heidegger, for example, recognizes that 'will to power is the fluctuating nexus of preservation and enhancement of power'. He understands that this means that will to power fixates into complex forms or constructs of domination (*Herrschaftsgebilde*) which are, to be sure, finite in their 'positions and configurations', but which may, nevertheless, prevail for a long time.[95] Without some principle of temporal demarcation, or periodization, without an account of actual social formations ('nodal points' and 'concentrations of power'), the radical liberal democratic appeal to 'constant overcoming', it seems to me, is empty and blind.[96]

In Nietzsche, there are both strategies of subversion and strategies of reconstruction, and neither are implemented to generate ephemera. It may be said, listening to Laclau and Mouffe, that 'neither absolute fixity nor absolute non-fixity is possible', but that 'partial fixations' are possible, 'otherwise the very flow of differences would be impossible'.[97] In this sense, Nietzschean 'identity', or 'strong will' (*virtù*), would constitute a 'partial fixation' or a 'nodal point' which has organized itself antagonistically against an oppressor. It does not have to be a full presence, but can be thought of as a 'hegemonic articulation'.

If we follow certain critics of the radical liberal democratic reading,[98] and simply make use of Nietzsche's critique of democracy, then the result, in effect, is to arrest Nietzsche at a certain stage of his political philosophical development; namely, the stage at which he incorporates all the vocabulary of the aristocratic or conservative liberal critique (Burckhardt, Taine, even Mill). But Nietzsche emerges with a more radical solution, a Machiavellian militancy (rooted in a reading of *The Prince*), which seeks the authoritarian potential within democracy, similar to that of the founders of mass psychology and elite theory. This is where the account I provide will take us in the following chapters. Such an account has the advantage of unleashing perspectives, effectively quarantined by the radical liberal democratic reading, which may better describe our own political *topos*, and actual governance (political psychology, communications, biometrics, tactics etc.) – beyond 'Pensée nomade', but not beyond 'Societies of Control'.

3
Nietzsche and Aristocratic Liberalism

I sometimes think of [Taine] and Burckhardt as my only readers. We are at root all three committed to one another as three radical nihilists – although I myself still do not doubt that I shall find the way out and the hole through which one arrives at 'something'.

Letter to Erwin Rhode, 1887

The radical liberal democratic reading or deconstruction of Nietzsche's theory of the subject, perspectivism and agonism elicits from the Nietzschean corpus liberal individualism, pluralism and tolerance, libertarian opposition to inner and outer constraints, antistatism and antitotalitarianism, and aristocratic, elitist meritocracy, excellence or self-perfection. The radical liberal democratic readers recognize, correctly, that Nietzsche was antidemocratic, a critic of the democracy of his own period; but they also claim that he was a proponent of a democracy yet to come, that he recognized that democracy presented conditions that made genuine excellence possible. I will take up this latter point in Chapter 4. They see Nietzsche's criticism of democracy solely focused on the levelling effects of the egalitarian ideal, that the principle of equality levels society to the rank of its lowest members, and that in opposition to these effects Nietzsche advances liberal, libertarian and elitist values.[1] It is a valid perception to a certain extent; but Nietzsche's criticism of democracy exceeds the mere concern for its possible levelling effects because it assails the very foundations of democracy and democratic theory. Aside from the principle of equality, which undermines 'every increase in culture' (A 43), Nietzsche rejects outright the principle of the sovereignty of the people. He recovers the decisionistic and personalistic element in the concept of sovereignty lost with the theorists of the French Revolution. He is not a democratic or republican reformist. But in the process of this recovery, Nietzsche traverses and becomes complicit with a distinct strand of European liberalism, namely, aristocratic liberalism.

In this chapter I would like to consider Nietzsche's connection to the political critique of the so-called 'Aristocratic liberals', particularly, Alexis de Tocqueville (1805–59), Jacob Burckhardt (1818–97) and Hippolyte Taine (1828–93), the notion that Nietzsche can be categorized as a 'late-blooming' aristocratic (or conservative) liberal.[2] In the following text, I focus on his critique of the state, egalitarianism and individualism, how this critique is similar to, and saliently differs from, the aristocratic liberal critique. I will argue that Nietzsche assimilates all the vocabulary of the aristocratic liberal critique, that he is oriented towards similar issues around equality, the state and the individual, but that he radicalizes this critique in so far as he is an apologist for, and a proponent of, centralized rule (pan-European hegemony), an unconditional opponent of democratic equality and the proponent of an individualism (Renaissance-inspired) that entails hierarchy and domination, and is advanced in strict antiegalitarian terms. It should be noted that I do not take the aristocratic liberals I discuss as mirror-images, as there are nuances which divide them. My reading is selective, along the lines of ideal types, and locates only the profound strains which connect their critique to the Nietzschean one.

1. Excursus

Nietzsche, as his letter of 1887 cited in the epigraph above indicates, counted Taine and Burckhardt as his only readers and aligned himself with them, in a qualified sense, as a radical nihilist. For Nietzsche, radical nihilism represents a disavowal of any 'metaphysical world' (WP 12 Nachlaß 1887–88 KSA 13 11[99]), of any 'morality incarnate' (WP 3 Nachlaß 1887 KSA 12 10[192]), of any conception of goodness or justice in themselves, and of any notion of progress, which Nietzsche considers illusory. Radical nihilism is a philosophy of power which conceives values in relation to the power of those who posit them, in relation to interests, and never in the abstract. Values are understood 'only in the perspective of what tends to preserve certain types of human communities' (WP 789 Nachlaß 1885–86 KSA 12 2[206]). They are always involved with power. Thus it must be the case that Nietzsche found these ideas within the writings of both Taine and Burckhardt.

To Burckhardt, in 1886, Nietzsche writes, 'I know nobody who shares with me as many [premises] as you yourself . . .', expressing sympathy for Burckhardt's scepticism regarding humanization, or democratic human rights, as a condition for the advancement of culture and the 'enlargement of the human type'.[3] Nietzsche, who sat in on Burckhardt's lectures on culture, religion and the state at the University of Basel during the winter of 1870–71, does share many premises with Burckhardt (aside from the premises of radical nihilism) including the Lamarckian notion of the inheritance of acquired characteristics, the rejection of the Paris Commune of 1871, the idea of a necessary antagonism between culture and the state, that the state should be subordinate to culture – cultural elitism – that growth in culture occasionally requires the energies of evil, that culture is transmitted through great individuals, that the ends of culture should be the production of free and creative individuality, as well as the Machiavellian-inspired conception of the state as a work of art (*Der Staat als Kunstwerk*), that it possesses no intrinsic legitimacy, no moral basis, that it is the product of calculation and expediency, that it is not founded on a social contract but on acts of force, cunning and violence, taking their cue from the Italian petty tyrants.[4] Burckhardt differs from Nietzsche, for example, in his rejection of militarism, about which Nietzsche equivocated, and in his idea that 'power is in itself evil', although Nietzsche agrees with this in *Daybreak*, but not after, where he writes that 'the love of power is the demon of men' (D 262) and refers to the 'fanaticism of the *lust for power (Machtgelüst)*' (D 204).

With respect to Taine, Nietzsche read the first two parts of *The Origins of Contemporary France* (1875–92) on the *ancien régime* and the Revolution in 1878 or 1879, but not the third part on the modern regime.[5] He did, however, read Taine's articles on Napoleon which appeared in *Revue des deux mondes* in February and March of 1887, which form a part of the modern regime.[6] Nietzsche would have been sympathetic towards Taine's idea of the need for authority and an order of rank in society, towards his discourse on the atavism of instincts, his high estimation of psychology, his deterministic and naturalistic outlook, his theory of 'race' over Enlightenment universalism, his description of the masses in the French Revolution (their psychology of *ressentiment*) and his general attack on the abstract axioms of Rousseau's *Social Contract* (1762), such as the doctrine of the goodness of human nature.[7] He would also have agreed with Taine's view, although Taine is ultimately critical of Napoleon, that Napoleon was a representative and 'continuator' of the Renaissance (GS 362).

In a letter to Franz Overbeck from 1887, Nietzsche not only refers to himself as a student of the thought of Taine, but also of de Tocqueville.[8]

What Burckhardt, Taine and de Tocqueville share, as aristocratic liberals, is a critique of the results of the Enlightenment and French Revolution of 1789: the abolition of privilege, the rejection of tradition and authority, the affirmation of rationalist and ahistorical values, the cosmopolitan ideal, the sovereignty of the people, the principle of equality, and the dominance of the press and public opinion (the emergence of public opinion as a political force). For the aristocratic liberals, the principal trends developing from the Enlightenment and the French Revolution are the increasing centralization and expansion of state power, and concomitant social atomization or 'individualism', and the 'despotism' or 'tyranny of the majority'. They are critics of democracy and the Jacobin heritage of democratic radicalism. Their pre-eminent concern is with how the principle of equality may suppress individual freedom and diversity, in so far as equality implies a normative uniformity which further implies the expansion of governmental control. De Tocqueville, for his part, in *Democracy in America* (1835), 'sought to expose the perils with which equality threatens human freedom'.[9]

The aristocratic liberals, however, are not unconditional opponents of democracy or egalitarianism, but reject it in the form of universal suffrage (de Tocqueville is ambivalent but not adamant on this point). This translates into an antimajoritarian antipathy for the expanding powers of the labouring masses and the middle classes in the democratic state which, furthermore, conveys a rejection of the values they associate with these classes: the commercial spirit and the drive for material comfort and well-being, as well as mediocrity and conformity in opinion and practice. Their principal adversaries, however, are the working classes and the socialists who defend them.[10]

Nietzsche continues, from his essay on the *Greek State* (1871), the aristocratic liberal critique of the social and political tendencies inherited from the Enlightenment and the French Revolution. Like de Tocqueville, Nietzsche views the French Revolution as the 'continuation of Christianity' (WP 94 Nachlaß 1884 KSA 11 25[178]) transferred through the doctrines of equality, pity and the abstract conception of the person or universality. In *Daybreak*, Nietzsche associates the French Revolution with the transmission of the doctrine of 'individual empathy and social feeling' or pity (D 132). In *The Gay Science*, Nietzsche cynically refers to the French Revolution as having 'aimed at the "brotherhood of nations" and a blooming universal exchange of hearts' (GS 362). It 'placed the sceptre in the hands of "the good human being" '(GS 350). The French Revolution represents the rise of the lower and middle classes whom Nietzsche, in the element of class warfare, refers to as 'the lower kind of spirit and body' (WP 60 Nachlaß 1885 KSA 11 34[43]). It 'destroyed the instinct for a grand organization of society'; it levelled a society constructed upon special claims and privileges, and *order of rank* (WP 90 Nachlaß 1888 KSA 13 15[8]); 'its instincts are against caste, against the noble, against the last privileges' (WP 184 Nachlaß 1888 KSA 13 14[223]). The French Revolution was 'the last great slave rebellion' (BGE 46) – in this remark, the conflation of 'type' with socioeconomic 'class', usually denied to exist in Nietzsche, is plainly evident. Nietzsche is also an enemy of the system of universal suffrage 'through which the lowest natures prescribe themselves as laws for the higher' (WP 862 Nachlaß 1884 KSA 11 25[211]). When Nietzsche, in a notebook entry from 1884, declares that a war on the masses is required, a component of the revaluation of all values, he specifically targets the pervasive social tendency which is working in favour of universal suffrage (WP 861 Nachlaß 1884 KSA 11 25[174]).

2. The state

Nietzsche is generally thought to be antistatist, against all states and accumulations of state power which oppress the individual. However, this is not the case. Rather, he is opposed to the modern democratic (or socialist) centralized state 'dominating and determining culture'.[11] According to Burckhardt, as he contends in his lectures from 1870–71, the 'first *perfected* example of the modern State with supreme coercive power exercised on nearly all branches of culture' is found in the *ancien régime*, 'in the France of Louis XIV'.[12] The democratic republic which follows merely perpetuates the despotism of the *ancien régime* in so far as it furthers the centralization and expansion of the state, as de Tocqueville also argued in *The Old Régime and the French Revolution* (1856).

For Burckhardt, the character of the modern democratic state is coercive power and control of the individual, imperialism, capitalism, the dominance of the press and the military, the degradation of political leadership, as well as nationalism and the 'equalization of rights'.[13] Burckhardt sees the modern democratic and nationalistic state tending towards despotism through the increasing political participation of the masses and their increasing demands for equal rights in the realms, for example, of education and employment.[14] The masses are the 'wage-earners', the 'progressive element' who strive for a 'universal State' which, if achieved, would mean, according to Burckhardt, the end of all liberty and 'initiative'.[15] Burckhardt sees the democratic programme tending towards economic socialism and the welfare state, and a general culture dominated by the rights of the majority. And from this 'despotism of the masses', he anticipates 'a future tyranny which will mean the end of history'.[16]

Burckhardt's political thought concentrates on the tension or antagonism between the state and culture which, in his terms, means primarily the tension between the expansive and centralizing democratic, egalitarian and majoritarian state and individual freedom. For Burckhardt, individual freedom – conceived as intellectual freedom and cultivation, and religious tolerance, for example, along classical liberal, elitist and humanist lines – is the necessary condition for culture. The state and culture so defined, however, cannot be reconciled, which means that the democratic participation of the masses cannot be reconciled with individual freedom but can only inhibit it.[17] Ultimately, Burckhardt argues for the decentralization of state power and the maintenance or development of independent small states.[18]

Given the general nature in much of the secondary literature of the commentary on Nietzsche's antistatist attitude, it is important to emphasize that Nietzsche, even though he may occasionally speak from the general standpoint of the interests of the individual against the state and against the background of a general proposition that what is 'great in the cultural sense' has been '*anti-political*' (TI Germans 4), when he criticizes the state has particular state formations or forms of government in mind.

From his inaugural lectures at the University of Basel (1872) to *Twilight of the Idols* (1888), Nietzsche establishes himself, like Burckhardt, as an elitist opponent of the Bismarckian *Kultur-Staat* and 'the democratism of "culture" made "universal" and *common*', which he sees as its consequence. It is this 'democratism of culture' which has, at least partially, according to Nietzsche, caused the general decline of German culture.[19] All higher culture and education should be a privilege of the exceptional few (TI Germans 5), as there is a natural hierarchy in the realm of the intellect. When Nietzsche says that culture and the state are antagonists, as Burckhardt does, he does so in a context in which he specifically condemns the cultural state as an error (TI Germans 4). And when he calls himself antipolitical, as he does in *Ecce Homo*, he does so in a context in which he distinguishes himself as 'more German' than 'mere citizens of the German *Reich*' (EH WW 3) which, as he says elsewhere, is established on the 'threadbare'; and decadent ideas of 'equal rights and universal suffrage' (WP 748 Nachlaß 1887–88 KSA 13 11[235]). When Nietzsche says he is anti-political, he means he is anti-statist and pro-cultural, but he may also mean, more specifically, that he is antisocialist and antidemocratic in conformity with a convention in German conservative political philosophy. He does not mean he is apolitical.[20]

In Nietzsche's inaugural lectures at the University of Basel, and in the *Untimely Meditations* and notes from this period (1872–74), Nietzsche deprecates, more than once, the 'adoration' or 'apotheosis' of the modern nation state, which he correctly sees as a tendency of the Hegelian philosophy, critically noting the appropriation of this philosophy by the Prussian state in particular. Against this philosophy, Nietzsche asserts that the state should be subordinate to culture. By 'culture' Nietzsche means the production of exemplary human beings to whom belong a certain sense of freedom and creative individuality (value creation) or 'genius'. Nietzsche never says that the state should be abolished; rather, he says that it should provide 'the basis for a *culture*'. Its purpose should be 'a nobler form of humanity' and it should regard itself only as a '*means*' to this end (Nachlaß 1873–74 KSA 7 30[8]). Nietzsche's ideal of governance is radically aristocratic, and every 'healthy aristocracy', according to Nietzsche, views itself as 'the *meaning* and highest justification' of the state and not as its function (BGE 258). The state should not regard itself as 'the highest goal of mankind' (UM III 4). What it must work towards is the production and 'protection of a few individuals in whom humanity will culminate'; this means that it should not subordinate itself to the 'egoism of the masses' (Nachlaß 1873 KSA 7 29[73]) or submit to public opinion.[21]

Likewise in *Human, All Too Human*, Nietzsche does not call for the abolition of the state but rather criticizes, and calls for resistance to, dangerous and excessive 'accumulations of state power', the perfection and completion of the state which would 'enfeeble' and 'dissolve' the individual, and decisively ruin the necessary conditions for the production of 'great intellect' or 'genius' which he sees in the programme of the socialist ideal of the 'perfect state' (H 235). The socialist ideal, according to Nietzsche, is despotic and of a totalitarian character in so far as it intends to transform the individual into 'a useful *organ of the community*', and in so far as it requires the 'complete subservience of the citizen to the absolute state'. In opposition to this ideal, as a counterpoise, Nietzsche, at this stage (1878–80), with Bismarck's antisocialist laws in effect, campaigns for '*as little state as possible*' (H 473).

Like the aristocratic liberals, Nietzsche regards the democratization of society as an inevitable, irreversible process, 'for *all* parties are nowadays obliged to flatter the "people" and to bestow on it . . . liberties of every kind through which it will in the end become omnipotent' (WS

292). However, unlike the aristocratic liberals, at least in *Human, All Too Human*, Nietzsche regards modern democracy not as furthering the centralization and expansion of the state but as 'the historical form of the *decay of the state*'. In *Human, All Too Human*, Nietzsche says that the democratic conception of the state, of popular sovereignty, leads 'to distrust of all government', diminishes respect for law, discourages the execution of social projects which require 'decades or centuries' to nurture, and liberates not the *individual* but the 'private person'. All these features of the democratic state will ultimately further 'the decline and *death of the state*'. But Nietzsche does not wholly welcome this '*decay*' (although he favours it over socialist accumulations of state power). He concludes, rather, that the existence of the state (he does not say which one, although, in context, he appears to have sympathies for Bonapartist legitimation) should be preserved and the 'destructive experiments', which would lead to its '*death*', resisted (H 472).

Another aspect of socialism and the socialist ideal which Nietzsche criticizes – he also rejects, at various points, its doctrine of the abolition of private property and its terroristic methods – is the value it places on well-being, material comfort and happiness, its 'desire to create a comfortable life for as many as possible' (H 235). This aspect of the socialist ideal is also shared by anarchists and democrats and all the 'slaves of the democratic taste', as Nietzsche writes in *Beyond Good and Evil* (BGE 44). In other words, once Nietzsche has made a distinction between the consequences of the socialist and democratic conceptions of state, as he does in *Human, All Too Human*, one representing its completion, the other its decay, the two terms tend to merge in the Nietzschean corpus, along a chain of equivalence, encompassing in general the ideals of democratic culture and the principles of the French Revolution – popular sovereignty, equality, pity and social empathy, as well as the drive for comfort and universal security – as is clear, for example, from his interpretation of socialist systems in *Daybreak* (D 132); property rights remaining the variable. When Nietzsche criticizes 'state idolaters', it is always to criticize those whose programme it is to institute 'measures for making life better and safer', socialists and democrats who wish to establish 'Chinese conditions' in Europe (GS 24).[22] Nietzsche is consistently opposed, in accordance with his agonistic conception, to those whose objective is 'common security', the crux of Hobbesian political philosophy, who would, through this objective, obliterate 'all the sharp edges of life' (D 174, 179). He shares this perspective with Taine, who criticizes the 'Englishman's' (the democrat's) 'private comfort and public security'.[23]

In *Thus Spoke Zarathustra*, in his frequently quoted and construed as generally antistatist, as if anarchist, passage on the state as the 'new idol', Nietzsche's specific target is the modern democratic state, the state that says, '*I, the state, am the people*'.[24] In this passage, Nietzsche singles out for criticism – he does not cite its *decay* as he does in *Human, All Too Human*, but rather its cold monstrosity – some of the characteristics of the modern democratic state criticized by Burckhardt in his lectures of 1870–71: the centralization of power ('I, the regulating finger of God'), imperialism (the assimilation of 'peoples'), capitalism (money as the 'lever of power') and the dominance of the press ('newspapers'). Thus it should be understood that when Nietzsche says where the state '*ceases*' in this passage, he means it is where *this* state '*ceases*' that one may find 'the bridges' to the *Übermensch*. Not just *any* state, but the state formation or form of government founded on the sovereignty of the people (Z New Idol), the state which protects the rights of the majority, which institutionalizes popular power. And this indicates that the *Übermensch* is not an abstraction, but conditional on such material transformations, and further points to the political, revolutionary component in the revaluation of all values.

As is well known, Nietzsche is also a relentless adversary of nationalism promoted by the liberals of his day. Why he is an adversary of nationalism is expressed through his opposition to the anti-Napoleonic German Wars of Liberation (1813–15), which gave birth to German nationalism and represented an attempt to reestablish the Holy Roman Empire (its major agitators, Johann Fichte and Friedrich Schleiermacher, advocated state patriotism but this was their principal aim). In Nietzsche's opinion, the German Wars of Liberation forestalled the development of a European union, the federation Napoleon had wished to establish.

In general terms, Nietzsche is a supporter of an anti-Enlightenment and antidemocratic cosmopolitanism or internationalism which would maintain an order of rank, as opposed to a principle of universality, between nations with Europe at the centre. During the period of *The Birth of Tragedy* (1872) however, under the influence of German Romanticism and the Wagnerian culture of Bayreuth, Nietzsche expressed a nationalistic aspiration for the renewal of culture and politics in Germany, but soon became disillusioned with the prospect, probably because of the anti-Semitism within the Wagner circle. Subsequently, Nietzsche cultivates an antinationalist (and anti-German) position and proclaims himself a *good European*. The ideal of the good European is the 'amalgamation of nations' (H 475) and the 'mutual blending and fertilization' of cultures (WP 748 Nachlaß 1887–88 KSA 13 11[235]). It is distinctly antiracist and, at times, pro-Jewish and pro-Russian, as these groups are viewed as indispensable elements in the governance of the European union Nietzsche foresees and advocates.

For Nietzsche, nationalism is racist and *'anti-cultural'*. When he censures nationalism as *'petty* politics' (EH CW 2), it is to criticize the 'separatist policies' (BGE 256) which encourage the European nations 'to delimit and barricade themselves against each other' (GS 377). This represents a reversal of Nietzsche's position in *The Greek State* where he reproaches liberalism's obstruction of political separatism. The social and political forces behind nationalism, as Nietzsche identifies them, are 'dynastic and democratic' (BGE 208). In opposition to this European system of a multitude of 'petty states', Nietzsche advocates, as a *good European*, the political and economic union of Europe. In any event, this is the *'synthesis'* towards which Europe is inevitably moving, for it *'wants to become one'* (BGE 256). This position does not contradict Nietzsche's agonistic doctrine, it merely represents an imaginary redistribution of geopolitical forces.

It is at this juncture that Nietzsche extricates himself from the aristocratic liberal critique of the state and its preference for the decentralization of state power. The aristocratic liberals reject all forms of centralized state power, whether in the form of the *ancien régime*, the Republic or otherwise. It is instructive to invoke the analysis of Burckhardt here in order to see the contrast. Burckhardt, without going into intricate detail, saw democracy eventually developing towards military despotism. He based this prediction on the pattern of the French Revolution, the logic which led from Rousseau to Napoleon, namely, the popular assault on authority and the Napoleonic Caesarism or autocracy which curtailed it.[25] Napoleon, who concentrated all administrative power in his hands,[26] demonstrated to Burckhardt the susceptibility of the democratic programme to despotism which he rejected.

Nietzsche, conversely, submits that the only justification for the French Revolution was that it made Napoleon possible (WP 877 Nachlaß 1887 KSA 12 10[31]). Nietzsche admires Napoleon, not only for his personality or character, which he both praises and castigates,[27] but also for his political policies and tactics or political techniques. Strictly speaking, it is an error to interpret Nietzsche, even though he contributes to its historiography, as continuing the Napoleonic cult of personality or genius. In fact, he criticizes it, associating it with Thomas Carlyle (D 298). Just as there is 'concrete political meaning', as Lukács says, in Goethe's and Hegel's attachment to

Napoleon,[28] there is 'concrete political meaning' in Nietzsche's attachment to Napoleon as well.

Napoleon represents 'the problem of the *noble ideal as such* made flesh' (GM I 16). He is an 'enemy' of 'modern ideas', which is code in the Nietzschean corpus for French revolutionary principles, and a 'continuator' of the Renaissance, as Taine remarked in his essays on Napoleon in the *Revue des deux mondes*. Unlike Hegel, Nietzsche does not see Napoleon as a purveyor of liberal democratic values, does not link him with the political heritage of the French Revolution, does not see him as a conduit of Jacobin ideology. Rather, for Nietzsche, Napoleon represents the 'rapturous counterslogan' of the 'supreme rights of the few' against 'the mendacious slogan of *ressentiment*', the 'supreme rights of the majority' (GM I 16).

Nietzsche is entirely aware of Napoleon's despotic methods. Unlike Chateaubriand, Nietzsche is not disgusted by Napoleon's manipulation of the Church (the *Concordat* of 1801) in spite of his contempt for Christianity. Napoleon's esoteric approach to politics or to democracy, whether in his plans for the Foreign Missionary Society of Paris or in his use of the plebiscite, prefigures Nietzsche's own which I will discuss in Chapter 4. Nietzsche's model of governance is Bonapartist in conception: autocratic will in the guise of popular rule. Bonaparte is the model for the Nietzschean commander; not only his *virtù*, his ethics of martial valour, but his political institutions and techniques of power. Nietzsche understands well that Napoleon manipulated the democratic process, the electoral system, that he abandoned the concept of popular sovereignty and undermined the principle of equality (through the formation of an imperial nobility), that he was opposed to Parliament and party politics but maintained their simulacra, a manoeuvre Nietzsche admires in respect of tactics. There are strong points of convergence between the Bonapartist and Nietzschean orders: the privileging of executive power, the 'new nobility', technocratic rule, the myth of the general will. But most visibly, Nietzsche embraces Napoleon because he wanted 'to create a unity out of Europe, a political and *economic* unity for the sake of a world government' (EH CW 2). In other words, because Napoleon was a *good European*.

So Nietzsche, unlike Burckhardt and Taine, does not object to Napoleonic Caesarism or autocracy as such, nor to the centralization or concentration of administrative power it represented. As his plan for political organization is developed, Nietzsche's radical aristocratic philosopher-legislators are situated above the state and rule society and culture indirectly through its subordinate mediation; they employ political leaders as their instruments. As envisaged in *The Anti-Christ(ian)*, Nietzsche's ideal radical aristocratic regime includes a political authority exercised through a state apparatus; an executive branch and 'guardians of the law' who maintain 'order and security', though Nietzsche articulates almost nothing specific about state policy (A 57); it remains a formalistic construct. Nietzsche is not opposed to a 'grand organization of society', with all the trappings of legitimacy, which, in his view, necessitates social hierarchy and inequality of conditions. He is inspired by the Hindu law of Manu, incorporating Platonic modifications and Machiavellian precepts. His preferred model of government is a highly centralized model in which individuals are conceived as instruments of the dominant ideology of cultural production, their functions precisely delimited and coordinated. Nietzsche reproduces in his ideal radical aristocratic regime, in terms of its practical coordination of individuals, a structural feature of the despotic socialist state he so reviles in *Human, All Too Human* and *Daybreak*. His ideal regime conceives the regulation-exclusion of the majority of individuals – a legitimation of their own dispossession – justified, variously, through a discourse on instincts, nature or will to power. He has no objection to new forms or sedimentations of slavery or subjection.[29]

As early as *Human, All Too Human* (1878–80), Nietzsche says that the 'great task' of the 'good Europeans' will be 'the direction and supervision of the total culture of the earth' (WS 87). In *Beyond Good and Evil*, he states that the solution to the 'European problem' lies in 'the cultivation of a new caste that will rule Europe' (BGE 251). Both formulations valorize centralized rule; both of them clearly imperialistic.

Both Burckhardt and Nietzsche subscribe to the view that the state possesses no intrinsic legitimacy, no intrinsic moral basis. But unlike Burckhardt, who considered the thought with anxiety, Nietzsche seems to relish the implication that the state may become an instrument of the will to power for whomever has the strength to seize its control (kratocracy).[30] In fact, Nietzsche imagines his ideal 'new aristocracy' of philosopher-legislators and commanders at the *end* of the process of the democratization of Europe, as the inheritors of a future Europe, who 'employ democratic Europe as their most pliant and supple instrument for getting hold of the destinies of the earth' (WP 960 Nachlaß 1885–86 KSA 12 2[57], WP 132 Nachlaß 1885 KSA 11 35[9]).[31] Such is Nietzsche's vision of *die große Politik*, which seeks the authoritarian potential within democracy (as I stated, the governmental prototype or precursor is Bonapartist autocratic will in the guise of popular rule)[32] and which situates the task of the revaluation of all values in the context of the theme of anticipated wars for the dominion of the earth (BGE 208), a scenario made popular by Napoleon Bonaparte.[33]

3. Egalitarianism

In *Democracy in America*, de Tocqueville's intention was to expose the dangers with which equality threatens human freedom. For de Tocqueville, the dangerous tendency of the increasing demand for equality of conditions is that it could result in a 'despotism' or 'tyranny of the majority', a concentration or centralization of power whereby the individual would be subordinated to 'the general will of the greatest number' to such an extent that his liberty would be impeded or suppressed.[34]

But the aristocratic liberals do not unconditionally oppose equality – for de Tocqueville, who is ultimately a discerning supporter of democratic institutions and political democracy, equality may lead to freedom[35] – but do reject it in the form of universal suffrage which would imply strict majoritarian rule (again, this point should be qualified with respect to de Tocqueville). This rejection of universal suffrage translates into an attack on the working class, the collective electoral power placed within their grasp, and on 'proletarian taste and culture' in general.[36]

Nietzsche is also an enemy of universal suffrage and the democratic advancement of the European worker who, in his opinion, should have no right to vote, just as he is opposed to the emancipation of women. But since the German *Reich* is founded on equal rights and universal suffrage (WP 748 Nachlaß 1887–88 KSA 13 11[235]), since it already 'accords all equal rights' (EH CW 1), in the aftermath of the 1848 revolutions, Nietzsche's reflection is not on the dangerous tendencies which may accompany the increasing political participation of the masses and their increasing demands for equality, as those dangerous tendencies have already been realized. As Nietzsche writes in *Thus Spoke Zarathustra*, this 'present . . . belongs to the mob' (Z Higher Man 19). It is dominated by the utilitarian (Benthamite) and majoritarian principle of 'the happiness of the greatest number', which represents the 'greatest danger to the noble type' and to the advent of the *Übermensch* (Z Higher Man 3). It is because the majority have been victorious that Nietzsche conceives as a primary role for his *new nobility* a concerted reprisal against 'all mob-rule and all despotism' (Z Law-Tables 11). This reprisal, at base, means reestablishing, in opposition to universal suffrage and equality of rights, *order of rank*, which 'formulates the supreme law of life' against which all 'modern ideas' (read principles of the French Revolution) are impotent (A 57). It is continuous with Nietzsche's earlier conception of the *oligarchs of the spirit* whose role is to oppose any attempt 'to erect a tyranny with the aid of the masses' (H 261). Recall, too, that the revaluation of all values is aimed at the 'nonsense of the greatest number', that it represents a counterattack against the 'animalization of man into the dwarf animal of equal rights and claims' (BGE 203). The revaluation of all values has a definite political dimension.

Nietzsche, as de Tocqueville and Burckhardt would agree, considers the Christian concept of 'equality of all souls before God' as 'the prototype of all theories of equal rights' (WP 765 Nachlaß 1888 KSA 13 15[30]). In this sense, the French Revolution represents a continuation of Christianity. The Christian 'always lives and struggles for *"equal rights"* ' (A 46). The Christian God is 'the God of the "great majority" and the democrat among gods' (A 17). Nietzsche makes this connection clear in *The Anti-Christ(ian)* where he writes, 'this falsehood, this *pretext* for the *racune* of all the base-minded, this explosive concept which finally became revolution, modern idea and the principle of the decline of the entire social order – is *Christian* dynamite' (A 62).

Two points should be immediately understood here. First, any treatment of Nietzsche's critique of Christianity, if it is to be sound, must include reflection on the relation between Christian morality and modern politics, for Nietzsche himself does not underestimate the connection. Second, Nietzsche's *new nobility* should not be conceived as something entirely distinct from the aristocratic societies of the past; it must necessarily preserve some of their features, such as caste and privilege. Otherwise, Nietzsche's critique of the French Revolution and his reference to the ensuing 'decline of the entire social order' would not be intelligible. Nietzsche's aristocratic radicalism is inspired by certain past aristocratic social orders, for example, 'of the pattern of Rome or Venice' (TI Expeditions 43) or of the 'French seventeenth and eighteenth century' (GM I 16). At the very least, Nietzsche is committed to *aristocratic* inequality of conditions which is evident when he contrasts 'equality' with 'noble' or 'aristocratic', for example, when he writes that the principle of equality is the 'most malicious outrage on *noble* mankind ever committed', or when he says that the 'aristocratic outlook has been undermined most deeply by the lie of the equality of souls' (A 43).

Nietzsche's critique of democratic culture assumes all the vocabulary of the aristocratic liberal critique, but his rejection of the democratic claim to equality is unconditional. Nietzsche sees absolutely no corrective to the *décadence* of democratic culture in democratic institutions themselves, as did de Tocqueville, for example, but completely disconnects the concept of democratic equality from the concepts of freedom and justice.[37]

Assuming aristocratic liberal analysis, Nietzsche asserts that the 'slaves of the democratic taste' are *'levellers'*[38] whose principal and decadent goal is security, comfort and well-being (BGE 44).[39] The 'democratic movement', Nietzsche writes, 'is not only a form of the decay of political organization but a form of the decay . . . of man, making him mediocre and lowering his value' (BGE 203). This levelling and homogenization, in Nietzsche's assessment, 'constitutes *our* greatest danger' (GM I 12).[40] Other points of the aristocratic liberal analysis of democratic culture are absorbed by Nietzsche's own: the incapacity to think long-term,[41] the suspicion of authority and tradition (which Nietzsche shares to a certain extent)[42] and the decline or degradation of political leadership.[43]

Nietzsche's Machiavellian-inspired immoralism negates the Christian-Rousseauesque 'good man' and the morality of *décadence*. It should be noted that one aspect of Nietzsche's definition of *décadence*, as he defines it in *The Case of Wagner*, is *'equal* rights for all' (CW 7), which indicates that Nietzsche's critique of morality – and this is also evident in Nietzsche's critique of *ressentiment*, it cannot be stated more strongly – is also a critique of political doctrine.

The demand for equality of rights, Nietzsche says, is an expression of envy, *revenge* or *ressentiment*, the *ressentiment* of the 'ill-constituted, rebellious-minded, under-privileged' (A 21), which issues primarily from the lowest classes, the masses and the majority, and their anarchist, democratic and socialist agitators, all 'heirs of the Christian movement' (BGE 202). Nietzsche shares the fear the aristocratic liberals have of the constituent power of the multitude, their *becoming a political subject*. The doctrine of equality, or the belief in the 'supreme rights of the majority', has been the principal 'weapon' utilized 'against everything noble', against the 'aristocratic outlook' (A 43), from the first (Judeo-Christian) to 'the last great slave rebellion', the French Revolution, which Nietzsche refers to as a *'ressentiment* movement' (GM I 16). For Nietzsche, *ressentiment* has its most prominent expression in modern political and social institutions, including the Bismarckian *Reich*, in all modern political theories and state constitutions which declare the natural equality and power of the people in *praxi*.

When Nietzsche says that the doctrine of equality is an expression of *ressentiment*, he is making an assertion, probably inspired by Taine's reading in *The Origins of Contemporary France*, about the psychology of revolution and the behaviour of revolutionary masses, the envy of the 'downtrodden' and the 'weakest' against the 'well-constituted' and the 'fortunate' (GM III 14), the conspiracy of those who would make 'the ruling class responsible for their character' (WP 765 Nachlaß 1888 KSA 13 15[30]). But Nietzsche also sees in the will to power of the will to equality, namely, in the democratic movement, a reactive, repressive and imperialistic assault on 'all who are not as we are', meaning a general assault on cultural differences, which also defines its *ressentiment*. As Nietzsche sees it, the democrats, socialists, anarchists and anti-Semites are resentful in their 'instinctive hostility to every other form of society' (BGE 202). The democratic movement is characterized by Nietzsche as a form of tyranny. Behind the will to equality is concealed a 'secret tyrant-appetite' which claims a monopoly on the concepts of goodness, justice and virtue (Z Tarantulas). In Nietzsche's view, the democratic movement is engaged in a repression of and a 'war on all that is rare, strange, privileged, the higher man, the higher soul, the higher duty, the higher responsibility, and the abundance of creative power' (BGE 212). But the will to equality does not only represent a direct assault on the noble type, it also represents, more generally, under the guise of 'civilization' (the civilizing mission) or 'humanization' (human rights), a homogenizing process which threatens all of humanity, whereby cultures become increasingly more detached from the conditions under which they have originated. The imperialistic (and even racist) demand of democratic *virtue* requires that these cultures 'change their character, shed their skin and blot out their past'. The tyrannical will to equality represents the levelling and destruction of fundamentally distinct cultural types. It attempts to make human beings 'more and more alike' (WP 315 Nachlaß 1887 KSA 12 9[173]).[44] It constitutes an 'actual rendering similar' (TI Expeditions 37); 'they teach virtue as an ideal *for everyone*' (WP 317 Nachlaß 1887 KSA 12 10[109]).

This is precisely Nietzsche's concern when he criticizes the abstract conception of the person, the fictive individual of Rousseau's social contract theory, in texts such as *The Greek State* or *On the Genealogy of Morals*, the imperialistic or colonial construction of the doctrine of 'one normal human type' (where 'normal' means 'equal'), which he believes is 'the greatest danger that has yet confronted humanity' (GS 143).

Nietzsche is an unconditional opponent of the democratic principle or doctrine of equality and equal rights. As he writes in *Thus Spoke Zarathustra*, 'I don't want to be confused with these preachers of equality' (Z Tarantulas). Elsewhere, regarding 'the Rousseauesque *morality*' of the doctrine of equality, Nietzsche writes, 'there exists no more poisonous poison' (TI Expeditions 48). The doctrine of equal rights is a symptom of decline whose effect is to erase the natural *pathos of distance* between different human types, cultures and social classes. From as early as *Human, All Too Human*, Nietzsche dissociates the claim to equality and equal rights from the claim to justice (H 451). Rather, what is at stake is not justice but power and the willingness to use immoralistic means to achieve it. For Nietzsche, the violence of the French Revolution, its release of 'savage energies' (H 463), the Jacobin Terror, is a confirmation of this. Although, ultimately, Nietzsche is more disturbed by the 'truths' of the Revolution than by its violence, probably because of his compromise with *Realpolitik*. The doctrine of equality and the claim to equal rights represents the '*end* of justice' (TI Expeditions 48) because it represents the unjust violation of 'every special claim, every special right and privilege' (BGE 202). In this critical context, Nietzsche attempts to articulate a just conception of right (or privilege), in the interests of promulgating the idea of a *noble egoism*, as that which is conditioned or determined by the instincts (physiology) or nature (typology) of each being. It cannot fail to impress as a neoconservative appeal to maintain what has already been constituted. As has been pointed out, Nietzsche has his own historical preferences regarding formations of domination. But at the same time, Nietzsche advances a strong appeal to the right to resist, a natural right unimpeded by natural law (say, in the Hobbesian sense), governed only by 'precepts of health' and a 'voluntary discipline'. In his compromise with *Realpolitik*, he comes to equate right with power (as Spinoza did) and power with legitimacy, where the sovereign decides the exception.

For Nietzsche, equal rights are essentially 'inaccessible' (EH WW 5) simply, and justly so, because human beings are not all equal, neither in terms of natural talents and assets, intellectual capacities nor tables of values. As Nietzsche writes in *Thus Spoke Zarathustra*, 'men are *not* equal: thus speaks justice' (Z Scholars). Nietzsche's argument proceeds from a spacious empirical description of natural inequality (also found in democratic theory) to a conception of justice which simply endorses it in a circular fashion. *Contra* Rousseau, Nietzsche sanctions natural subordination and formulates a concept of 'natural vocation' (A 57), which he ultimately derives from 'natural law'. The problem is that he does not effectively argue as to why natural inequality should prevent the European worker from obtaining the right to vote or the right to higher education, or improvement in working conditions or higher wages, for example, except that it is not in accord with the worker's *instincts*, ultimately not in accord with *nature* or *life*. As Nietzsche says in *On the Genealogy of Morals*, the idea 'that every will must consider every other will its equal – would be a principle *hostile to life*' (GM II 11). This has the effect, of course, of naturalizing a social order (with historical precursors) and social prejudice, based on inequality of conditions and political exclusion.[45] And this is where Nietzsche's argument fundamentally remains, where it settles: with a precise set of doctrinaire preconceptions, imperatives and slogans which say: *human beings should not become equal, master and servant should not be repudiated, there should be more war and inequality, inequality of rights is the sole condition for the existence of rights*.[46] Another problem is that Nietzsche never indexes *which* special claims, rights and privileges have been violated by the principle of equality (with the exception of selective education or the whole existence of other cultures or the diminution of the political power of an historical class) which reduces the effectiveness of his revaluating counterattack, making it somewhat nebulous and essentially schematic or formalistic in terms of social reconstruction.

Furthermore, Nietzsche's determination of the nature of each being does not move beyond the circularity of master and slave typology, and master and slave morality or politics (good–bad, anti-Christian–Christian, ascending–descending) – this sharp division of political space; and does not fundamentally move beyond the assertion (or political credo) that 'what is fair for one *cannot*... for that reason alone, also be fair for others' (BGE 228), that there should not be one morality for all. Nietzsche's aristocratic conception of justice is articulated as 'equality for equals, inequality for unequals' (TI Expeditions 48), which implies only that the noble type naturally recognizes its equals and exchanges and cedes honours, rights and privileges in its social relations with them (BGE 265). Nietzsche's conception of justice, with this classical (Aristotelian) conception of proportional equality, projects the segregationist construction of radically distinct spheres of life, each guided by different moralities and laws, with deep divisions maintained between classes and types.

Another aspect of Nietzsche's argument against equality is that it has undermined 'the *precondition* of every elevation' and 'every increase in culture' (A 43). His view, as Burckhardt was convinced as well,[47] is that democracy produces mediocrity (*Vermittelmässigung*) and represses the exceptional type. Nietzsche is convinced that only a *pathos of distance*, inequality and the 'ingrained difference between strata' can provide the conditions for the complete enhancement of humanity (BGE 257).

But Nietzsche is not exactly clear on this question of the conditions of the repression of the exceptional type. On the one hand, he indicates that the democratic movement and the doctrine of equality must be repudiated in the interests of the mere *appearance* or *possibility* of the exceptional type (upon whom the enhancement of humanity depends), which is to say, variously, the 'philosopher', the *'new philosophers'*, the 'commander', the *'strong* human being', the 'spiritual *tyrants'*, the 'higher sovereign species', the 'master race'. This repudiation involves, for example, the affirmation of slavery, the precondition of every higher culture, the prescription of laws for the future and the affirmation of war and inequality, among other agonistic doctrines, advanced by the free spirits in the *interregnum*.

On the other hand, Nietzsche says that the process of democratization must not be, and *cannot* be, obstructed, but should even be hastened (WP 898 Nachlaß 1887 KSA 12 9[153]) like the advent of nihilism. This is because, according to Nietzsche, the same democratic conditions that produce the levelling and mediocrity of the human being, 'that leads to the production of a type that is prepared for *slavery'*, are also likely 'to give birth to exceptional human beings'.[48] Nietzsche does not explain precisely why this follows, but the democratic conditions to which he refers are 'supra-nationality' (where did *'petty* politics' go?), 'power of adaptation', 'absence of prejudice' and 'manifoldness of practice, art and mask' typical of democratic education. Democratic conditions will produce both 'workers who will be poor in will' and 'in need of a master and commander' (BGE 242) *and* the *new philosophers* and commanders, the exceptional human beings envisaged by Nietzsche, who force 'the will of millennia upon *new* tracks' through a revaluation of all values (BGE 203) and reestablish *order of rank*. However, they exploit and overcome this education (but it is primarily in the development of techniques of dissimulation pointed at a more vulnerable psychology and ambiguous identity) Nietzsche's stronger type are stronger in will, more responsible, more self-assured, more goal-directed (WP 890 Nachlaß 1887 KSA 12 9[17]).

In spite of Nietzsche's lack of explanation as to those features of democratic education he cites, and why they will produce or provide conditions for new commanders, beyond the fact of simple genealogical transmission, it is my view that these two positions regarding the process of democratization do not constitute a mere inconsistency or contradiction, but rather present a total position of antagonism and solution which ratifies Nietzsche's search for the authoritarian potential *within* democracy and which makes programmatic the perspectival or spectral-syncretic governmental practices he endorses (adaptability, art and mask). 'Art and mask', or deception, allow for more comprehensive forms of domination to emerge (cf. BGE 61). However, such practices may be located in various epochs and are not strictly a feature of democratic culture (they apply to the Romans, the Jesuits and to Machiavelli).

Whatever the blind spots in Nietzsche's vision, his point, addressed to the free spirits, is that there are conditions both to create and exploit in the interests of the genesis of the commander, and in the interests of the formation of the political society they desire. For this philosophy seeks the commander, whose model is arguably Napoleon Bonaparte, who, as I pointed out above, introduced his own methods of masking and manipulation. And whatever the blind spots, his propagandizing and lack of argument, it is clear that Nietzsche's consistent object of invective and reprisal are '*degenerate*' socialist and democratic ideals (BGE 203), 'the so-called 'truths' of the Revolution' or 'Rousseauesque *morality*' (TI Expeditions 48).

4. Individualism

The principal aristocratic liberal value is the individual, free from all coercion and the imposition of the values of the masses and the major-ity.[49] The individual is sovereign. For the aristocratic liberals, the dangerous tendency of the increasing demand for equality is that it could result in a 'tyranny of the majority' whereby the individual would be subordinated to the general will of the greatest number to such an extent that his liberty would be impeded. But the aristocratic liberals are not advocates of an unqualified individualism; rather, they valorize a particular conception of individualism.

De Tocqueville, for example, criticizes the atomistic individualism, characteristic of democratic ages, which 'merges with egoism' and private interest, and 'disposes each citizen to isolate himself from the mass of his fellows'.[50] According to de Tocqueville, the equality which gives each citizen independence ultimately renders him isolated from the rest of society. Equality 'tends to isolate men from each other',[51] encloses each citizen within himself, makes him forgetful of his ancestors and his descendents, and indifferent to the public and public virtue.[52]

De Tocqueville and the other aristocratic liberals are antagonistic towards the self-interested, bourgeois form of individualism which preoccupies itself solely with personal ends and personal ambition, with its own well-being, comfort and security, and which dissociates itself from any wider social and political commitments or responsibility. The aristocratic liberals argue for a conception of the self-development of the individual which involves his liberation from coercion and conformity, egalitarian tyranny and the drive for material comfort. They argue for decentralized units of power, the inviolability of the individual and property, and a definition of individual liberty which presupposes active political and social engagement (which, none the less, does not accommodate the doctrine of universal suffrage).[53]

Nietzsche adopts virtually all the vocabulary of the aristocratic liberal critique of democratic individualism (the democratic individual de Tocqueville describes is of a kind with the '*last man*' of *Zarathustra*), but he does not adhere to the same liberal ideals. He does not propose the same solution to this dangerous form of individualism which, for the aristocratic liberals, lies strictly in education or *Bildung*, in the humanistic tradition. Recall that Nietzsche includes as part of his definition of *décadence*, in a quotation that encapsulates the primary targets of his political critique, 'anarchy of atoms' and 'freedom of the individual' (CW 7).

In the *Untimely Meditations*, Nietzsche critically refers to our age as an 'age of atoms, of atomistic chaos' (UM III 4) and pejoratively employs the expression 'atomistic revolution' (UM IV 6). The aristocratic liberal critique clearly constitutes the background of this phraseology. Like the aristocratic liberals, Nietzsche disparages not only the isolation and bourgeois self-interest of the individual in democratic culture, the 'private person', but also the abstract and ahistorical conception of the individual. Nietzsche conceives the individual as physiologically and organically situated in relation to particular historical and social circumstances, communities, institutions and practices. This view is expressed in acute opposition to the Christian, Cartesian (modern) and classical liberal conception of the individual, as well as to the abstract, fictive individual of Rousseau's social contract theory, also excoriated by Taine and Burckhardt.[54]

The Nietzschean individual is neither hollowed-out nor abstract, whereby the 'uniqueness of his being has become an . . . uncommunicating atom' (UM III 3). Rather, Nietzsche defines the individual in terms of practical activity,[55] just as he defines freedom in terms of 'great deeds' (UM III 8), but combined with the idea that the individual should consecrate himself to something higher than his own self-interest. This means that each individual, from the standpoint of the Nietzschean programme, should consecrate himself to a community which is united by a radical aristocratic ideal of culture, which legislates, as the principal task of each individual, the *'promotion'* of the production of individual great men (UM III 5).[56]

This imperative constitutes an implicit critical response to the social values of Christianity which, according to Nietzsche, encourage 'the most *private* form of existence' and presuppose 'a narrow, remote, completely unpolitical society' (WP 211 Nachlaß 1887 KSA 12 10[135]). Because of its fixation on the afterlife, Christianity diminishes the importance of 'public spirit' (A 43); and because of its *ressentiment*, it demonstrates a lack of 'public openness' (A 21). Nietzsche sees these tendencies (atomization, lack of public spirit and public openness) in democratic culture as well, except that the fixation on the afterlife is replaced by a preoccupation with personal well-being and security. Democratic culture liberates the 'private person' and not the *individual* (as Nietzsche carefully qualifies), discourages social projects which require decades to nurture, produces distrust of and indifference towards government and law (H 472) and is a purveyor or vector of *ressentiment*, for example, with respect to other cultures, particularly non-Christian cultures.

Like the aristocratic liberals, Nietzsche's principal value, in the most general terms, is the individual. Nietzsche's general position, particularly between *Human, All Too Human* and *Beyond Good and Evil*, is that the individual should take precedence over the community. Nietzsche defines the individual in opposition to 'the herd men (*die Heerden-Menschen*)' (GS 23) and tends to idealize the 'independent spirituality' which destroys 'the self-confidence of the community' (BGE 201). In *Daybreak*, in the style of the aristocratic liberal critique, Nietzsche deprecates those who are dominated by the opinions of the 'great majority', who possess no 'real ego' but only a 'pale fiction' they are 'incapable of annihilating' (D 105). This 'pale fiction' refers to the 'neutral substratum' and 'one normal human type' presupposed by democratic social contract theory. During this period in particular Nietzsche is radically individualistic in so far as he affirms a *'plurality of norms'* (GS 143) and 'diverse prescriptions' for diverse individuals (GS 149). There are 'innumerable healths of the body', he declares in an anti-Kantian register, and each individual must devise his own right and 'peculiar virtue' (GS 120). For *external* nonpersonal prescriptions (or morality) can only undermine the happiness of the individual. The defining desire of this radical aristocratic individualism is to *'become those we are* – human beings who are new, unique, incomparable, who give themselves laws, and create themselves' (GS 335).

Nietzsche articulates his conception of the individual in opposition to the Christian value of selflessness and self-abnegation, and to the 'private person' who emerges as a 'consequence of the democratic conception of the state' (H 472). Nietzsche's criticism of Christian self-abnegation (which implicates Schopenhauer as well) amounts to a criticism of the Christian education in *virtue* which reduces the individual to 'a mere function of the whole', or a 'public utility', through which the individual is deprived of his 'noblest selfishness and strength for the highest autonomy'. It is an education which dominates him '*to his own ultimate disadvantage*' but in the interests of the common or 'general good' (GS 21). This critique recalls Nietzsche's critique of socialism in *Human, All Too Human*, which points out, and inveighs against, socialism's reduction of the individual to 'a useful *organ of the community*'.

But, more specifically, Nietzsche idealizes those individuals who are agents of change, 'powerful and influential', who exercise 'judgements of taste' and 'enforce them tyrannically', who 'coerce many' until new habits and new needs are developed (GS 39). These are the individuals who 'carry the seeds of the future' and who are 'the authors of the spiritual colonization and origin of new states and communities' (GS 23). In other words, the free spirits and the philosopher-legislators who are born or predestined for the art of command or, at least, make themselves appear so (cf. GS 40). Thus more than simply possessing autonomy from the dominant ideology of the majority and mass culture, the individual Nietzsche idealizes, as in Machiavelli, is a lawgiver and a legislator, a founder and a *commander*.

Aside from possessing character traits, according to the semiotics of Nietzschean *virtù* ethics (and it is a *virtù* ethics not a virtue ethics), such as politeness, honesty, resoluteness and fidelity, independence, *immorality*, self-mastery and abundance of creative will (BGE 212), the individual Nietzsche idealizes, namely, the *higher type*, experiences *itself* as determining values, as *value*-creating (BGE 260). The higher or noble type is a legislator and a commander who is governed by a 'private morality', who is not afraid to enter into an adverse or antagonistic relationship with the existing social order, but who, none the less, can achieve his most complete expression only in the political or public realm in the form of rule.

Nietzsche praises the individualism of the Renaissance, an epoch he views as 'the climax of this millennium'.[57] This Renaissance concept of individualism, or Renaissance, which is to say Machiavellian, *virtù*, demands that 'one should *persist* in one's *own* ideal of *man* ... should impose one's ideal on one's fellow beings and on oneself overpoweringly, and thus exert a creative influence';[58] that is how an individual acquires value.

With Burckhardt, Nietzsche would agree that the ends of culture should be the production of free and creative individuality, and that culture is transmitted through great individuals. But Nietzsche has a unique conception, as did Burckhardt, of what greatness, creativity, freedom and individuality are. When these terms are positively claimed by Nietzsche they always apply to the anti-Christian and antimodern type, to what is pagan.

Freedom is a privileged concept in Nietzsche's philosophy in so far as the Nietzschean individual is a *free* individual, a *free* spirit. Nietzsche says he is opposed to the 'modern concept of freedom' which, in his view, represents the 'degeneration of instinct' (TI Expeditions 41). Nietzsche's free spirit is described in terms of scepticism and suspicion of authority. He is a *nomad*, but he is stabilized in hegemonic articulation, so to speak, by the values of the revaluation which are fiercely anti-democratic and antiliberal. Nietzsche opposes his conception of freedom to the liberal democratic conception and connects it to the 'aristocratic communities of the pattern of Rome and Venice' (TI Expeditions 39).

Scepticism and suspicion of authority are clearly modern conceptions, so what aspect of modern freedom does Nietzsche reject, and what is the character of the freedom he affirms?

Nietzsche associates his concept of freedom with the 'will to self-responsibility', the preservation of a *pathos of distance*, Stoic indifference to hardship and privation, the readiness to sacrifice oneself or others to a cause, the agonistic preservation of a state of war – because the free individual is a '*warrior*' and the experience of freedom occurs when 'the manly instincts that delight in war and victory', namely *virtù*, 'have gained mastery over the other instincts'. According to Nietzsche, freedom, or sovereignty, should be measured – as Machiavelli would agree and contrary, for example, to the Hobbesian conception of freedom as freedom from opposition – in individuals or nations, where there is present the greatest danger of servitude, 'where the greatest resistance is constantly being overcome', where there is the greatest effort expended 'to stay *aloft*' which compels strength of spirit (TI Expeditions 39). Nietzsche refers to this agonistic conception of freedom, which requires resistance and opposition, as a form of 'positive power' and associates it with 'the classic type of the *sovereign* man' or the 'tyrant', and with epochs that were *inhumane*. In this sense, freedom is possession of power and the desire to overpower (WP 784 Nachlaß 1887

KSA 12 10[82]). In any case, such freedom has never been attained in liberal democratic societies, as there is nothing more detrimental to this sense of freedom, according to Nietzsche, than liberal democratic institutions. Therefore, these societies have never been *great*. Liberal democratic institutions do not promote freedom because they do not promote war (a category which includes *inequality*) as Nietzsche had disparaged them for in his essay on the *Greek State*. They suppress all '*illiberal* instincts' while favouring the instinct for happiness and well-being, while promoting a levelling (equalizing) process or '*reduction to the herd animal*'. It is, rather, the past aristocratic commonwealths of the pattern of Rome or Venice, for example, 'those great forcing-houses for strong human beings', which understood freedom as Nietzsche declares he understands it: not as something that should be *given*, but 'as something one has and does *not* have, something one *wants*, something one *conquers*', something one earns (TI Expeditions 38).

Nietzsche's concept of freedom is such that it is for the very few and a privilege of the strong. His idea of freedom is subordinate to questions of power. The question of the degree of freedom that an individual can possess is subordinate to the question of the degree of power that an individual can exercise over other individuals. The Nietzschean response is not highly nuanced in retrospect. A sacrifice of freedom and a regime of inequality and slavery for some is advanced as the basis for the emergence of a '*higher type*' (WP 859 Nachlaß 1886–87 KSA 12 7[6]).

The Nietzschean individual is a '*noble egoist*' who is as selfish and self-interested as the democratic individual, but towards ends that exceed mere preoccupation with material comfort and security. The noble egoism Nietzsche defines has political repercussions in so far as it is defined in opposition to *decadent* expressions of pity and altruism (TI Expeditions 39) and in so far as the egoism of the noble soul accepts the fact that others must be subordinate to it by nature. For Nietzsche, the state of nature, as in Hobbes, is one of 'ruthless inequality' (WS 31). Nietzsche's very definition of egoism, and of life as will to power, is that it is always furthered at the expense of others, 'the expense of other life' (WP 369 Nachlaß 1884 KSA 11 26[93]). This is why Nietzsche can legitimately condone the 'willingness', which he associates with 'greatness', to inflict suffering without remorse (GS 325).

The Nietzschean individual is finally not opposed to all ideas of community. In *Twilight of the Idols*, Nietzsche describes the will which is the condition for viable social institutions and the 'grand organization of society', an expression which implies inequality of conditions and social hierarchy. It is 'anti-liberal to the point of malice'; it is *aristocratic* in so far as it affirms 'tradition', 'authority', 'centuries-long responsibility' and *'solidarity* between succeeding generations' past and future (TI Expeditions 39). What tradition and authority is made explicit in Nietzsche's revaluation and reversal of values: pagan, Roman, Renaissance.

For Nietzsche, society should exist for a 'choice type of being' (BGE 250) and for the production of 'valuable individuals' which necessitates the sacrifice of 'countless individuals' (WP 679 Nachlaß 1886–87 KSA 12 7[9], GS 325, TI Expeditions 34). Nietzsche does not explicitly prescribe what this sacrifice entails, beyond the fact that it precludes certain rights and that it involves the reduction of many human beings to slaves and instruments (BGE 258). It stands opposed to Christian 'universal love' for the 'underprivileged' and 'degenerate' (WP 246 Nachlaß 1888 KSA 13 15[110], A 7), and politically represents an assault on fundamental human rights and the welfare state. While Nietzsche espouses his radical aristocratic individualism, he also espouses the doctrine of the necessity of slavery, that slavery is the condition for 'every enhancement of culture' (BGE 239). It fundamentally means that all bodies are seen panoramically in his conception of political organization.

As was stated above, Burckhardt thought of freedom in terms of intellectual freedom and cultivation, religious tolerance and freedom from coercion along traditional liberal and humanistic lines. Like Nietzsche, he thought that the increasing participation of the masses through democratic processes would inhibit individual freedoms. Like Nietzsche, he thought, in elitist terms, that higher culture and education should be the privilege of the exceptional few. But Nietzsche's conception of culture implies an antiliberal and antihumanist conception of freedom which legitimates the coercion and control of many human beings. Its precept is that strength must express itself as strength and cannot be subject to any social contract which interprets weakness as freedom, which imagines 'that the strong man is free to be weak' (GM I 13). Because they can, they will. And whatever 'strength' is for Nietzsche, it is 'command', and 'command' is 'law'. For the strong, no rights are transferred. In this context, it is absorbing to note that Burckhardt later expressed disdain for Nietzsche's glorification of the *Gewaltmenschen* or outlaws of history. Strictly speaking, Burckhardt had reservations about the arbitrariness of power Nietzsche's philosophy condones, even though his work on the Renaissance may have contributed to its inspiration, and consequently rejected it for its 'tyrannical trait'.[59]

In his notebooks, Nietzsche says that his 'philosophy aims at an ordering of rank: not at an individualistic morality' (WP 287 Nachlaß 1886–87 KSA 12 7[6], cf. H P 6). This implies, first, that he is opposed to an individualism, or individualistic morality, which posits the equality of individuals, since the 'vanity' of the individual is that 'every other should count as its equal' (WP 783 Nachlaß 1885 KSA 11 40[26]). For Nietzsche, individualism and the demand for equality of rights are the same, or interrelated phenomena, in modern Europe. Second, it implies that the 'leaders' and the 'herd', the commanders and the masses or the multitude, require fundamentally different valuations for their own actions. They should not be governed by the same morality. The commanders should possess exceptional rights, immunities, dignities and privileges. However, the establishment of an order of rank means precisely the governance of the masses by a dominant ideology of cultural production in which the masses or the multitude acquire value in so far as they serve this production. So there is a certain normative uniformity in its general economy.

At times, Nietzsche may appear liberal inasmuch as he appears to support the development of diverse individuals. For example, he writes that 'the individual, each according to his kind, should be so placed that he can achieve the highest that lies in his power' (WP 763 Nachlaß 1887 KSA 12 9[34]). But the operative clause here is 'each according to his kind', and it has something of Plato's myth of the metals attached to it. You achieve the highest that lies in your power as long as you remain in your place. Nietzsche's concept of order of rank, in fact, is not unfolded beyond the formulation of a dual typology of master and slave, although there are subdivisions in terms of social labour, and remains steadfast in an anti-Hegelian position of nonrecognition. He restricts the 'nature' or 'instincts' of each being accordingly, which justifies their social position. Nietzsche regards every individual as representing either 'the ascending or descending line of life', claiming 'extraordinary value' for the egoism of the former and parasitical status for the latter (TI Expeditions 33). Such a scheme simply reproduces the Christian–noble, modern–antimodern, democratic–antidemocratic antithesis; and divides political space accordingly.

In the most comprehensive declaration of his own political identity, Nietzsche says that he, and those political forces he identifies with (it is not an imaginary community), are not conservative, do not wish to 'return to any past periods', are not liberal, do not believe in progress and are opposed to equal rights and to the idea of a '*free* society'. They reject the democratic and socialist ideal of 'no more masters and no servants'. They oppose the idea of the establishment of a 'realm of justice and concord', for that implies the 'deepest levelling', favouring instead 'war' and 'danger'. They are anti-Christian and antihumanitarian, against the 'religion of pity' and for sacrifice and 'a new slavery'; for every enhancement of the human being also entails a new kind of enslavement (GS 377). These are the salient political features of the 'new order' they seek to reveal.[60]

I have claimed in this chapter that Nietzsche assimilates all the vocabulary of the aristocratic liberal critique of democratic society. Thus it can be said, following Kahan, that Nietzsche is a 'late-blooming' aristocratic liberal. But he conspicuously differs from them as well on all key issues of their critique. In fact, he is more radical and more draconian, in both assessment and solution, with respect to those democratic social tendencies which the aristocratic liberals see merely as potentially dangerous tendencies. They do not reject liberal democratic institutions *ex toto*.

Like the aristocratic liberals, Nietzsche rejects universal suffrage (de Tocqueville qualified), but unlike them, he is clearly not an opponent of centralized government, not an opponent as they are, for example, of Napoleonic Caesarism (autocratic will in the guise of popular rule). Nietzsche even affirms the idea of a world government of Bonapartist inspiration, a global system (empire) on which the revaluation of all values is conditional. The aristocratic liberals are also concerned with the question of political leadership, but do not support any form of tyranny, as exemplified by Burckhardt's later decisive rejection of and dissociation from Nietzsche.

Unlike the aristocratic liberals, Nietzsche is an unconditional opponent of the democratic doctrine of equality. He is strictly for hierarchy and order of rank in society (in Bonapartist terms, the patriarchal family, property and titles of nobility). Nietzsche invests no credibility whatsoever in democratic institutions or ethics, beyond instrumental purpose, where they are subordinate to radical aristocratic politics. Rather, he advocates their subversion by a new nobility, accompanied by a political conception of the masses as inert and passive, predisposed to Taine's description of the crowd in the French Revolution, as pliable, raw material for control and manipulation. Nietzsche regards the masses, in all their potential, as machine-like and militarized, as soldier-workers (WP 763 Nachlaß 1887 12 9[34]), and the democratic state merely as an instrument of the will to power for whomever has the strength to seize control of it and redirect it (kratocracy).

Unlike Taine and Burckhardt, as Nietzsche considers them, Nietzsche wants to 'arrive at something', by which he means a *vita activa*, active legislation, a legislation of new values. This desire is encapsulated in Nietzsche's conception of the individual, who is only an individual in so far as he is a legislator or a lawgiver, who represents the coincidence of philosophy and political power. The coincidence of philosophy and political power in the figure of the Nietzschean philosopher-legislator is evident in the very fact that because he possesses *virtù* he must necessarily impose his will, his values, on another, as the Renaissance conception implies. He legislates *politically*, because the revaluation of all values is clearly political in its implications (cf. BGE 202), the successful execution of its goals is entirely conflated with a specific form of social and political organization. His spirit is *'world-governing'* (cf. EH WC 6, WD 1). The 'genuine philosophers' are *'commanders and legislators'* who determine the goals of humanity (BGE 211). Their activity is not cloistered or solitary.

Nietzsche does not consider all human beings as *individuals*, or as sovereign, in the aristocratic liberal sense. Rather, he justifies exploitation and recommends slavery for some. He also seems divided on the issue of tolerance, given his extreme antagonism towards Christianity, and freedom of thought, given his views on education and the press. Nietzsche's conception of justice (*Gerechtigkeit*) is not centred on the person who, for Nietzsche, possesses no inherent value or sanctity. Rather, Nietzsche defines justice as the 'function (*Funktion*)' of a 'panoramic power (*umherschauenden Macht*)' which 'preserves something that is more than this or that person (. . . *mehr ist als diese und jene Person*)' (KSA 11, 26[149]).

Nietzsche's work proceeds in the spirit of the revocation of democratic rights and the legitimation of the dispossession or nonrecognition of certain human beings. The aristocratic liberals, to the contrary, believe that all individuals should be free from coercion and control. They would condemn Nietzsche because he does not forbid 'acts injurious to others', to borrow a phrase from Mill.[61] That Nietzsche does not do so is clear from his definition of the individual or the ego and its relations. Mill, for example – and this chapter may have easily accommodated a more extensive treatment of Mill given his political concerns, even though he was an adversary of universal suffrage and of the welfare state and antisocialist – nevertheless saw value in educating the poor and in reducing their poverty. Like de Tocqueville, Mill is far more receptive than Nietzsche to the injustices which afflict the poor and labouring classes.[62]

Nietzsche exhibits certain ideological similarities with the aristocratic liberals. However, on closer examination, he is radically different from them. He is ideologically more like the Italian neo-Machiavellian elite theorists (Pareto, early Mosca) and to the French founder of crowd or mass psychology (Le Bon), all of whom considered Taine's *Origins of Contemporary France* an eventful and pivotal work. It is in relation to these political movements that Nietzsche may be more accurately situated as the final chapter shall explicate.

4
Nietzsche and Machiavellianism

at bottom the masses are willing to submit to slavery of any kind, if only the higher-ups constantly legitimize themselves as higher, as born *to command.*

(GS 40)

perfecting consists in the production of the most powerful individuals, who will use the great mass of people as their tools . . .
(WP 660 Nachlaß 1885–86 KSA 12 2[76])

Therefore . . . is a new nobility *needed: to oppose all mob-rule and all despotism.*

(Z Law-Tables 11)

Hohepunkte der Redlichkeit: Macchiavelli, der Jesuitismus . . .
(Nachlaß 1884 KSA 11 25[74])

Nietzsche's radicalization of the aristocratic liberal critique, his resolve to 'arrive at something', a resolve he sees lacking in his allies Burckhardt and Taine, leads him to embrace a conception of politics he associates with Machiavelli. Not the republican freedom and the appreciation of the political capacities of the masses found in the *Discourses* which, in any case, Nietzsche does not appear to have read, but rather the authoritarian practices found in *The Prince*. Nietzsche did not read Machiavelli as Spinoza or Rousseau did, as someone who revives republicanism and defends democratic freedoms (Spinoza and Rousseau read *The Prince* as a book for Republicans, designed to educate the people), but adheres to what has been called the 'vulgar' conception of Machiavellianism.[1] Rousseau would have considered Nietzsche to be a 'superficial and corrupt' reader of Machiavelli. What Nietzsche adapts from Machiavelli are his conceptions of *virtù* (at the operational basis of his ethics) and immoralism (at the operational basis of his political conception) based primarily on a reading of *The Prince*.[2]

Nietzsche derived his knowledge of the Renaissance and of Machiavelli from a variety of sources.[3] Perhaps most importantly Jacob Burckhardt's *The Civilization of the Renaissance in Italy* (1869), which would have introduced Nietzsche to the idea of the 'state as a work of art' and to the idea of the *political artist*; and from which he would have learned that Renaissance culture, which saw the emergence of the *individual*, outgrew 'the limits of morality, religion and law'; that from the point of view of its 'cult of historical greatness', or *personality*, vices were matters of indifference in spite of which Renaissance heros achieved their greatness'.[4] Then Emile Gebhart's *The Origins of the Renaissance in Italy* (1879) or his book, heavily annotated by Nietzsche, *The Italian Renaissance and the Philosophy of History* (1887). From both these books Nietzsche would have acquired a strong definition of *virtù*: that it has nothing in common with virtue *per se*, that it combines 'great qualities' with 'great vices'.[5] Then, perhaps, Pasquale Villari's *Machiavelli and His Times* (1877–82),[6] from which Nietzsche would have learned that, for Machiavelli, *durability* is the supreme value in matters of state; that the pagan spirit is opposed to 'private morality'; that *virtù* means 'courage and energy for both good *and* evil';[7] that the 'people in the hands of its legislator' are like 'soft clay in the hands of the sculptor',[8] a notion that dominates *The Prince* and is an image Nietzsche evokes in the name of Zarathustra (EH Z 8), to say something of his *praxis*. From these sources Nietzsche would have understood something about the contents of Machiavelli's other principal works – namely, *The History of Florence*, *The Art of War* and the *Discourses* – but there is no evidence to suggest that Nietzsche read any work by Machiavelli other than *The Prince*.

Nietzsche would have been familiar also with the passages on Machiavelli in Lange's *History of Materialism* and Ueberweg's *History of Philosophy*. Lange's brief remarks focus on Machiavelli's point regarding the importance for the princes of a republic of conserving religion even if they consider it to be false.[9] Ueberweg's commentary points to the discrepancy between *The Prince* and the *Discourses* as being one between absolute power and republican freedom, but notes that this discrepancy is solved when it is understood that, for Machiavelli, periods of decadence or corruption require despotic remedies, implicitly understanding that it is the notion of the 'return to beginnings' which unites the two books. He also says that Machiavelli teaches the doctrine that the ends justify the means.[10]

With Machiavellian *virtù*, which is characterized by courage, daring, strength of will and political capability, Nietzsche associates that 'active force' which operates in the 'artists of violence and organizers who build states' (GM II 18), whose 'work is an instinctive creation and imposition of forms' (GM II 17); political artists such as Cesare Borgia (1475–1507), the Duke of Romagna featured in *The Prince*,[11] whom Nietzsche considers to be a kind of *Übermensch* (EH WGB 1), the *anti-Christ* who might have restored noble values to the papal throne (A 61), or Napoleon Bonaparte, the 'synthesis of the *inhuman* and *superhuman*' (GM I 16). Thus, for Nietzsche, as for Machiavelli, *virtù* is the power that forms states and is a necessary quality possessed by his envisaged philosopher-legislators and commanders.

In *Twilight of the Idols* Nietzsche praises the 'realism' of *The Prince* (TI Ancients 2) and in his notebooks refers to Machiavellianism as 'perfection in politics' (WP 304 Nachlaß 1887–88 KSA 13 11[54]). This Machiavellian realism and perfection which Nietzsche praises, and which he also locates in Thucydides and the Sophists, refers to Machiavelli's analysis of the nature of power and, specifically, to his description of the techniques for the manipulation of power that Nietzsche subsumes under the rubric of 'immoralism', which further encompasses the idea that the state is founded on violence, force and fraud and not on a social contract, as the case of Romulus illustrates for Machiavelli, that it has no inherent moral legitimacy, that it is entirely the product of calculation and expediency or prudence over moral considerations. What Nietzsche understands by the 'Machiavellianism of power' is *Realpolitik*. Like Machiavelli, Nietzsche subordinates morality to political practice.

In this chapter I will comment on Nietzsche's relation to Machiavelli, his adaptation of Machiavellian *virtù* and immoralism, and to disciples of Machiavelli such as Gustave Le Bon (1841–1931), one of the founders of crowd or mass psychology, and the elite theorists Vilfredo Pareto (1848–1923) and Gaetano Mosca (1858–1941), all contemporaries of Nietzsche. Like Nietzsche, they reflected on the dangers of mass movements, namely, democratic or socialist, and on the possibility of mass manipulation through the use of appropriate and practical political techniques.[12] In opposition to the view of Peter Bergmann, who says that of 'all Nietzsche's contemporaries, Nietzsche's position most closely resembles that of the anarchists' (in spite of Nietzsche's many criticisms of anarchism and of one of the formulators of anarchist doctrine,

Bakunin),[13] I will argue, conversely, that of all Nietzsche's contemporaries Nietzsche's ideological position, the trajectory of his political reflections, is more closely related to that of the neo-Machiavellians. It is with them, and not with the anarchists, that he shares deeper ideological premises.

I will begin with a general review of the philosophical parallels between Nietzsche and Machiavelli as a background to Nietzsche's Machiavellian discipleship. Subsequently, I will engage, in more specific terms, Nietzsche's adaptation and implementation of Machiavellian *virtù* and immoralism in his moral and political philosophy, concepts which are also present in neo-Machiavellian political theory. *Virtù* for Nietzsche means political, legislative capability, overcoming of resistances, freedom from morality and reconciliation with evil, traits which apply to the Nietzschean conception of leadership exemplified by Napoleon Bonaparte. Immoralism constitutes a thesis regarding the subordination of morality to politics, but also refers to the political technology with which Nietzschean *virtù* is armed. It becomes the principle of action of the Nietzschean *tractatus politicus*, for the free spirits and new philosophers. I will claim that immoralism is Nietzsche's breakthrough which radicalizes the aristocratic liberal critique, a practical move towards the possibility of new regimes.

I will also claim that Nietzschean political theory does not ignore the necessity of the principles of legitimacy, as he recommends the use of myth and religion, and authors a noble lie in the guise of natural law – will to power and order of rank.

I will claim that Nietzsche expresses an applied interest in the power religious and political ideals exercise over human beings, in the strategies and tactics employed by priestly-philosophical power-structures, and supports the utilization of practical political techniques to control the constituent power of the democratic masses. I will argue that it is his search for the authoritarian potential within democracy, his similar adaptation of Machiavellian *virtù* and immoralism, his understanding of political power, and his characterization of the masses, which situates him within the ideological constellation of the neo-Machiavellians.

I will conclude with a few remarks distinguishing Nietzschean political doctrine from the anarchist political doctrine of Bakunin.

1. Philosophical parallels[14]

Martin Heidegger writes that by the time Nietzsche wrote *Twilight of the Idols*, he 'had clear knowledge of the fact that the metaphysics of the will to power conforms only to Roman culture and Machiavelli's *The Prince'*.[15] Similarly, Charles Andler recognizes in Nietzsche 'un disciple de Machiavel'.[16] These views are opposed to the view of Karl Jaspers, for example, who claims that there is 'no practical political technique like Machiavelli's' in Nietzsche's writings.[17] I will suspend for now the question of the presence of a practical political technique in Nietzsche's work and comment instead, in this section and the two that follow, on the evidence for Nietzsche's Machiavellian discipleship.

First of all, as mentioned above, Nietzsche praises Machiavelli for his realism and immoralism and completely embraces Machiavelli's conception of *virtù* in opposition to the Christian morality of self-abnegation. But there are present in Nietzsche's work other philosophical parallels with Machiavelli as well, which I will broadly review drawing from both *The Prince* and the *Discourses*. Keith Ansell-Pearson, who develops a more comprehensive delineation of these parallels than anyone in the Anglo-American literature, draws five points of comparison between Nietzsche and Machiavelli which includes the two points alluded to above. First, an aesthetic conception of politics which views the state as a work of art made by the personality or *virtù* of the prince; second, the view that morality is rooted in immoral foundations; third, a relativistic conception of good and evil (for Nietzsche there should be different moralities for different types); fourth, the idea that human beings construct illusory, transcendental worlds in order to live in a world of radical flux and contingency; and fifth, the advocacy of a politics of controlled violence.[18]

Other points of comparison may be added. For example, both Nietzsche and Machiavelli author a critique of Christianity which deplores it for encouraging weakness, humility and contempt for worldly objects, to the detriment of, in Machiavelli's terms, 'grandeur of soul' and 'strength of body' (DL 2 II), but at the same time consider religion, morality or myth to be an indispensable political tool in the hands of rulers or princes, as Numa Pompilius and the Roman ruling class exemplify for Machiavelli. Nietzsche begins to articulate the importance of myth and mythic horizons for society in *The Birth of Tragedy*.

Both believe in the inconstancy and finitude of every regime, the perpetual cycles of degeneration which afflict them, the return of the same conflicts (for Nietzsche, between master and slave), but praise and affirm the wills of heroic and creative individuals who attempt to overcome these cycles, or attempt to overcome *fortuna*, and work to establish something durable and lasting such as the *Imperium Romanum*. (P VI, A 3). Nietzsche acknowledges, and he seems to agree with him, that for Machiavelli, the form of government is of only minimal importance, that the 'great goal of politics should be *permanence*' or durability (H 224).[19] This acknowledgement introduces an esoteric, eclectic or spectral-syncretic element into Nietzsche's political philosophy, a willingness to use whatever ideologies are at hand in the interests of deeper and more distant goals. This means that certain political or religious ideologies may be used for ends which are antithetical to them.

Both recognize the greatness of ancient Rome and Roman culture (both consider the principal conflict in values to be that between the values of Rome and Judea), but Machiavelli's appreciation of ancient Rome and Roman republicanism, though it has points in common with Nietzsche's, is supported by a more spacious discussion. While Nietzsche praises Rome's tolerance, secular status, durability, realism and aristocratic values, which in 1887 he links to the 'salvation and future of the human race' (GM I 16), Machiavelli praises its mixed constitution through which the people were allowed increased power and authority over political affairs (DL 1 VI). Unlike Nietzsche, Machiavelli holds popular opinion and judgement in high esteem, their capacity to pronounce on particular issues (DL 1 LVIII), and, unlike Nietzsche, condemns the tyranny of Caesar (DL 1 X), whom Nietzsche admires (GS 23). Nietzsche does not support the institutionalization of popular power.

Both possess a pessimistic conception of human beings, believing them not inherently good (P XVIII); in Nietzsche's case, *contra* Christianity, Rousseau and socialist doctrine, although Nietzsche says that human beings are neither fundamentally good nor fundamentally evil (H 56). Both believe that human beings are power-maximizing and that the expansion and growth of power is necessary for survival, although Nietzsche does not consistently see the aim of the will to power as self-preservation (GS 349). Both wish to take human beings as they are (P XV); Nietzsche in opposition to Rousseauian and egalitarian ideals (TI Expeditions 32), to the 'fantasist and utopian' character of Platonism (D 496), its flight from reality (D 448) and to Christianity's 'instinctive hatred *for* actuality' (A 39). In fact, Nietzsche's professed '*cure* from all Platonism' is Thucydides and *The Prince* of Machiavelli, for Thucydides and Machiavelli are closely related to Nietzsche, as Nietzsche himself recognizes, through 'their unconditional will not to deceive themselves' (TI Ancients 2), through their realism.

Both subscribe to a doctrine of action or *praxis* over contemplation, convey a militaristic ethos (P XIV, TI Expeditions 38) and contest that freedom may flourish only under agonistic conditions where there is conflict and struggle between princes, nations and individuals, where there is great resistance to be overcome. Both adhere to the value of having opponents or enemies (P XX).

Both see the great human being in the figure of the centaur, half-man, half-beast. Recall the narrative in *The Prince* about how the ancient princes were educated under the discipline of Chiron the centaur (P XVIII, H 241).[20] Both believe that there existed a stronger type of human being, worthy of imitation, in the ancient world (P VI, WP 957 Nachlaß 1885 KSA 11 37[8]).

Both reject classical natural law and natural right. It is the analysis of power, the subordination of life to questions of power, which occupies the centre of their thought, and power and politics have an instrumental character for both. Nietzsche's conception of the will to power incorporates two ideas found in *The Prince*: first, that there is 'inevitable harm inflicted on those over whom the prince obtains dominion', and second, that the 'desire to acquire possessions is a very natural and ordinary thing' (P III).

Both seek *new modes and orders*, a *revaluation of all values* against decadence and corruption. Both view the masses as pliable material (P XXVI, GM II 17), advocate patriotism, although in Nietzsche it is articulated in terms of an imperial pan-Europeanism (P XXVI, EH CW 2).

A Machiavellian perspective, its ether, dominates the Nietzschean corpus: the 'destroyer of morals', the 'friend of evil', the 'new nobility' and the 'commanders' of *Thus Spoke Zarathustra*; the 'individuals' and founders of new states in *The Gay Science*; the communications theory in *Daybreak*; the 'genius of culture', the 'lawgiver' and the 'free spirits' of *Human, All Too Human*; the defence of the *coup d'état* of Louis Bonaparte in Nietzsche's early Germania club essay, *Napoleon III as President* (1862); the 'artists of violence' in *On the Genealogy of Morals*. It is evident that Nietzsche read *The Prince* very carefully, it is so deliberately transfused to his corpus that many of its ideas are articulated without acknowledgement, Nietzsche so pervasively incorporates them. And everything Nietzsche says about the Renaissance refers to *The Prince*.

We can see Nietzsche's neo-Machiavellian solution, its development and fruition, in his book, *Beyond Good and Evil*; how it develops from Nietzsche's praise for Machiavelli's style and, subsequently, through his *'esoteric'* affirmation of independence as something for the 'very few', or for those *'immoralists'* who have overcome Christian morality; through reflections on deception and perspectivism, the affirmation of 'masks and cunning', and the new philosophers who want to 'remain riddles'; through a reference to Cesare Borgia as the 'healthiest of all tropical monsters and growths'; through a justification of the *eternal* order of command and obedience; through his ideal of the *'genuine* philosopher' who is a *'legislator'* and a *'commander'*, 'beyond good and evil', the 'most concealed, the most deviant'; through an affirmation of aristocratic society and an *order of rank*; through codes of the seizure of certain rights characteristic of *masters* (kratocracy) and the end of popular power; the projection of a new configuration of domination; all against the backdrop of an assault on Europe's democratic move- ment; the 'overcast sky of the beginning rule of the plebs' (cf. BGE 28–287). And at the nucleus of this book, a method for the 'ability to rule'; a principle concerning the need for some form of ideology as a political tool, or pretext, for purposes of social control and cohesion: the 'philosopher as *we* understand him, we free spirits . . . will make use of religions' and 'whatever political states are at hand' to advance his 'project of cultivation and education' (BGE 61, P 18).

Nietzsche sees in the Renaissance 'the climax of this millenium' and lauds the individualism of that epoch.[21] The Renaissance for Nietzsche represents the antithesis to the modern concept of humanization, to the morality of pity and to the theory of equal rights (TI Expeditions 37). It was 'the last *great* age' (EH CW 2) in its attempt to revalue Christian values, in its endeavour 'to bring about the victory of the opposing values, the *noble* values'. There has been no greater, 'more fundamental, more direct' war against Christianity. And it possessed 'a *possibility* of a quite unearthly fascination', namely, *'Cesare Borgia as Pope'*, an event which would have accomplished, in Nietzsche's view, the complete abolition of Christianity (A 61). Certainly, when Nietzsche refers to the values of the Renaissance – its individualism, its anti- Christianity – he has Machiavelli in mind, and perhaps even more so when he writes that the 'superiority' of Renaissance culture over medieval culture consisted solely in 'the great amount of *admitted* immorality' (WP 747 Nachlaß 1887 KSA 12 10[176]).

There is evidence for Nietzsche as a disciple or student of Machiavelli in the many direct and indirect references Nietzsche makes to him, par- ticularly to *The Prince*. As shown above, there are many philosophical parallels between Nietzsche and Machiavelli, but Nietzsche clearly acknowledges his indebtedness to Machiavelli only with respect to Machiavellian immoralism (realism) and *virtù*, clearly implements these ideas in his philosophy of morality and politics. In *Beyond Good and*

Evil, referring to *The Prince*, Nietzsche praises the *'allegrissimo'* of Machiavelli's style and Machiavelli's 'dangerous thoughts' (BGE 28). So it is to these 'dangerous thoughts', to *virtù* and immoralism, that I will now turn my attention.

2. *Virtù*

In *Daybreak*, Nietzsche broadly states his preference for the Greek and Roman 'morality of antiquity' whose most basic virtue he reads as 'personal distinction' (D 207). Nietzsche never departs, in his own thinking on morality, from this affirmation of personality or, in his terms, 'noble egoism'. In this sense, he consistently advocates, in opposition to the Christian morality of self-abnegation and to Christianity's conception of the 'good man', a virtue or character ethics which is more Roman and clearly more Renaissance-inspired than Greek for its emphasis on strength, virility, war, will and passion rather than on reason and rational harmonization.[22] Nietzsche repudiates the Greek tradition in ethics: Platonism, Aristotelianism and Stoicism (although there are features of each of these philosophies to which he is amenable).

What Nietzsche appropriates from the Renaissance, and more specifically from Machiavelli, and implements in his philosophy of morality and politics, is the notion of *virtù*. (Nietzschean ethics, to be precise, and as I stated previously, are *virtù* ethics not virtue ethics.) It is only beginning in 1885 and after that Nietzsche employs the term *virtù* – an italianization of the Latin word *virtus* – to describe the Renaissance individualism he praises.[23]

For Nietzsche, *virtù* means all of what it meant for Machiavelli: energy, courage, daring, strength of will, valour and political capability, intelligence and excellence. Nietzsche's own direct, verbatim references to *virtù* comprehend it as the possession of 'some ability and using that to create' (WP 75 Nachlaß 1885 KSA 11 34[161]), as the 'maximum of strength' (EH WC 1), as 'proficiency' (*Tüchtigkeit*) – in the sense of the feeling of an increase in power and the overcoming of resistances, which is Nietzsche's conception of 'happiness' and 'goodness' (A 2) – and as 'freedom from morality' (WP 304 Nachlaß 1887–88 KSA 13 11[54]), even as 'criminality' (WP 740 Nachlaß 1887 KSA 12 10[50]). *Virtù*, as Nietzsche writes, is 'moraline-free' (WP 317 Nachlaß 1887 KSA 12 10[109]).

It is antimoral or anti-Christian in so far as it is not posited as an ideal for everyone, but is 'rare' and 'aristocratic' (WP 317 Nachlaß KSA

12 10[109]). It constitutes a strength of soul which Nietzsche associates with the egoism of the noble type and the higher human being, for example, the soldiers Borgia or Napoleon, who were more whole than the Christian because they did not attempt to suppress the beast, the evil or the inhuman within themselves (BGE 257), and who were consequently more *natural*. For Nietzsche, the Renaissance or Machiavellian conception of *virtù* implies that an 'increase in the terribleness of man' is a necessary 'accompaniment of every increase in culture', that 'the higher and the terrible man necessarily belong together', an insight Nietzsche affirms as fundamentally at odds with the Christian, Rousseauian and socialist ideal of the 'good man' (WP 1017 Nachlaß 1887 KSA 12 10[5]). The Nietzschean new philosophers and legislators, contrary to this ideal, will possess an immoral mode of thought which will allow them to cultivate the good and the bad qualities in themselves to their fullest extent.

In the interests of further exposition, I now want to make some critical remarks on Bonnie Honig's reading of Nietzschean *virtù*.

In her comparison of Machiavellian and Nietzschean *virtù*, Bonnie Honig is erroneous on two points. First, her observation that for Nietzsche, as opposed to Machiavelli, *virtù* is strictly 'an instrument of self-fashioning' and is essentially nonpolitical. As Honig writes, *virtù* in Nietzsche's view 'is an individual excellence in the service, not of founding a republic, but of the strategic disruption of the impositional orderings of the herd and of the alternative construction of the self as a work of art'; and second, her observation that Nietzsche does 'not set his account of *virtù* in an account of institutions'.[24]

Honig is correct in implying that Nietzsche does not wish to found a republic, and in saying that Nietzschean *virtù* serves 'the strategic disruption of the impositional orderings of the herd' (namely, democratic and socialist); as Nietzsche writes, *virtù* does 'all that is generally forbidden', it is 'the real *vetitum* within all herd legislation' (WP 317 Nachlaß 1887 KSA 12 10[109]), and thus a verbal amulet for the free spirits. However, Honig is wrong in thinking that this 'strategic disruption', in theory, merely has as its *telos* the 'alternative construction of the self as a work of art'.

Nietzschean *virtù* is egoistic and immoralistic. It is opposed to contentment and peace and to pity for the 'ill-constituted and weak' (A 2), which has profound political consequences. And because it refers to the ability or capacity which is a precondition for the necessary practice of deeds, it is inherently political in so far as the Nietzschean self – the noble type – must necessarily impose itself on the other, can achieve its most complete expression only in the political or public realm in the form of rule. The egoism which belongs to the nature of a noble soul carries with it the conviction that 'other beings must be subordinate by nature and have to sacrifice themselves' (BGE 265). In short, the perfectionism which accompanies Nietzschean 'self-fashioning' cannot be separated from the perfectionism which uses 'the great mass of people as . . . tools' (WP 660 Nachlaß 1885–86 KSA 12 2[76]). It must be thought in connection to the political regime, order of governance and state apparatus which most adequately supports it. As with Machiavelli, Nietzschean *virtù* is ultimately that 'active force' which operates in the 'artists of violence and organizers who build states' (GM II 18). Complete 'self-fashioning', in the Nietzschean sense, implies the development of 'new states and communities' (GS 23). His 'strategic disruption' has consequences for the configuration of political space.

Nietzschean *virtù* refers to that 'excess of power' which 'experiences *itself* as determining values', as '*value-creating*' (BGE 260). So more than simply representing autonomy from and resistance to the 'impositional orderings of the herd', the Nietzschean individual possessing *virtù* is a lawgiver, a legislator and a *commander*. When Nietzsche affirms the individualism of the Renaissance, he is affirming the idea that 'one should *persist* in one's *own* ideal of *man*' and that 'one should impose one's ideal on one's fellow beings and on oneself overpoweringly, and thus exert a creative influence'.[25] In this sense, Nietzschean individualism can never be nonpolitical. It comports itself towards society and societal institutions as a whole.

Honig is also wrong when she says that Nietzsche does 'not set his account of *virtù* in an account of institutions'. First of all, and briefly, when Nietzsche writes that '*manly virtù, virtù* of the body is regaining value', he does so in a context in which he explicitly states his approval of 'the military development of Europe' (WP 127 Nachlaß 1884 KSA 11 26[417]), and thus it can be said that he does set his account of *virtù* in an account of military institutions. Furthermore, Nietzsche praises Napoleon Bonaparte as among the 'great artists of government' (WP 129 Nachlaß 1885 KSA 11 36[48]), a 'continuator' of the Renaissance (GS 362) who recalls the Italian *condottieri* of the fifteenth and sixteenth centuries. Napoleon represents a 'return to nature' which is, as Nietzsche declares, essentially *immoral* (TI Expeditions 48). He is Nietzsche's *new prince* and a man of *virtù*. Thus it can also be submitted that Nietzsche sets his account of *virtù*, by extension, in an account of Bonapartist institutions or Bonapartism.

Like Machiavelli's prince, the Nietzschean individual possessing *virtù*, the noble type, the commander, as he is idealized, impresses or stamps his personality on a pliant and malleable mass of people. For Zarathustra, 'man is . . . an un-form, a material, an ugly stone that needs a sculptor' (EH Z 8). Nietzsche's politics of *virtù* implies that such 'sculpting' necessarily entails the use of immoralistic means for the goals it aims to achieve. The willingness to use such immoralistic means are an intrinsic part of Nietzsche's conception of political leadership and politics in general, a conception radically at odds with the aristocratic liberal conception, an essential aspect of the disruptive strategy to break through to 'something'.

'*Not* contentment,' Nietzsche writes, 'but more power; *not* peace at all, but war; *not* virtue, but proficiency (*Tüchtigkeit*) . . . *virtù* . . . moraline-free' (A 1). To turn an Althusserian phrase, *virtù* prepares the philosopher-legislator to 'act immorally'.[26]

3. Immoralism

Two of Nietzsche's earliest references to Machiavelli, the first, a notebook entry from 1873, quoting B. G. Niebuhr,[27] and the second, from *Human, All Too Human* (1878), comprehend Machiavellian politics as *perspectivism*, as a *perspectival art of governance*. The first reads: 'At times you have to hold each single human being sacred, at other times you can and should treat them as a crowd, it comes down to knowing the time' (Nachlaß 1873 KSA 7 29[189]). The gist of the second is that 'the *form* of government is of minimal importance' – which is to say, any pure or simple form – the 'great goal of politics should be *permanence*' or durability (H 224). Thus Nietzsche appears to agree with Machiavelli that no simple or pure form of government can function effectively (P XIX), that different times require different remedies (P XVIII, XXV). The new prince must be able to operate between a variety of positions.[28] But Nietzsche also understands that this means that the prince 'who knows how to command' (P IX) 'must learn how not to be good' (P XV), must learn how to 'manipulate the minds of men' (P XVIII) and must 'know how to make good use of both the beast and the man' (P XVIII), which the parable of Chiron the centaur in *The Prince* instructs. And Nietzsche's next overt reference to Machiavelli and *The Prince*, which may also be found in *Human, All Too Human*, repeats precisely this instruction: The '*Genius of culture* . . . uses lies, power, the most inconsiderate self-interest . . . but his goals, which shine through here and there, are great and good. He is a centaur, half animal, half human' (H 241).

Nietzschean immoralism is Machiavellian perspectivism and Nietzschean perspectivism is Machiavellian immoralism. The first part of this formula means that the free spirits, or the new philosophers, have 'access to many and contradictory modes of thought' (H P 4); have 'the capacity to employ a diversity of perspectives and interpretations' (GM III 12); for them, 'all that is and has been becomes a means . . . an instrument' (BGE 211) in setting new goals for the human community. The second part of this formula means that Nietzschean perspectivism must be thought along with the *art of dissimulation.* In other words, the new philosophers must use concealment, infiltration, secret implementation of policy and masking techniques, which is emphasized, implicitly, when Nietzsche equates Machiavellianism with Jesuitism (Nachlaß 1884 KSA 11 25[74]) and further, if we can assume that he is talking about 'we immoralists', when he writes, 'Our true essence must remain concealed, just like the Jesuits' (Nachlaß 1881 KSA 9 11[221]).

Nietzsche is hyperbolic when he writes 'I am the first immoralist' (EH WD 2), for he has the example of Machiavelli and *The Prince* before him, to which he often refers. Nietzsche states that his term *immoralist* – and by extension, *immoralism* – entails two negations which are clearly interconnected: first, the negation of the conception of the 'good man' (Christian, Rousseauian and found in English moral doctrine), and second, the negation of Christian morality (EH WD 4).

These negations essentially translate into the idea that in a higher culture and in a higher and more whole human being, as was shown with respect to the individual possessing *virtù*, the higher and terrible necessarily belong together, the *inhuman* and the *superhuman* (exemplar: Napoleon), that the energies of evil contribute to the preservation and advancement of culture.[29] As Nietzsche writes in *Ecce Homo*, 'to demand that all should become "good" human beings . . . would deprive existence of its *great* character' (EH WD 4).

The affirmation of the indispensability of evil and evil instincts is general throughout the Nietzschean corpus. For example, Nietzsche identifies Zarathustra as 'a friend of evil' (EH WD 5) and asserts that it is the 'strongest and most evil spirits' who have 'done the most to advance humanity'. By 'evil' Nietzsche means all forms of transgression, both violent and nonviolent, the violation and subversion of 'old boundary markers' and 'old pieties' either through destructive war and 'force of arms' or through the establishment of 'new religions and moralities' (GS 4); the desire to dominate in all that is daring and new.

But Nietzsche's philosophy of immoralism goes beyond these two negations to encompass a general proposition about the nature of all morality and politics, namely, that morality is rooted in immoral foundations and that the state possesses no inherent moral legitimacy, that it is entirely the product of calculation and expediency over moral considerations, that it is founded on usurpation and violence, force and fraud and not on a social contract, a theory Nietzsche dismisses as mere 'sentimentalism' (GM II 17). The whole realm of 'legal obligations' and the 'moral conceptual world' is rooted in 'blood and torture' (GM II 6), inquisitions, the persecution of heresy and schisms. He gives radical expression to this general proposition in *Twilight of the Idols* when he writes: '*every* means hitherto employed with the intention of making mankind moral has been thoroughly *immoral*' (TI 'Improvers' 5).

What Nietzsche says about the nature of morality is that it is political in motivation. It is motivated by self-interest and power, guided by an instrumental rationality in which the ends proposed justify or measure the value of the means (P XVIII). Like Machiavelli, Nietzsche subordinates morality to political practice and comprehends the *praxis* of all morality and politics, whether Christianity or Bismarckian policy, in terms of the 'Machiavellianism of power' or *Realpolitik*.[30] As Nietzsche formulates it, all 'virtues' achieve domination and power exactly as a political party does: through 'immoral' means, through 'slandering, inculpation, undermining of virtues that oppose it and are already in power, by rebaptizing them, by systematic persecution and mockery' (WP 311 Nachlaß 1887 KSA 12 9[147]).[31] Even Martin Luther, according to Nietzsche, was as much a Machiavellian disciple 'as any immoralist or tyrant' (WP 211 Nachlaß 1887 KSA 12 9[147]). Immoral means have been exploited by all moral and political systems in coming to power.

Nietzsche's understanding of politics as guided by self- and class-interest, and ultimately by the sacrifice of principle for immediate advantage, is vividly demonstrated in his discussion of nationalism in *Human, All Too Human* where he writes that nationalism is 'a forcibly imposed state of siege' imposed by a minority – 'princely dynasties' and 'certain classes of business and society' – on the majority, and who manipulate the latter through 'cunning, force and falsehood' (H 475). Such an observation may have come from either Marxists or neo-Machiavellian elite theorists, but Nietzsche more closely resembles the elite theorists in so far as he interprets transformation in society primarily as the result of the application of force and fraud – as a result of political rather than economic power – and in so far as he views the masses, the majority of people, as essentially nonlogical or nonrational, with an inability or marked incapacity to comprehend complex political and social issues. I will revisit this point below when I discuss Nietzsche's relation to the neo-Machiavellians.

Nietzsche states that the very *'purpose'* of his critique of morality is to demonstrate that morality rests on immoral foundations (WP 272 Nachlaß 1887 KSA 12 10[154]). Furthermore, he is convinced that such a demonstration will be sufficient to break the 'tyranny of former values' (WP 461 Nachlaß 1888 KSA 13 14[134]). This critique is undertaken most rigorously in the *Twilight of the Idols* and *The Anti-Christ(ian)* where it focuses on the use by philosophers, priests and moralists of the *pia fraus* (pious fraud) and 'holy lies' for the purposes of social control. Nietzsche's primary examples are Plato's *Republic* and the *Laws of Manu*, as well as Confucius and the Jewish and Christian teachers, such as St Paul. Never, Nietzsche says, did these 'improvers of mankind' doubt 'their *right* to tell lies' nor 'their possession of *other rights*' (TI 'Improvers' 5). They merely assumed them. But, ultimately, Nietzsche says nothing against the use of such immoral means, says nothing against their indispensability, only the ends they serve (A 55). As Nietzsche writes, 'the point is to what *end* a lie is told . . . [that] "holy" ends are lacking in Christianity is *my* objection to its means' (A 56). As Nietzsche also says, making the same point and recalling Machiavelli's discussion of Romulus: 'It does indeed make a difference for what purpose one lies: whether one preserves with a lie or *destroys* with it' (A 58), just as it 'makes a difference . . . whether it is Homer or the Bible . . . that tyrannizes over mankind' (H 262). This perspective is in effect, as well, at that point at which Nietzsche will no longer condemn the violence, as he did in *Human, All Too Human*, or the *immorality* of the French Revolution, but only its 'Rousseauesque *morality*', its principle of equality (TI Expeditions 48).

The logic of his position is essentially circular. On the one hand, he wishes to show that 'everything praised as moral is identical in essence with everything immoral', but on the other hand, he says that 'everything decried as immoral' is higher than everything considered moral and that 'a greater fullness of life necessarily . . . demands the advance of immorality' (WP 272 Nachlaß 1887 KSA 10[154]), for example, the *lie*. Nietzsche's commitment to this position is clearly evident in an unpublished outline for a political treatise (*Ein tractatus politicus*) which affirms the 'perfectionism' of Machiavellian politics, although he says that it can never be truly achieved only 'approximated'. Its central idea is that the domination of any system of virtues is never attained through virtuous means, that the 'moralist' must be an immoralist in practice, that he must be free from both morality and truth for the sake of his goal of power. Like Machiavelli's prince, the 'moralist' must learn well the art of 'dissimulation', or techniques for the assertion of power; everything must be done with the 'appearance' of virtue, truth and goodness (WP 304 Nachlaß 1887–88 KSA 13 11[54], P XVIII).

There is a general consensus in the literature on Nietzsche and Machiavelli that Nietzsche readily accepts Machiavelli's 'concessions to immorality in the reform of political life'.[32] However, there is some question, or confusion, as to whether or not Nietzsche actually condones the 'pious fraud', whether or not he, or his projected regime, requires the appearance of virtue, truth and goodness. Leo Strauss says Nietzsche has absolutely no use for it, as does Conor Cruise O'Brien, who says that Nietzsche is free from 'the trammels of that appearance of piety which was binding on Machiavelli's *Prince*'.[33] This view is moderated by Geoff Waite who sees the theme of the will to Machiavellian and Jesuitical concealment, the problem of the relation between 'esoteric and exoteric statement', clearly operative in Nietzsche's political philosophy, although Waite does not strictly say that Nietzsche or the philosophers of the future, for whom Nietzsche writes, necessarily require the mask of piety or the mask of mediocrity which the mediocre majority is sure to believe.[34]

Nietzsche, however, writes of his 'delight in masks and the good conscience in using any kind of mask' (GS 77). In his notebooks, he associates the very ability to wear masks with '*strength of will*' (WP 132 Nachlaß 1885 KSA 11 35[9]). Like Machiavelli, he seems to agree that the form of government (or ideology) is only of minimal importance in *governing* (H 224); the true goals are elsewhere. As Nietzsche explains in *Beyond Good and Evil* – and it attests to the inherently tactical and spectral-syncretic nature of Nietzsche's political philosophy – the 'philosopher as *we* understand him, we free spirits . . . will make use of religions' (or the pious fraud) and 'whatever political and economic states are at hand' to advance his 'project of cultivation and education' (BGE 61). Elsewhere he records, 'shrewd exploitation of the given situation is . . . our best, most advisable course of action' (WP 908 Nachlaß 1884 KSA 11 25[36]). Sometimes, depending on the situation, the Nietzschean lawgiver expects arduous sacrifice from those lower in the order of rank, and sometimes he treats them politely and moderately.

For Nietzsche, the affirmation of 'reality' is a necessary characteristic of the stronger, noble type (EH BT 2), of the free spirits and commanders; the '*pia fraus* offends the taste of the free spirit' (BGE 105). But Nietzsche is not beyond recommending the use of myth or religion, or the production of a noble lie for the weaker type, weak in will, who are the majority of people in need of belief and external regulation. Even though Nietzsche praises the Renaissance for its *'admitted* immorality' – although he is surely only speaking of *The Prince* itself and not what *The Prince* recommends – his grand politics of *virtù* expediently and prudently seizes all the rights of the 'improvers of mankind', all the techniques for the manipulation of power, including deception, fear and the mask of piety or any ideology if necessary. Such a view is fully consistent with the 'genius of culture' who Nietzsche envisages in *Human, All Too Human*, the Machiavellian 'centaur' directed by 'ruthless self-interest' who manipulates falsehood and force in the interests of good objectives (H 241), just as Cesare Borgia did when he united the Romagna (P XVII).

Frederick II, King of Prussia, in his *Anti-Machiavel* (1740), which criticizes Machiavelli's theory that evil is necessary in politics, refers to *The Prince* as 'one of the most dangerous works ever to be disseminated'.[35] Machiavelli was condemned by the Church as well, viewed as a threat, and the Jesuits listed him on the *Index Librorum Prohibitorum*. However, as Prezzolini states, 'in Protestant countries a popular equation between Jesuitical and Machiavellian was reached' in the maxim, attributed to both the Jesuits and Machiavelli, 'the end justifies the means'.[36] This equation is apparent in Ueberweg's section on Machiavelli in his *History of Philosophy* (where Machiavellianism is tied to ecclesiastical practice) and, as was indicated above, is reflected in Nietzsche. It encodes his preoccupation with tactics.

But the first unapologetic vindications of Machiavelli emerge in Germany in the seventeenth and eighteenth centuries, in the works of Gasper Schoppe and John Frederick Christ, for example.[37] And Machiavelli's ideas, particularly, his patriotism, are taken up with renewed enthusiasm in the nineteenth century in the works of Fichte and Hegel. They defend Machiavelli's patriotism with respect to Germany's position under occupation by Napoleon's forces, drawing an analogy between the Italy of Machiavelli's time and the Germany of their own.[38] In *The German Constitution*, Hegel criticizes the polemic of Frederick II, arguing against those who would interpret Machiavelli's work as a foundation for tyranny and oppression.[39]

Meinecke claims that German political theories made increasing compromises with Machiavellianism or *raison d'état*.[40] None the less, they could not deviate from Christian ethics. Hegel initially justifies Machiavellian methods in founding a state, *virtù* against Christian ethics, but ultimately does not see such methods as 'universally applicable'.[41] And for Treitschke, the principal architect of power policy in Germany during the Bismarck era, the state is subject to moral law, or so he says.[42] Nietzsche approvingly refers to the nineteenth century as more natural in its position 'in *politicis*' because it 'sees problems of power' and does not 'believe in any right that is not supported by the power of enforcement'; it feels 'all rights to be conquests' or equates right with power (WP 120 Nachlaß 1887 KSA 12 10[53]). Nietzsche is an acolyte of this naturalistic version of the doctrine of right and political power, and, accordingly, his political philosophy displays an uninhibited compromise with Machiavellianism, not with respect to German nationalism or the Bismarckian state, but with respect to another kind of revolutionary force.

4. The right to rule and the process of legitimation

The experimental 'counter-force' Nietzsche speaks about in *Daybreak*, who believe that society should be an experiment in command and obedience, who seek the commander and the formation of a *new nobility*, are immoralists 'who do not regard themselves as being bound by existing laws and customs', who repudiate *contracts*. They are legitimated by the power of their own collective will and 'private morality'. They *create for themselves a right* (D 164) in accordance with the principles they have and the strength and power they possess. They simply *designate* their rights.

The death of God is accompanied by a sense of exhilaration (GS 342) because now 'mankind can do with itself whatever it wishes' (AOM 179), because the future is now 'dependent on a human will' (BGE 203). The Nietzschean legislators and commanders are like those 'autocratic human beings' of past generations whom Nietzsche imagines as he travels through Genoa and its regions, human beings who 'wished to live on', who built their houses 'to last for centuries'. They were human beings of strong will, characterized by an 'insatiable selfishness of the lust for possession', who 'refused to recognize any boundaries', and who despised the law (GS 291).

Such is the character of the philosopher-legislators and elite commanders Nietzsche envisages. When they arrive to organize the ruling structure they desire, to delimit and coordinate its functions, their imposition will be guiltless (GM II 17). Their aim is to restore, in opposition to the decadent theory of equal rights and to the morality of pity, to the political theories and state constitutions which espouse these (TI Expeditions 37), *pathos of distance* and order of rank.

For Nietzsche, the state is essentially an instrument of power for whomever has the strength to seize its control. The Nietzschean noble lawgiver and legislator, by Nietzsche's own account, possesses 'criminal' features, submits only to the law which he himself has given (D 187), represents 'a new strength and a new right' (Z Creator), possesses the 'characteristic *right*' to create and legislate values (BGE 261) as his *virtù* demands. However, Nietzsche's aristocratic radicalism, this ideal of self-assertion, does not eschew the gestures of political legitimacy and self-justification.[43] In the process of the legitimation of his aristocratic radicalism, Nietzsche does not provide us with a *holy* lie (although he recommends its use) but rather with a *noble* lie in the guise of natural law, exoterically communicated.[44]

Nietzsche insinuates that he is doing this himself when he criticizes the Stoics for imposing their morality on nature, but subsequently provides an apology for such an imposition explaining that philosophy 'always creates the world in its own image' since it is 'the most spiritual will to power, to the "creation of the world", to the *causa prima*' (BGE 9). And more directly, concluding his criticism of those who are making 'concessions to the democratic instincts', when he suggests that 'somebody might come along who, with opposite intentions and modes of interpretation, could read out of the same "nature" . . . the tyrannically inconsiderate and relentless enforcement of claims of power', or will to power (BGE 22), exactly as Nietzsche does. Like the Stoics he criticizes, Nietzsche reads 'the canon of [his] law in nature' (BGE 9).

The Nietzschean noble lie – or ideological justification – is will to power or order of rank, eternal recurrence and the origins of political society, the future and the exemplary human being, all founded on or conveying the conception that *life* or *nature* is *immoral*. Nietzsche describes nature as 'wasteful beyond measure, indifferent beyond measure, without purposes and consideration, without mercy and justice' (BGE 9), a description that is not reducible to, but finds a definite rapport with, the general economy of Nietzsche's social and political philosophy, particularly its assault on the liberal democratic interest in security and the general welfare.

Nietzsche's noble lie arguably does not possess the salutary features of the Platonic noble lie (*gennaion pseudos*), for it conveys with it the necessity of poverty, hardship, exploitation and self-sacrifice (a sort of Stoic asceticism). It should be said that Nietzsche criticizes not only *holy* lies such as are found in Platonism and Christianity – he even defends them as in the case of the *Laws of Manu* – but also *secular* lies such as the theory of equality (WP 464 Nachlaß 1885 KSA 11 37[14]). Ultimately, however, all lies have the same purpose, the same rationale, as Nietzsche says, which is to 'make the law *unconscious*' (A 57).

Nietzsche's noble lie is not salutary and, like Plato's (the myth of the metals taken from Hesiod) and Machiavelli's, is publicly or exoterically communicated. Nietzsche recognizes that Plato arrogated to himself the 'right to tell lies' (WP 141 Nachlaß 1888 KSA 13 15[42]) and recognizes the 'cold-blood reflection' on political technique in Plato's *Republic* (WP 142 Nachlaß 1888 KSA 13 15[45]). In Plato's *Republic*, the virtuous guardians control the foundational narrative and use 'persuasion or compulsion to unite all citizens'.[45] But, although they contrive to invent fictions, they reject 'representation' or role-playing;[46] they reject dissimulation. This is why Nietzsche, in my understanding, says Plato is not Machiavellian (WP 304 Nachlaß 1887–88 KSA 13 11[54]), because Plato wants to be what he appears to be.

Nietzsche publicly communicates his noble lie, but his writing is designed for selective consumption, for initiates of the hidden god, Dionysus. Nietzsche does not want to be read by the 'people' (WS 71). He wants a style that creates a distance, which is not accessible to everyone, but which only opens 'the ears of those whose ears are related to ours' (GS 381). (Although he displays a willingness to forge objective alliances with forces he ultimately opposes.) There is no esoteric teaching in Nietzsche, nothing hidden from view, for he publicly recommends the use of esoteric methods in politics, both noble and pious frauds, the mask of orthodoxy, even though he exposes many of the tactics of priestly-philosophical power-structures (which he employs) in the process. Lampert is incorrect when he says that, for Nietzsche, 'it's all over with the pious fraud because of the youngest virtue, honesty'.[47] This is because, for Nietzsche, honesty, integrity or *Redlichkeit* is coupled with Machiavellianism and Jesuitism (Nachlaß 1884 KSA 11 25[74]). The honesty of these doctrines pertains to their honesty about the political techniques that Nietzsche agrees need to be employed.

In his own system of ideological justification and legitimation, Nietzsche's final recourse is always to *life* or *nature*; that is its normative ground, the formula of Nietzsche's ideological rationalizations. For example, Nietzsche says that order of rank, or social hierarchy, expresses 'the supreme law of life' and 'sanctioning of a *natural order*' (A 57). Recall that the egoism of the noble type finds itself reflected in the 'primordial law of things' (BGE 265). But, for Nietzsche, life is will to power (BGE 13), the most pervasively deployed term or formula of ideological justification in the Nietzschean corpus. The formulation of the hypothesis of will to power attests to the inherently political *modus operandi* of Nietzsche's philosophy, in so far as it grounds this philosophy.

Its antidemocratic political rationale is made evident in *On the Genealogy of Morals* when Nietzsche opposes the hypothesis of will to power, or the 'theory that in all events a *will to power* is operating', specifically and exclusively to the 'democratic idiosyncrasy which opposes everything that dominates and wants to dominate' – the 'modern *misarchism*' (hatred of rule or government) which has permeated the 'sciences' and 'taken charge of all physiology and theory of life' (GM II 12), to 'the democratic prejudice in the modern world toward all questions of origin' (GM I 4).

In modern sociology, Nietzsche sees this democratic appropriation working through the theory of adaptation (a theory he associates with Herbert Spencer) which, in Nietzsche's view, robs life of the 'fundamental concept . . . of *activity*', ignores the will to power – 'the essence of life' – and the 'essential priority of the spontaneous, aggressive, expansive, form-giving forces that give new interpretations and directions' (GM II 12). In modern biology, similarly, Nietzsche sees the imposition of humanistic 'moral evaluations' which privilege altruism (as Spencer does) and depreciates order of rank, war and the drive to dominate. Nietzschean sociology or biology, conversely, and ideally conceived, proposes a theory of the will to power which negates the concept of the adaptation of 'inner' circumstances to 'outer' circumstances, favouring instead the notion of a will to power 'working from within' which 'incorporates and subdues more and more' of that which is external (WP 681 Nachlaß 1886–87 KSA 12 7[9]).

Nietzsche's first-order proposition is that the will to power governs all 'organic functions' and 'instinctive life'. It constitutes the essence of life and the 'intelligible character' of the world (BGE 36). It is 'the *primordial fact* of all history' (BGE 259). Nietzsche's second-order proposition is that life 'aims at the *expansion of power*', at 'growth' and 'superiority' (GS 349) and, in so doing, 'operates . . . in its basic functions, through injury, assault, exploitation, destruction'. Nietzsche's doctrine of the will to power broadly justifies all 'processes of subduing' and 'counteractions' (GM II 11), all acts of consolidation and *overcoming*, whether through arms, trade, commerce, colonization or ideas (WP 728 Nachlaß 1888 KSA 13 14[192]).

However, Nietzsche is much more specific regarding the doctrine's political repercussions. Accepting the doctrine implies the defamation of the concept of 'equality before the law' (and the rule of law) and the praise of authority, autocracy, privilege (order of rank) and concomitant 'claims of power' (BGE 22). It absolutely rejects, as a '*fundamental prin-*

ciple of society', the principle of 'placing one's will on par with that of someone else', which is considered by Nietzsche to constitute 'a will to the *denial* of life'. It is incompatible with any political doctrine which envisages social conditions free of exploitation, such as Marxism, anarchism and socialism, because exploitation is an essential and functional 'consequence of the will to power, which is after all the will of life'. According to its logic and its principle, it must condone or be silent about, depending on what ends are served, all that is '*essentially* appropriation . . . overpowering of what is alien and weaker; suppression . . . imposition of one's own forms . . . exploitation' (BGE 259). It must, in principle, violate all mutual contracts against injury.

The doctrine of the will to power provides legitimation and justification for Nietzschean *virtù* and immoralism, for exceptional rights and privileges. Nietzschean *virtù* evokes and encompasses the qualities of the future Nietzschean lawgiver, whose creative and artistic will shall be able to fashion human beings according to its antidemocratic and anti-Christian principles and, important for Nietzsche as for Machiavelli, 'prevail through long periods of time'. Only two doctrines impede his advent: the doctrine of equal rights and the doctrine of pity. It is the task of the free spirits, inspired by the immorality of the Renaissance, to undermine these doctrines in preparation for a reversal of values. Nietzschean immoralism incorporates the tactical concept that new values will have to 'appear in association with the prevailing moral laws, in the guise of their terms and forms', and that in order for this to happen, 'many transitional means of deception' will have to be devised (WP 957 Nachlaß 1885 KSA 11 37[8]). For the *genuine philosophers*, who are commanders and legislators, 'all that is and has been becomes a means for them, an instrument' in setting new goals for the human community (BGE 211).

Ernst Bloch says that Nietzsche recognized only positive law and techniques of domination.[48] He does not point out, however, that one of Nietzsche's techniques of domination is the introduction of nature as a noble lie (which grounds his 'legal' order), like the priests who want the whole course of nature in their hands, out of which he reads order of rank and order of castes. It logically follows that a Nietzschean genealogist should see only positive law where others see natural law, should not see nature as anterior to the state, should consistently see rights in terms of interests as they were seen by the school of historical law in Germany. We should expect a Nietzschean genealogist to speak consistently of utility or of convention rather than of a law of nature, as say Hume or Bentham did. But Nietzsche, in the manner of all priestly-philosophical power-structures, speaks not only the language of 'ancient' drives but also the language of 'eternity'.

The Nietzschean process of legitimation exceeds the deployment of the doctrine of the will to power. As was pointed out above, it also sees deployed the narratives of future promise, of the exemplary human being and of the violent origins Nietzsche considers to be at the basis of every *higher* culture (BGE 257), as well as the doctrine (or earthly religion) of eternal return which mythicizes the conflict between *master* and *slave*. This doctrine may plausibly be argued as 'a principle of rhetorico-political manipulation',[49] governed by a political motive and usage which may parallel that operative in Louis Auguste Blanqui's treatise, *L'Éternité par les astres* (1872),[50] where the same doctrine is pressed into the service of the political ideal of 'regular Anarchy'.[51] As a rhetorical tactic, Nietzsche's doctrine of eternal return simulates a priestly discursive control-function because 'eternity' is religio-moral sign-language. As the interventionist tactic of the 'convalescent', it is the device of political technology, the appropriation of the past and future. In both Blanqui's treatise and Nietzsche's doctrine, the point is to *will* the return against enemy projections of the future.

In the remaining two sections I will examine Nietzsche's reflections on control and manipulation and how these reflections ultimately situate him within the ideological constellation of the founders of mass psychology and elite theory.

5. Control and manipulation

Nietzsche's reflections on the methods of social control may be found throughout his corpus. They are formed, most visibly, by readings of Plato's *Republic* – the noble or '*necessary lie*' of the myth of metals at the foundation of the Platonic state (UM II 10) – the Hindu *Laws of Manu*, Christian scripture, the tactics of the Jesuits and Machiavelli's *The Prince*, that 'basic book of public conspiracy';[52] or, in other words, through examination of the concepts at the basis of all 'priestly-philosophical power-structures' including the 'demagogic' democratic state, as well as mediological reflections on Wagnerian theatre. But these reflections do not merely constitute empirical descriptions of the forms of communication and control in various societies. Rather, they comprise a practical search and implicit practical recommendations for a political technique (or political technology) wholly determined by Nietzsche's understanding of politics and his view of the necessity for an aristocratic social system of command and obedience whose members are divided into active and passive, a minority which legislates and a majority, weak in will, in need of belief and external regulation. Nietzsche fully accepts the Machiavellian doctrine 'that one who deceives will always find those who allow themselves to be deceived' (P XVIII).

Deception – or the *lie* – is the principal *immoralistic* practice and political technique Nietzsche ascribes to the priestly-philosophical power-structures he examines as he constructs his critique of the holy lie. In the Nietzschean analysis, deception is something consciously and practically employed in all ideology, myth and religion, including state-sponsored ideology such as patriotism and duty (WP 717 Nachlaß 1887–88 KSA 13 11[407]). It is implemented to arouse belief or faith, not reason or rational processes. In saying this, my intention is not to diminish the importance of Nietzsche's analysis of originary violence – the originary violence of the *Ur-Staat* – or the forms of punishment he associates with the 'morality of mores' or *mnemotechnics* in *On the Genealogy of Morals*; they are equally important. Rather, I wish to emphasize that Nietzsche, entirely in accord with the psychological orientation of his philosophy, expresses a strong and applied interest in the power religious and political ideals exercise over human beings. Nietzsche's interest is applied inasmuch as he supports the development or utilization of a practical political technique – which involves the maintenance and manipulation of already existing religious and ideological schemata – for his own political purposes. In this respect, Jaspers is erroneous when he claims that there is no practical, Machiavellian political technique in Nietzsche's philosophy, if only because Nietzsche advises the use of techniques already at hand.

The *virtù* of the free spirits and the *genuine philosophers* is armed with the capacity to employ diverse perspectives and interpretations.

Nietzsche is engaged in a war of spirits, an information war, a war of values and, because it is *noble*, depreciates 'the cruder instruments of force' (GS 358) in favour of a more *spiritual order* or more comprehensive forms of domination. In Machiavellian terms, Nietzsche would rather be a fox than a lion, his war of spirits is a war of cunning. This is also why he is interested in the psychology of belief, the need for belief which characterizes *weakness* (A 54), because he knows that 'it is easier to augment belief in power than to augment power itself' (WS 181). Nietzsche's fascination for the founders of religion, such as St Paul or Calvin, revolves around the cultural historical question of the secrets they possessed about domination and power; in effect, how they were able to change the 'shape' of a soul, reconstitute sensation in the body, and rule over it (D 113, 76); how the priestly type was able to hypnotize the 'entire nervous and intellectual system' (GM II 3) with the sole purpose, guided by their own *will to power*, of tyrannizing over masses (A 42). In *Human, All Too Human*, Nietzsche refers to the 'tactics and organization' of the Jesuits, their 'infamous arts' which reduced human beings to instruments (H 55). The overall fascination Nietzsche has for these secrets and these arts leads him, in subsequent work, in a more direct and less mystified manner, to catalogue the rhetoric of power, the discursive strategies and rhetorical devices employed by those who possess power, the 'conditions *under* which the priest comes to power' (A 55). Nietzsche's question is: 'What gives authority when one does not have physical power in one's hands?' (WP 140 Nachlaß 1888 KSA 13 14[189]). His primary case studies are the pagan, Hindu, Platonic, Jewish and Christian priesthoods – priests of both paganism and *décadence* – the *aesthetic* practice of the priest, the art of the holy lie; how the priest *seduces* with his morality, how he shrewdly takes possession of signs, symbols and concepts such as *God, truth, love, wisdom* and *life* making them synonyms of himself (A 44), how he 'stays master' through 'forms of systematic cruelty' and doctrines such as *Last Judgment, eternal damnation, sin* and *immortality of the soul* (A 38), how he makes himself, his values and practices, the *norm*.

In his notebooks, Nietzsche writes of the measures priestly-philosophical power-structures generally employ. He says that in order to prevail these structures support themselves through a discourse of 'spurious origin', 'by a pretended relationship with powerful ideals already existing', 'by the thrill of mystery, as if a power that cannot be questioned spoke through it', 'by defamation of ideals that oppose it' (a point he repeats in a number of places in his published work) and 'by a mendacious doctrine of the advantages it brings with it' (WP 343 Nachlaß 1886–87 KSA 12 7[6]). Guided by *Realpolitik*, permitting themselves the use of all immoralistic means to 'pious ends', these structures 'arrogate to themselves the right to tell lies'. What they require is the appearance of unconditional authority, that they hold 'the whole course of nature in their hands, so that everything that affects the individual seems to be conditioned by their laws'; they require the appearance of the possession of 'a more extensive domain of power whose control eludes the eyes of its subjects', for example, as with Christianity, 'power of punishment in the beyond' (WP 141 Nachlaß 1888 KSA 13 15[42]).

Elsewhere, Nietzsche reflects upon other methods and procedures of artifice and manipulation which range from the employment of words which are 'ambiguous and suggestive' and which appeal to 'future hope'

(AOM 95), to the shock tactics and *'permanent false alarm* of the press' (AOM 321) and the 'exaggeration' which characterizes modern writing (H 195), to control of time and history on the part of the pagan-Roman, Jewish and Christian priesthoods who knew how to transform everything into their own prehistory.[53]

According to Nietzsche, the point of all priestly-philosophical power-structures and systems of morality, the arts of persuasion and 'enchantment' which they employ, is to paralyse the 'critical will' (D P 3), to achieve a 'complete automatism of instinct', to make the law *'unconscious'*. Thus their rhetoric is such that it will never provide the reasons for the 'utility of a law', it must stand as a broad imperative designed to prevent 'the perpetuation *in infinitum* of the fluid condition of values'. This is generally accomplished through the appeal to revelation, tradition and divine authority. As Nietzsche writes, the 'authority of the Law is established by the thesis: God *gave* it, the ancestors *lived* it' (A 57).

Nietzsche sees the same arts or system of procedures operative in democratic society. In *The Case of Wagner*, he comments on the technical economy of Wagnerian theatre, observing in it the model of democratic demagogy coincident with the *Reich*; reading both, as he reads the aims of asceticism and priestly-philosophical power-structures in general, through the model of hypnosis (as Le Bon conceived the relation between leader and masses). The aim of Wagner's musical theatre, Nietzsche says, is to move and persuade the masses (*die Massen*), to 'induce intimations' rather than 'thought', to 'agitate the nerves', to stimulate the unconscious, 'reaching the body, the spine, the intestines' (CW 6). What Wagner and, by inference, democratic forms of communication want is 'effect' not 'truth' (CW 8). It is in this book, which may be read, in part, as a manual of propaganda or mediology, that Nietzsche coins the phrase 'the theatre is a revolt of the masses', meaning modern democratic politics is theatre (CW PS). Indeed, all modern political movements – anarchism, democracy and socialism – betray this 'demagogic character and the intention to appeal to the masses' (H 438).

In his earliest publications, Nietzsche asserts that all healthy, complete and creative cultures require myth to sustain them (BT 23); that every 'mature' nation or human being requires an 'enveloping illusion' or a 'protective and veiling cloud' (UM II 7). In his later publications, Nietzsche will say only that the masses or the majority requires this, that such a requirement contradicts the more enlightened and sovereign 'grand passion' of the free spirits and philosopher-legislators who can do without unconditional affirmations. It is essentially this view of the elite and the masses which connects Nietzsche to the ideology of the neo-Machiavellian elite theorists and to the founders of mass psychology. The masses, or the multitude, are weak, dependent and selfless *believers* who have to be used, who need someone who will use them, the constraint of 'external regulation', 'compulsion' and *'slavery'* in order to 'prosper', while the elite, Nietzsche's radical aristocracy, have the 'courage for unholy means', an immoralism which permits them to employ conviction or belief 'as a *means*' (A 54), using ideology as they see fit.

In the literature on Nietzsche, there are two opposing points of view which are relevant to the topic of control and manipulation of power, and to the question of the presence of a practical political technique in Nietzsche's writings. One view is expressed by Keith Ansell-Pearson, who argues, following Sheldon Wolin's discussion of Machiavelli, that although Nietzsche is 'a descendant of Machiavelli's aesthetic appreciation of power and politics', he is not concerned 'so much with mastery as with art, not manipulation but architectonic, political sculpture rather than political mastery'.[54] The opposing view, with which I am in agreement, is expressed by Daniel Conway, who argues that Nietzsche is a 'type of Christian priest' who 'intends to reproduce the priestly stratagems of St Paul', that 'everything he says about the priest is true of him as well'.[55] As tabulated above, Nietzsche does provide a description of the manipulative procedures, tactics and rhetorical devices of priestly-philosophical power-structures; the question, however, is whether or not he endorses such procedures for his own political ends.

I stated above that Nietzsche advises the use of political techniques already at hand, that he supports the utilization of a practical political technique which involves the maintenance and manipulation of already existing religious and ideological schemata, that he supports 'transitional means of deception' and the 'guise of moral laws', that he supports the use of *masks*, of mediocrity, of piety, of virtue, truth and goodness, that he implements, for legitimation purposes, a series of *noble* lies (one of which is order of rank, which claims as a law of nature, coterminous with Plato's myth of the metals, the impossibility of blending the classes together). Nietzsche understands, as did Numa, that myth, religion and ideology are indispensable political tools in the hands of rulers.

Contrary to what Ansell-Pearson suggests, Nietzschean political sculpture implies political mastery and manipulation. The pliant and malleable material it works on are, in principle, the majority of people, the masses who are in need of belief and external regulation. But Nietzschean political sculpture is, moreover, political opposition wherein the sense of mastery and manipulation is *reversal*, the control of mass movements through the use of appropriate political techniques – rule through *simulacra libertatis*.

One of Nietzsche's principal concerns is that history has been revised by the people, from the democratic standpoint of the *sovereignty of the people*, that it has been appropriated by a despotic 'mob' (Z Law-Tables 11). It is the *modus operandi* of the Nietzschean new nobility to oppose all 'mob-rule', in part, through appropriating this history. Their grand politics of *virtù* expediently seizes all the rights inherent to priestly-philosophical power-structures, all the practical techniques for the manipulation of power including the right to lie. As Nietzsche writes, our 'true essence must remain concealed, just like the Jesuits who exercised dictatorship in conditions of general anarchy, but who installed themselves in the guise of *tools* and *functions*'.[56] In other words, the new nobility accept as a standard of political behaviour the secret implementation of policy (*Arcana rei publicae*). If they are to be the 'subtle seducers' Nietzsche refers to in *The Gay Science*, then they must know how to arouse 'expectations . . . while making no effort to furnish reasons for their cause' (GS 38).

Nietzsche never condemns the lie as such, for 'the point is to what *end* a lie is told'. He condemns Christian means because of the ends they serve, but not the means he finds in the *noble* Hindu *Laws of Manu*, because he supports its ends; namely, its caste model of social organization, its conception of society as a pyramid, in which 'the *noble* orders, the philosophers and the warriors, keep the mob under control' (A 56), which is precisely what Nietzsche wants.

In order to achieve this control, Nietzsche endorses the use of not only state-sponsored religion, but also of 'whatever political and economic states are at hand' (BGE 61). In *Human, All Too Human*, Nietzsche suggests that the state requires religion in order to 'excite reverence', but moreover, because it 'guarantees a calm, patient, trusting disposition among the masses'. The ruling classes remain 'superior to it . . . using it as a tool'. This is something that not only Numa and Machiavelli grasped, but Napoleon Bonaparte as well: that power requires the legitimacy of priests (H 472). (Nietzsche is wholly cognizant of the fact of Napoleon's concern with appearances.) In *Beyond Good and Evil*, Nietzsche continues this trajectory of thought. Dicussing the art of governance, he claims the necessity of religion 'as a bond' which delivers subjects over to their rulers, which may provide them 'an inestimable contentment with their situation' (BGE 61). However, the religion Nietzsche is confronted with is the religion (ethos or morality) of democracy and democratic institutions. Thus he supports the development of these institutions, although not in the dangerous form of socialism, because 'they enhance weakness of will'. Democratic institutions 'prepare a type of man that must one day fall into our hands, that must *desire* our hands' (WP 132 Nachlaß 1885 KSA 11 35[9]).

Nietzsche – and this constitutes a central component of his political vision – anticipates a future democratic Europe populated by a mass of 'workers . . . poor in will' and in need of a *commander*; a type directly produced through the process of democratization who is 'prepared for *slavery* in the subtlest sense' (BGE 242). (Because of the democratic ethos of toleration, an ambiguous identity is produced with the need to please.) Because Nietzsche's search for a political technology takes place within a moment of European democratization, and is aimed at the *becoming a political subject* of the multitude, their constituent power, it can be said that Nietzsche seeks the authoritarian potential within democracy itself, wherein democratic Europe is treated as a tool or instrument in the formation of a new order, guided by the tenet that the masses are not suited for philosophy, rather what they need is holiness (CW 3), or the pious fraud, as Nietzsche writes in 1888. The 'new virtue' of honesty does not prevent him from asserting the importance, 'for the present', of supporting 'the religions and moralities of the herd instinct' (WP 132 Nachlaß 1885 KSA 11 35[9]).

6. Nietzsche and neo-Machiavellianism (Nietzsche's Machiavellian militancy)

Nietzsche's search for the authoritarian potential within democracy, his reflections on control and manipulation, his desire to control the *mob*, which are significantly informed by a reading of the Machiavellian conceptions of *virtù* and immoralism, situate him within the ideological constellation of the neo-Machiavellian founders of mass psychology and elite theory (Le Bon, Pareto and Mosca), all of whom reflected on the dangers of democratic and socialist mass movements and on the possibility of manipulating those mass movements through practical political techniques. They also emerge from the aristocratic liberal tradition, following de Tocqueville in his critique of the Jacobin revolution and Taine in his conception of the masses; but they are radicalized along Nietzschean lines.

Le Bon, Pareto and Mosca wrote a political psychology, sociology and political science which is methodologically more coherent, expository and argumentative than Nietzsche's philosophy (which relies on the seductive power of the aphorism and is topically dispersed), containing, among them, a more complex analysis of the distribution of power in society, but which is ideologically of the same character. In Pareto, for example, as in Nietzsche, can be found an antimetaphysics, a recognition of the contingent character of ethical and legal systems, a critique of natural law, social contract theory and universal suffrage (or majority rule), a critique of equality and the idea of progress (in favour of cycles of ascent and decline), and of the 'epidemic of humanitarianism' which Pareto tendentiously traces to the French Revolution and its 'neo-Christian democratic sentiments'.[57]

Like Nietzsche, Pareto is critical of the 'submissiveness' of contemporary rulers to the people, which is to say, to the demands of the working classes or proletariat who are driven by envy and a *ressentiment* against culture and intellect. In *Mind and Society*, he praises Nietzsche for daring to 'speak ill of the god People'.[58] Like Nietzsche, he sees democratization as an essentially irreversible process, but programmatically observes, along acknowledged Machiavellian lines, that it may be manipulated through control of public opinion, through persuasion and the use of religion, morality and myth.[59] Although Pareto, in contrast to Nietzsche, demonstrates more commitment to the use of 'cruder instruments' of force. Even though Pareto says that the general will is 'not observed in reality', that popular representation and universal suffrage is a fiction, because it is always elites or 'aristocracies' who rule, he none the less recommends that the 'residues in the masses' be exploited and persistently criticizes humanitarian ideology (democratic, socialist, Marxist, Kantian) as a principal cause of the 'decay' and 'decadence' of the ruling classes.[60] Implicit to Pareto's 'science', esoterically styled, is the imperative to reform, revalue or replace the ruling or governing classes, and the rationalization of the potential to 'mislead the subject class' into serving whatever elitist interests are established.[61]

It should be said that Pareto does argue for a 'circulation of elites', as does Nietzsche in *Human, All-Too-Human* (H 439), and that any elite should draw, based on extraordinary physiological and psychological characteristics, energy, aptitude and intelligence, from all classes. It is an argument for selection, arguably influenced by Social Darwinism, against humanitarian doctrines or systems which favour 'the weak, the vicious, the idle, the ill-adapted'.[62] Pareto affirms, typical of aristocratic liberalism, the potential mobility of individuals from the lower classes, but not the lower classes themselves. As far 'as these lower classes themselves are concerned' he writes, 'they are incapable of ruling; ochlocracy has never resulted in anything save disaster'.[63] Like Nietzsche,

Pareto argues, in his case in direct opposition to Marxism, for the onto-logical necessity of exploitation, that exploitation is intrinsic to life.

Mosca, like Nietzsche and Pareto, also constructs a polemic against the 'absurd metaphysics of social democracy'.[64] His principal targets are Rousseau and democratic doctrine, socialist and anarchist reform, and the 'dictatorship of the proletariat'. He views the granting of universal suffrage as a 'mistake'.[65] Mosca seeks a new mode of political organiza-tion somewhat vague in its contours. Like Nietzsche, he hopes for a new 'moral and intellectual aristocracy' who will shape the 'minds' of their contemporaries, 'forcing their programs upon those who rule the state'.[66] Like Nietzsche, he justifies minority rule and order of rank. According to Mosca, political power 'never has been, and never will be, founded upon the explicit consent of majorities', but 'always will be exercised by organized minorities',[67] or a ruling class. All human orga-nization requires 'ranking and subordinations', that there should be some who, by nature, command and others who obey or 'can be brought to obey'.[68] Along with this justification, this 'political formula', Mosca's *The Ruling Class* constitutes an attempt to refute the idea of uni-versal equality and justice, the idea of a classless society and the end of exploitation, and the optimistic or Enlightenment conception of human nature.[69]

In Le Bon, too, there are similar themes. His mass psychology is informed by a Machiavellian interest in the methods and rules of the art of governance, in how charismatic leadership (*virtù*) may control and manipulate the masses, through myth and imagery, *spiritually* and *unconsciously*. He is also critical of the principles of the French Revolu-tion and the *ressentiment* of the lower classes.[70] Like Nietzsche, he sees in the principle of equality the disdain of all authority and superiority. Like Nietzsche, he says that 'natural laws do not agree with the aspira-tions of democracy',[71] rather with class war, and that 'government of the crowd' or 'mob rule' must be resisted.[72] but Le Bon's work justifies authoritarian leadership, claiming the essential 'credulity' of the masses who, without a leader, remain 'an amorphous entity incapable of action'.[73]

In Le Bon's book, *The Crowd*, there are two dominant ideas. First, the idea that the masses think in images (sentiments and nonrational asso-ciations of ideas) and are influenced by 'theatrical representations', as Nietzsche implied in *The Case of Wagner*, rather than by reason and argu-ment (it accompanies the question as to how individuals are fused into a crowd); and that it is imperative that contemporary leaders come to understand, as Napoleon did, the psychology of the masses – their imaginations and the *religious* form of their beliefs, that the masses are essentially servile and thirst for obedience, that they are open to *suggestion* – as well as the power of certain words and formulas.[74] As Le Bon writes, haunted, as was Nietzsche, by the Paris Commune, 'it is necessary to arrive at a solution of the problems offered by their psychology or to resign ourselves to being devoured by them'.[75] And second – and here the ideological orientation of Le Bon's discussion is more apparent – the idea that the 'religious' beliefs which must be opposed, solved and redirected are the beliefs or dogmas of popular sovereignty and universal suffrage, dogmas that possess 'the power that Christian dogmas formerly possessed'.[76] Like Nietzsche and the elite theorists, Le Bon is critical of the 'capitulation' of contemporary leaders to the demands of the masses.[77]

All the neo-Machiavellians argue that civilization is the achievement of organized minorities, that society is a *pyramid*, as Nietzsche conceives every 'higher culture', that the masses are dominated by nonrational, unconscious forces and cannot be influenced by reasoning or logic, but rather through the use, for example, of 'magical' words or repetition, and that the practice of power is based on force, fraud and manipulation by elite leadership, that manipulation, in the process of obtaining popular consent which is required in order to govern, is a necessity. They are antidemocratic, anti-Rousseauian, antiegalitarian and antisocialist and adhere to the Machiavellian distinction between 'the few and the many', the ruler type and the ruled type.[78] The ruler type possesses *virtù*, while the majority or the masses are conceived as passive instruments, uncreative and mediocre. The neo-Machiavellians further argue that freedom can only result from the agonistic interaction of social and political elites, that there should be no commitment on the part of elites, outside of maintaining power, to any particular political programme. Le Bon writes, the 'political system which a nation adopts is not a matter of great importance'.[79] They argue for a spectral-synthetic (dissimulative and esoteric) application which not only harks back to Machiavelli, but to Napoleon Bonaparte.[80] (Strictly speaking, Le Bon was critical of the dictatorship of Napoleon, but subscribed to the Napoleonic form of government, autocracy based on popular consent, plebiscites without discussion, authoritarian democracy.)[81]

As with Nietzsche, the political ideals of the neo-Machiavellians are, variously, autocratic, aristocratic and authoritarian, although Mosca later came to vindicate representative democracy and liberal institutions.[82] They offered somewhat more than simply 'tacit' support[83] for a manipulative conception of political authority. As Ettore Albertoni writes, elite theory clearly operated as 'a political doctrine or ideology' which radically put into question the expansion of democracy. It was 'intended to aid the organization and rise to power of a new class'.[84] More radical than the aristocratic liberals, de Tocqueville, Burckhardt and Taine, they believed that the democratic process would, rather than simply could, lead to socialism and degenerate into despotism. Thus they opposed the interests of the working class and the extension of the voting franchise, the real participation of the masses in democratic processes. They follow de Tocqueville in his critique of the Jacobin revolution and its assault on individual freedom and Taine in his conception of the masses.[85] However, the elite theorists and Le Bon, more systematically, unlike the aristocratic liberals, but like Nietzsche, introduce a scientific basis to their psychological analysis. For Le Bon, in order to defeat socialism, it is imperative to know 'the psychology of its disciples'.[86]

It was Taine who characterized the masses of the French Revolution as *canaille*, who criminalized them, countering the Rousseauian 'myth' of the good human being, who claimed them to be passive instruments of Jacobin leadership, who described them as lacking any social identity. In Taine's view, the revolutionary masses were 'recruited from the human waste which infects all capital cities', they formed a mob 'dictatorship' which, according to their nature, consisted of acts of violence. It was Taine who formulated the general principle, in a work seminal for the elite theorists, that the 'human herd' is 'accustomed to being led'.[87]

Nietzsche describes political culture in terms which share the essential presuppositions of Machiavellian and neo-Machiavellian political theory. He consistently adheres, for example, to the Machiavellian distinction between the ruler type and the ruled type, elite and masses, that there can be no human organization without ranking and subordinations. Nietzsche also conceives of political power as *immoralistic* in nature, as possessing inherent manipulative potential, and shares a similar definition of *décadence*.

Robert Nye, in commenting on the 'elite–mass' dichotomy in elite theory, states that 'it can be persuasively argued that the legitimacy claimed for elite rule by these theorists follows from the particular nature of the mass rather than the elite'. What Nye means is that the elite theorists do not have a clear 'normative definition' of *elite*, but do have a clear conception of *non-elite*.[88] Nietzsche's own claims to legitimacy are also primarily embedded in reactive terms, anti-Christian and antidemocratic, with the masses (or the working classes) clearly and negatively, which is not to say correctly, conceived. Nietzsche shares many political ideas with the neo-Machiavellian elite theorists, but it is his conception of the masses, coupled with these ideas, which solidifies his connection to them.

Like Le Bon, Nietzsche recognizes that this is 'the age of the masses' (BGE 241), 'the century of the *crowd*' (BGE 256), and that these masses and crowds must be controlled. From *Human, All Too Human* and *Daybreak*, where his *'campaign against morality'* also constitutes a campaign against popular sovereignty, to throughout his post-Zarathustran writings, Nietzsche typically characterizes the masses, or the 'great majority', as 'unknowledgeable' (H 448), as 'ill-informed and incapable of judgement' (AOM 318), as dwelling in 'a fog of impersonal, semi-personal opinions' and 'poetical evaluations' (D 105), as immune to reason or rational argument,[89] as profoundly susceptible to the 'actor' and the theatrical methods which most effectively produce belief (Z Flies). He makes it quite evident that politics should not be entrusted to the masses (D 188), that they do not have the capacities to understand complex social and political issues.

In Nietzsche's view, as in Machiavelli's, the masses are passive 'raw material' who must be shaped (GM II 17), with an innate or instinctive need for obedience, with the 'fundamental conviction' that they '*must* be commanded' (GS 347), in need of a *commander* (BGE 199). Nietzsche wants to give incentive to the new ruling, aristocratic class he envisages, and so he writes: 'at bottom the masses are willing to submit to slavery of any kind, if only the higher-ups constantly legitimize themselves as higher, as *born* to command' (GS 40). He realizes that some form of legitimation, or 'political formula', is necessary, because he understands, like Machiavelli, that popular consent is required in order to govern, that government must appear to come from the people, that the prince or the ruling class must keep the populace in their favour and not incur their hatred, and that it is a 'duty for the *exceptional human being* to handle the mediocre gently' (A 57, P 19). It is an essential requirement of Nietzschean *perfectionism*. In the Nietzschean polity, the masses would acquire value only to the extent to which they would serve the ideology of the production of the higher type. The masses would be used as tools or instruments towards this end, for 'perfecting consists in the production of the most powerful individuals, who will use the great mass of people as their tools' (WP 660 Nachlaß 1885–86 KSA 12 2[76]).

And Nietzsche wants to give the new ruling, radical aristocratic class he envisages a method. This is clear from his reflections on priestly-philosophical power-structures I discussed above: the rules and methods for governance, the tactics political communications must employ. It is a question of political realism and a 'politician's insight' that he 'who wills the end must will the means' (WP 142 Nachlaß 1888 KSA 13 15[45]). It should be known, concerning practical political techniques, that the masses 'grovel on their bellies before anything massive' (BGE 241), that they desire 'to hear only the most elevated language' (D 189), that the rulers must *intoxicate* them with 'the prospect of conquests and grandeur' (D 188), 'patronize and applaud the virtues' that make them 'useful and submissive' (WP 216 Nachlaß 1887 KSA 12 10[188], P XVIII, XXI). They 'must receive the impression that a mighty, indeed invincible force of will is present; at the least it must seem to be present' (H 460). Under certain circumstances, it might even be necessary to strengthen socialism, employ it as a lever of power (H 446). If the masses are 'so greatly deceived', Nietzsche writes, mining Machiavellian doctrine, it is because 'they are always *seeking* a deceiver' (D 188, P XVIII). They are passively waiting to receive the imprint of the ruling class, to respond to the shaping hand of the political artist. Ideally, and this is entailed by Nietzschean perfectionism, what they serve they will serve *unconsciously*, with 'complete automatism of instinct' (A 57). This constitutes the most comprehensive form of domination because, as Le Bon would say, 'it cannot be fought against'.[90]

In this chapter I have argued that Nietzsche's radicalization of the aristocratic liberal critique leads him to embrace a politics inspired by Machiavelli's, *The Prince* and, particularly, by Machiavelli's conceptions of *virtù* and immoralism. Furthermore, in opposition to the idea that Nietzsche's political position 'most closely resembles that of the anarchists' of his period, I have argued that Nietzsche's political position, or ideology, is more akin to the neo-Machiavellians of his period. These neo-Machiavellians also incorporate aspects of the aristocratic liberal critique but radicalize it through the Machiavellian conceptions of *virtù* – which informs their idea of charismatic elite leadership – and immoralism – which informs their inquiries into practical techniques for political control.

Both Nietzsche and the neo-Machiavellians seek the authoritarian potential within democracy. In contrast to the aristocratic liberals, particularly Burckhardt and Taine, who were both very cynical regarding mass movements, they wish to provide incentive for a new aristocracy and prepare the ground for an active reversal. Like the neo-Machiavellians, Nietzsche is both antidemocratic and antisocialist, and also opposed to anarchism. But he is linked to them, via Machiavelli and Taine, primarily in his conception of the masses and in the philosophy of control he begins to develop through a reading of the tactics of priestly-philosophical power-structures and through reflection on Wagnerian opera. His breakthrough is not *virtù* as such, but immoralism. For Nietzschean perfectionism entails the mastery of the techniques of social control, because *virtù* is nothing without human beings to shape.

To those who claim that Nietzschean perfectionism implies a level of genuine excellence that democracy may contribute to, it can be said that the perfection or excellence Nietzsche describes (cf. BGE 200) should not appeal to democrats because it is only cynically supported by democratic institutions. What Nietzsche is saying is that democracy produces weakness of will and ambiguous identity, and that in the same age, and owing to the same conditions (provided by democratic education, adaptability, art and mask, etc.), a stronger type may appear to manipulate it. His obvious exemplar in this respect is Napoleon Bonaparte.

Nietzsche should be distanced from the anarchist doctrine of Bakunin, for example, to whom he critically refers, just as the anarchist Kropotkin distanced himself from Nietzsche. Kropotkin criticized the Nietzschean sovereign individual because he recognized that it could not exist without the oppression of the masses.

Bakunin may reject social contract theory and Christianity, he may, like Nietzsche (and the Marxists), emphasize the importance of the study of tactics, he may be Machiavellian in so far as he considers the recourse to immoral means as crucial in manipulating the masses to revolt, or in that he views the masses as essentially pliable material for manipulation by a conspiratorial and revolutionary elite. But Bakunin is opposed to Nietzsche in so far as he negates all forms of exploitation, oppression and domination, for which Nietzsche, as is evident in his hypothesis of the will to power, authors a justification. Unlike Nietzsche, Bakunin believes that freedom, which he considers to be an inalienable right, cannot be realized without equality, both educational and economic.

Bakunin is opposed to privilege and espouses the complete emancipation of the proletariat, the abolition of private property and the liquidation of the state, doctrines that are anathema to Nietzschean political philosophy.[91]

Nietzsche opposes universal liberty and equality. He envisages, rather, a new nobility or radical aristocracy who will seek to 'endure for millennia', who will not only be supreme in will, but in 'knowledge, riches, and influence', and who will redirect the constituent power of the democratic masses, employing 'democratic Europe as their most pliant and supple instrument for getting hold of the destinies of the earth' (WP 960 Nachlaß 1885–86 KSA 12 2[57]).

The militant, authoritarian conversion in Nietzsche, as it is projected, may be thought in terms of Bonapartist solutions: the pretence of democratic forms, while subverting democratic institutions, strengthening executive power through diverse machinations. For that is precisely the Nietzschean model of governance: *autocratic will in the guise of popular rule*. And *The Prince* is central to this political conception.

Epilogue

> *Then . . . something said to me voicelessly . . . 'You are the one who
> has unlearned how to obey: now you shall command! Do you know
> what it is all men most need? Him who commands great things.
> This is the most unpardonable thing about you: You have the power
> and you will not rule.'*
>
> (Z Stillest Hour)

Each phase of Nietzsche's philosophy is regulated by a *task* (*Aufgabe*).
However this task is defined, at whatever stage of his work, it is continually performed under the diagnostic presupposition of the *décadence*
and degeneration of life and culture, including politics and the politics
of *ressentiment*. In Nietzsche's early work, his primary task is the rebirth
of German culture. It is a task inspired by Schopenhauer, Wagner and
the ancient Greeks. Even then, this task possesses a political dimension
which addresses the democratization of the German educational system
and the question of the relation between culture and the state, the delineation of which appears to have been presented by Burckhardt.

Other fundamental oppositions begin to emerge at this early stage as
well: a position taken against Christianity, modernity, public opinion
and the public press, against the 'contemptible money economy' (UM
III 4), against the masses and the militant working classes, against whom
he declares war; and a position taken for the future of humanity, for the
naturalistic moral systems of Greek and Roman antiquity, and of the
Renaissance; for an active and sovereign individualism which strives
to be independent of state and society, but which needs a society to
support it and the political authority of a state to protect it.

When Nietzsche advances the 'individual' over the 'community' it is
not in the interests of individualism *per se* (of liberalism or anarchism),

rather, it is an assertion regarding where sovereign power should be invested, an actual struggle against popular power.

As Nietzsche's work develops, though he will not lose interest in the fate of German culture or the German state (primarily as a critic of Bismarck and German nationalism), his task is formulated in more global terms with clear political overtones encapsulated in the expression, *die große Politik*. This is the task of the revaluation of all values. It constitutes an extension of his *'campaign against morality'* initiated in *Daybreak*. The task of the revaluation of all values deepens the war against all decadent values, including decadent liberal democratic, socialistic and anarchistic political values. Ultimately, Nietzsche, like Plato, wishes to install philosophers as rulers and *lawgivers* – because a sovereign authority is necessary – but who must be, first of all and necessarily, *lawbreakers*, possessing a disruptive and dangerous capacity.

It may be instructive here, in the interests of synoptic closure and critical reflection, and because it touches on, and contradicts, some of the basic issues and claims of my study, to consider an essay by Thomas Brobjer which is an example of a continuing effort in Nietzsche studies to depoliticize Nietzsche. However, the bracketing it performs is quite tenuous, as I will show.[1]

In this essay Brobjer wishes to demonstrate that there is an absence of political ideals in the Nietzschean corpus. It opens with the claim that Nietzsche 'very rarely speaks explicitly of politics', although some pages later Brobjer says that Nietzsche does say things that are 'politically interesting' and which have 'political consequences', but that politics is not Nietzsche's 'main interest or motive'.

The main purpose of Brobjer's essay is to put into question those interpretations of Nietzsche which claim Nietzsche's affinity for the laws and society of Manu. He believes that the motive behind such interpretations is to 'force Nietzsche's thinking into categories into which it does not fit'. Yet at various points throughout the essay Brobjer himself characterizes Nietzsche's thinking in terms of the following political categories, most of which would be in accordance with the laws and society of Manu: elitism, hierarchy (order of rank and order of castes), antidemocratism, antisocialism, antistatism and antinationalism. Brobjer does not finally say, unequivocally, that the society of Manu is not an ideal for Nietzsche, but suggests that *if* it is an ideal for Nietzsche, 'it is so only to a very limited extent', and *if* it is an ideal, Nietzsche does not estimate it as highly as he does ancient Greece, the *Imperium Romanum* or the Renaissance. Brobjer believes that Nietzsche's 'main intention is not to establish [Manu] as an ideal but to criticize Christianity through it by contrast'. A 'more correct interpretation', he says, of Nietzsche's treatment of the laws of Manu in *The Anti-Christ(ian)* is not to see it as 'expressing Nietzsche's political ideal' but to see it 'as part of his critique of Christianity and modernity'.

Contrary to what Brobjer says, Nietzsche more than rarely speaks about politics – we may find political commentary in every one of Nietzsche's published works and throughout his notebooks as well – and does so explicitly, otherwise how could Brobjer himself identify those political categories into which he agrees Nietzsche's thought does fit? Second, if it is true that will to power is a fundamental Nietzschean philosophical doctrine (as Heidegger, for example, claims it is), and if we recall that Nietzsche establishes this doctrine or hypothesis in opposition to *democratic* theories of life, as he does in *On the Genealogy of Morals*, then we must consider that there is a political motive behind his philosophy. Finally, why does Nietzsche set up such oppositions as Manu–Christianity or noble–Christian if it is not to indicate what his ideals are? Nietzsche does not provide such oppositions for no reason, he provides them in the interests of a revaluation of all values.

As I argued in Chapter 1, Nietzsche's critique of Christianity and Christian morality is necessarily a critique of political doctrine because the critique of Christianity is necessarily a critique of 'the *fatality* that has crept out of Christianity into politics', a *fatality* which is manifest in modern social and political institutions. Nietzsche's critique of Christian teachings is also a critique of those teachings which have been 'expanded into political theory', namely, liberal, democratic, anarchist, communist and socialist political theory. This is made quite clear in Nietzsche's interpretation of *décadence* and in his delineation of *ressentiment*. In this vein, Nietzsche declares war on the masses which translates into an assault on universal suffrage; he criticizes representational or parliamentary constitutions; he criticizes the utilitarian formula of 'the happiness of the greatest number' which he considers to be an impediment to the advent of the *Übermensch*; he criticizes the democratization of education and the emancipation of women; he rejects the principles of the French Revolution, the principle of equality and the inalienable rights of the individual, as well as its principle of 'individual empathy and social feeling'. In *On the Genealogy of Morals*, he characterizes as symptoms of decline the 'advent of democracy, international courts in place of war, equal rights for women, the religion of pity' (GM III 25).

It is true that the society of Manu is not *the* political ideal for Nietzsche as he both accepts and rejects certain features it possesses.

For example, he rejects it for its racist aspect and considers corrupt its hereditary transmission of rule. It is not true, however, as Brobjer claims, that Nietzsche rejects its foundation in the *holy lie* or in *immoralism*; and it is not true, as Brobjer claims, that Manu's 'strong emphasis on the state (and on religion)' constitutes 'a contradiction to Nietzsche's individualism and belief in self-development'. What Brobjer says exactly is that 'it is *difficult* to believe that Nietzsche would *genuinely* accept and praise [its] strong emphasis on the state' and that 'it is *difficult* to believe' that Nietzsche would accept its foundation in a holy lie.[2]

Nietzsche recognizes that the law-book of Manu is founded on a 'holy lie', but is not critical of this fact as such. He is not opposed to immoralism or immorality *per se*, as I pointed out in Chapter 4; rather, it depends on what ends are served. As Nietzsche writes, and Brobjer does not quote this, 'the point is to what *end* a lie is told'. That 'holy' ends are lacking in Christianity is *my* objection to its means' (A 56). Second, Nietzsche does not reject all states or political constitutions; rather, he rejects the democratic and socialist states, the states which say 'I, the state, am the people' (Z New Idol). He praises, for example, the Greek state, the Roman state, the military (Bonapartist) state and his contemporary Russian state (under the autocrat Tsar Alexander III). Nietzsche's ideal is of rulers, as opposed to the people, using the state as their instrument, and this is an ideal he finds, for example, in the society of Manu where the noble class is situated above the state, ruling indirectly and beyond good and evil. Finally, the society of Manu does not contradict Nietzsche's individualism or his conception of self-development because the Nietzschean *individual*, whom Nietzsche opposes to the democratic *private person* and citizen, represents a claim to special dignities, immunities and privileges, is subject only to his *own* morality, and possesses a freedom (or *virtù*) which cannot belong to everyone as a right, but which is a privilege of the strong. And the self-development of the Nietzschean individual, the production of the exemplary human type, requires the order of castes or order of rank, which is a feature of the society of Manu, as its condition, a *pathos of distance*, inequality and ingrained differences between social classes. (Brobjer fails to mention that the self-development of the Nietzschean individual also requires the reduction of certain individuals to slaves and instruments.) Nietzsche praises this society for its pyramidal structure, the shape of every *higher* culture, and for its natural division of labour, that it stands on the broad base of a 'soundly consolidated mediocrity'. Nietzsche clearly opposes the society of Manu to Christianity, as Brobjer says, but particularly in so far as the noble orders of this society, unlike the priests of Christianity, were able to keep the 'mob' under control. This is also a Nietzschean political ideal and political imperative inscribed in what Brobjer refers to as that 'supremely apolitical book', *Thus Spoke Zarathustra*: 'a *new nobility* [is] needed: to oppose all mob-rule and all despotism' (Z Law-Tables 11).

Brobjer also believes that Nietzsche contradicts Manu inasmuch as Nietzsche affirms scepticism and the fluid condition of values, continual striving and competition, self-overcoming and experimentation. But scepticism and the fluid condition of values are properties only of the Nietzschean free spirits and their sphere of life in which convictions are viewed as *means*, and in which there is a necessary antagonism, in the interests of circulation and the prevention of stagnation, between the members of the *spiritual aristocracy* as Nietzsche envisages them. In addition, striving, competition (agonism) and self-overcoming all presuppose social inequalities, they are not compatible, as Nietzsche conceives them, with the principle of equality. The principle of equality, according to Nietzsche, represents 'the decline of the entire social order' (A 62). Lastly, the Nietzschean experiment is an authoritarian experiment in command and obedience, not an experiment in a democratic social contract. Thus it may be said that Manu contradicts Nietzsche only in its racial and hereditary stagnation, but not in its caste system or the social inequalities inherent to it, as Nietzsche affirms both (with a conception of justice along both Platonic and Aristotelian lines). In other words, Nietzsche does not criticize the society of Manu because it structured political exclusion as such, but because the basis of this exclusion was racist.

In claiming that politics is not Nietzsche's 'main interest or motive', Brobjer reiterates Nietzsche's remark that he is 'anti-political'; he refers to *Thus Spoke Zarathustra* as 'a supremely apolitical book', although he recognizes the critique of the state it contains; he refers to Nietzsche's contempt for reading newspapers because they are 'superficial and political'; he says that when Nietzsche refers to political persons such as Napoleon it is not because of their 'political significance'; he refers to Nietzsche's affirmation of culture over the state; and he says that Nietzsche's 'perspective was always personal, philosophical and cultural, and never, or very rarely, political in any ordinary sense of that word'.

When Nietzsche refers to himself as 'anti-political', it is arguable that he means that he is antidemocratic, following the conservative tradition in German political thought, as I suggested in Chapter 3. It cannot mean, given the political commentary and critique which pervades his work, that he is nonpolitical or apolitical. It also means that he is pro-cultural, that he wants culture to determine the state and not the state to determine culture (as with Burckhardt). In this sense Brobjer is correct, Nietzsche does affirm culture over the state. But Brobjer does not say that for Nietzsche this implies that the state should be a tool or an instrument for a cultured minority, and that this very idea deter-mines the kind of state and state constitution Nietzsche desires (drawn from ancient and pagan theories of state). Second, it can hardly be said that *Thus Spoke Zarathustra* is 'a supremely apolitical book', for aside from a critique of the state, which Brobjer acknowledges but does not qualify, it contains, for example, a criticism of contemporary rulers for making concessions to the masses (as I elaborated in this study), a cri-ticism of the principle of equality and the imperative, to which I referred to above, to oppose all 'mob-rule'. When Nietzsche criticizes 'newspa-pers', as he also does in *Thus Spoke Zarathustra*, it is because newspapers represent the dominance of public opinion, an outcome of the Enlight-enment and the French Revolution. They are the principal form of com-munication in the modern democratic state. Third, Brobjer is wrong when he says that Nietzsche does not refer to their 'political signifi-cance' when he refers to political persons such as Napoleon. On the contrary, when Nietzsche praises Napoleon he praises, for example, Napoleon's ideal of a European political and economic union ('for the sake of a world government'), as well as Napoleon's use of religion for legitimation purposes. Finally, Nietzsche's perspective was certainly 'per-sonal, philosophical and cultural', but in the Nietzschean corpus these categories do not exclude the political. For when we examine the 'per-sonal' Nietzsche we find someone who considers himself a 'destiny' and a 'world-governing spirit', and someone who is engaged not in grand *ethics*, not in grand *morality*, not in grand *philosophy*, but in grand *pol-itics* (*die große Politik*), as he refers to his own revaluation of all values. And when we engage the 'philosophical' Nietzsche we find, for example, the philosophical doctrine of will to power deployed in accordance with an antidemocratic rationale. And when we explore Nietzsche's con-ception of culture – the 'cultural' Nietzsche – we find, for example, a repudiation of the Bismarckian *Kultur-Staat* and the ideal of a higher culture which can only exist with the support of a particular political order, radically aristocratic in form. Political residues attach to virtually every philosophical doctrine in the Nietzschean corpus.

Brobjer reconstructs the Nietzschean order of rank placing Christian-ity in the lowest rank, Manu and the *Imperium Romanum* in the middle rank, and experimentation and new values, ancient Greece and the Renaissance in the highest rank. According to Brobjer, it is in the highest rank that Nietzsche's ideal truly lies. Although Nietzsche says that 'the Romans were the strong and noble, and nobody stronger and nobler has yet existed on earth or even been dreamed of' (GM I 16).

Nietzsche contrasts not only Manu, but also the *Imperium Romanum*, ancient Greece and the Renaissance with Christianity. It is out of these oppositions that his ideal emerges. Let us look at just some of the features Nietzsche associates with the Renaissance, a period Brobjer recognizes Nietzsche values very highly, and test Brobjer's argument for an essentially apolitical Nietzsche.

Nietzsche, as I stated in Chapter 4, lauds the Renaissance for its aristocratic values. The Renaissance represents a revaluation of Christian values, it represents a noble mode of evaluation. Nietzsche also affirms the individualism of the Renaissance and its idea of the individual as someone who imposes his ideals upon others, who does not remain *privatized*. This idea is encompassed in the Machiavellian conception of *virtù*, which Nietzsche reminds us is not an ideal for everyone and is free from the constrictions of morality. Nietzsche also praises the Renaissance for its opposition to the morality of pity and to the theory of equal rights, clearly political, and praises, as Machiavelli does, one of its products, Cesare Borgia. For Nietzsche, Borgia is evidence of the fact that evil (forms of moral, religious and political transgression) often contributes to increases and growth in culture.

With the Renaissance, Nietzsche primarily associates Machiavelli – *virtù* and immoralism, and '*admitted* immorality' – and Machiavellianism or the '*Machiavellianism of power*', which Nietzsche refers to as '*perfection in politics*', and which is at the epicentre of his own plan for a political treatise (*Ein tractatus politicus*). To complicate matters further for an apolitical reading such as Brobjer's, Nietzsche sees Napoleon (as did Taine) as a 'continuator' of the Renaissance, and even sets his account of *virtù* in military institutions and ultimately, by extension, in Bonapartism. Thus if Brobjer is going to place the Renaissance in Nietzsche's highest rank, not only must he place the '*Machiavellianism of power*' or immoralism there, he must logically place Napoleon there as well. And if he places Napoleon there, he must logically place the attributes (and political ideals) Nietzsche ascribes to Napoleon there as well. Following Nietzsche's statement in *On the Genealogy of Morals* of what Napoleon represents for Nietzsche, Brobjer must place in the highest rank the 'rapturous counterslogan', the 'supreme rights of the few', and place in the lowest rank the 'mendacious slogan of *ressentiment'*, the 'supreme rights of the majority' (GM I 16). Does Nietzsche set an account of *rights* in an apolitical discourse?

Nietzsche's political ideal emerges, not only through his anti-Christian, antimodern and antidemocratic polemics, but through his affirmation of certain features which, generally speaking, the society of Manu, ancient Greece, the *Imperium Romanum* and the Renaissance all share, and in some cases do not share. His political ideal is, generally speaking, a synthesis of these. Simply because the laws and society of Manu do not constitute *the* Nietzschean political ideal, because he rejects certain features which belong to these laws and to this society, it is too extreme to conclude, as Brobjer does, that there is an absence of political ideals in the Nietzschean corpus.

Nietzsche's critique of Christianity and modernity has a prominent political aspect as this study has shown. Brobjer does not seem to recognize that this critique reveals Nietzsche's own political ideals. Brobjer tells us that if 'we seek for more explicit political and social ideals in the writings of the late Nietzsche we will not find them for they do not exist'. Yet in Book V of *The Gay Science* (which is late Nietzsche, 1887), in the section *'We who are homeless'*, Nietzsche is quite explicit about his social and political ideals. I will quote it only in part:

> we are not by any means 'liberal'; we do not work for 'progress'; we do not need to plug up our ears against the sirens who in the market place sing of the future: their song about 'equal rights,' 'a free society,' 'no more masters and no servants' has no allure for us. We simply do not consider it desirable that a realm of justice and concord should be established on earth. . . . we think about the necessity for new orders, also for a new slavery – for every strengthening and enhancement of the human type also involves a new kind of enslavement. . . . We are no humanitarians. . . . [we do not] advocate nationalism and race hatred. (GS 377)

I indicated in my Introduction that, to a large extent, Nietzsche has been viewed as a political philosopher, or at least as a 'philosopher of power', who either justifies or does not justify a specific political order. Foucault says, 'Nietzsche is the philosopher of power . . . who managed to think of power without having to confine himself within a political theory in order to do so.'[3] But Nietzsche does confine himself within antiegalitarian political theory and pagan theories of state. There is an antidemocratic political rationale behind his development of the hypothesis of the will to power. It cannot be plausibly maintained that

Nietzsche has no politics or political ideals. Nietzsche's political commentary presupposes political theory, and this political theory is not liberal, democratic, anarchistic or socialistic at base. Rather, it germinally combines an argument for a caste system with Machiavellian technique. As I mentioned in Chapter 1, Nietzsche embraced the description 'aristocratic radicalism' applied to his philosophy by Brandes, who also noted its political aspects.

I also stated in my Introduction that the principal imperative guiding this study is to situate Nietzsche's political thought in relation to the political issues, critiques and movements of his own period, a project which is lacking in Nietzsche studies today. However, at the same time, I think it is important to be aware of contemporary reconstitutions or appropriations of Nietzsche's political thought, thus my criticism of the contemporary radical liberal democratic interpretation of Nietzsche.

In Chapter 1, I supported the view that Nietzsche reduces morality to politics and that there is a necessary interconnection between his critique of morality and his critique of egalitarian politics, that they are clearly and intrinsically linked through Nietzsche's concepts of *décadence* and *ressentiment*. I demonstrated that, aside from Nietzsche's direct engagement with political categories such as the social contract, there is a definite political dimension to virtually all the central themes and topics of his philosophy. After all, he does qualify his revaluation of all values as *die große Politik*, as I mentioned. And he also provides, along with his antidemocratic polemics, a qualified endorsement of the type of political regime he prefers (the template for a state apparatus) aristocratic and authoritarian in form.

I also demonstrated in Chapter 1 that Nietzsche is engaged in what amounts to class warfare, and that this position is deeply entrenched and encoded in his corpus, such that his conception of 'type' is often complicated, as it were, by a notion of social 'class'. He is consistently antiegalitarian, as is clear from his doctrine of right, a doctrine which also provides incentive for his *new nobility*. In addition, for example, I addressed the persistent question of Nietzsche's alleged pro-democratic position during the period 1878–82, but located no convincing arguments to support such an alleged position, except where his antisocialism expediently generates it. Throughout Chapter 1, by way of introducing the reader to the Nietzschean political landscape, I disclosed the basic oppositions, mediations and allegiances, the tenets and doctrines which govern his political thought as a prolegomenon to its political definition and identity or identification with which this study as a whole is concerned.

In Chapter 2, I criticized the contemporary radical liberal democratic reading of Nietzsche and challenged its central argument that there is a necessary discontinuity between Nietzsche's antifoundational philosophy and his aristocratic, authoritarian politics. I challenged their treatment of Nietzschean doctrines such as perspectivism and agonism and argued that Nietzsche's affirmation of the plurality, resistance and finitude these doctrines imply may be seen to be consistent with his politics of hierarchy and domination. I argued that the contemporary radical liberal democratic reading of Nietzsche cannot credibly demonstrate the aporetic structure it claims resides in Nietzsche's thought without major exclusions and censorship, and thus the attempt of this reading to appropriate Nietzsche for a radicalized liberal democratic political theory is profoundly compromised.

I want to emphasize as well that such readings, in excluding or rejecting Nietzsche's political prescriptions and polemics, quarantine in the process his *immoralistic* descriptions of political culture which are relevant to contemporary society; his interest in social control or the function of ideology; his analytic insights into the rhetorical strategies and tactics of priestly-philosophical power-structures and the mechanics of *theatrical* politics, which may teach us something about contemporary media and its impact on the political process. Perhaps such exclusions are performed because it is recognized that Nietzsche recommends such strategies and tactics in his own political recodification which does not dispose of laws, contracts or institutions.

I would suggest, as Frederick Appel does,[4] that rather than forcing Nietzsche to speak for democracy (or radical democracy), the result of which is problematic and contradictory, it is less problematic to take Nietzsche for who he is – an aristocratic radical, an authoritarian revolutionary – and to make positive use, if such use can be made, of his critique of democracy (its culture and its principles) and, I would add, of his critique of liberalism, anarchism and socialism, but without confining him there, as a mere critic of the levelling effects of egalitarian politics, which leaves him lying in state as a 'late-blooming' aristocratic liberal and misses his Machiavellian militancy.

As was shown, Nietzsche views all of these political doctrines as neo-Christian doctrines which are derived within modernity from the French Revolution. What Nietzsche rejects in the French Revolution are the principles of the sovereignty of the people and of equality, the idea of universal suffrage and the morality of pity, the abolition of privilege and the dominance of the press and public opinion. Nietzsche considers liberalism, democracy, anarchism and socialism to be doctrines of *ressentiment* because, essentially, they are imperialistic (and even racist) and constitute a form of repression of other types and societies. In this respect, they are destructive of organic communities and *peoples* when they impose on them the doctrine of one normal (*equal*) human type and the rationalist ideal of the absolute person, the *neutral* subject Nietzsche criticizes when he criticizes social contract theory. Nietzsche rejects all of these ideologies because they teach the doctrine of equality and promote the abolition of suffering so crucial to his concept of *nobility*.

More specifically, with respect to liberalism, Nietzsche rejects, for example, its conception of the individual and of individual freedom, its emphasis on well-being, security and material comfort, its opposition to war. With respect to democracy, Nietzsche criticizes, for example, its idea of the 'goodness' of human nature, its erosion of tradition, its weakening of respect for the law, its generation of distrust of all government, its production of a 'private person', its tendency towards majoritarianism and ochlocracy, and its inability to construct durable institutions, to undertake long-term projects (which Nietzsche also applies to liberalism) – in effect, the *decay of the power to organize*. Democracy also produces weakness of will, but this a positive feature for the Nietzschean *commanders* (once Nietzsche modifies his view that democracy impedes the rise of the commander). With respect to socialism, Nietzsche rejects, for example, its despotic and totalitarian character, its reduction of individuals to instruments, its utopianism or utopian ideal of the *perfect state*. Less schematically, he argues against its rejection of property rights, claiming that it is alien to human desire (that in order to *be* you must *possess*), and against its belief that social distress and social vices may be eliminated through institutions, or eliminated period. Nietzsche also rejects what he sees as its willingness to use violence and terrorism to achieve its ends. He accuses the doctrine of anarchism for the same reason, and also for its imperative (reading Bakunin) to destroy all traditional civilization. What Nietzsche rejects in all of these political doctrines is their repudiation of 'master and servant' and their faith in *community* as sovereign.

In Chapter 3, I suggested that Nietzsche's political critique has its foundation in the aristocratic liberal critique of democratic society. I claimed that Nietzsche assimilates all the vocabulary of the aristocratic liberal critique (levelling, mediocrity) but that he differs from them on all key issues (the state, egalitarianism and individualism), is more radical and dogmatic in his treatment, both in assessment and solution, of those democratic social tendencies which the aristocratic liberals see as merely *dangerous* tendencies. I indicated that, like the aristocratic liberals, Nietzsche rejects universal suffrage (de Tocqueville qualified) but that, unlike them, he is not an opponent of centralized government, not an opponent as they are, for example, of Napoleonic Caesarism. I indicated also that, unlike the aristocratic liberals, Nietzsche is an unconditional opponent of the democratic doctrine of equality, that he invests no credibility whatsoever in democratic institutions or ethics. Rather, he advocates their subversion. I further indicated that Nietzsche does not consider all human beings as *individuals* or as sovereign in the aristocratic liberal sense. Rather, he justifies exploitation and recommends slavery for some.

It may be asked: why does this study, given its declared interest in situating Nietzsche in relation to political or social movements of his own period, not discuss Nietzsche's relation to the left-wing Hegelians? In responding to this question I will rely on Karl Löwith's work *From Hegel to Nietzsche* and Zvi Rosen's *Bruno Bauer and Karl Marx*.[5] Löwith says that, among the left-wing Hegelians, Nietzsche concurs with Stirner's attempt at a 'new beginning' and Bauer's atheistic criticism of Christianity.[6] Löwith writes that Nietzsche is directly connected 'with the Hegelian school through his relationship to . . . Bauer' (1809–82). He points out that Nietzsche read Bauer's *Zur Orientierung über die Bismarcksche Aera* (1880) and that there are obvious correspondences between Bauer's *Entdecktes Christentum* (1843) and Nietzsche's *Anti-Christ(ian)*.[7]

Briefly, I am sceptical about Nietzsche's connection to Stirner (1806–56) in spite of the shared rhetoric of 'new beginnings'. I do not think that Nietzsche's noble egoism can be reduced to Stirner's private egoism because it does not reduce the entire social world to its own self. The Nietzschean individual, the *free spirit*, is not grounded in 'creative nothingness'.[8] Nietzsche, unlike Stirner, does not desire 'exemption from all authority' or release from the 'previous history of mankind'.[9] True, both Stirner and Nietzsche advance an anti-humanitarian doctrine, but the Nietzschean individual has a 'destiny' which lies in a future legislation which concerns all of humanity. Furthermore, the Nietzschean individual is grounded in an historical type (typology), is mediated by historical structures (genealogy) and requires an aristocratic social and political order to support it, a *sovereign authority*.

A more profound connection to Bauer is more probable, clearly for the reasons Löwith provides (the critique of Christianity and of bourgeois culture), but also because of Nietzsche's own acknowledgement of Bauer. In *Ecce Homo*, Nietzsche remarks that Bauer, after reading his early criticism of David Strauss, became one of his 'most attentive readers' (EH UO 2). In correspondence with both Brandes and Taine in 1887, Nietzsche refers to Bauer – the 'old Hegelian Bruno Bauer' – as a 'devoted' reader and counts him amongst his 'few readers'.[10]

Bauer and Nietzsche share an atheistic critique of Christianity, but they also share the view that 'philosophy must act in the political sphere'.[11] Both desire the subversion of existing political structures, but Bauer's political conception is radically different from Nietzsche's. First of all, Bauer views the state as inherently rational and sees its task in terms of the realization of freedom and reason.[12] Nietzsche, in contrast to Bauer, does not connect freedom with reason but with degrees of power. Bauer's political conception is influenced by the French Revolution. His conception of political liberty is the 'full liberation of man'. From his revolutionary-democratic standpoint he opposes all forms of tyranny. His political sympathies and ideals are distinctly republican. As Bauer writes, and this would be anathema to Nietzsche, the 'future belongs to the people; the truth is popular . . . the people and the truth are the same and, as such, the all-powerful ruler of the future'.[13]

Nietzsche's critique of Christianity develops into a critique of democracy, and it is for this reason, and on this level, that his relation to the aristocratic liberals must be viewed as more profound and more extensive than his relation to the left-wing Hegelians. In Löwith's own words, in 'Germany, J. Burckhardt continued de Tocqueville's line of thought about democracy'[14] and, as I suggested in Chapter 3, Nietzsche was clearly attentive to it.

In Chapter 4, I argued that Nietzsche's radicalization of the aristocratic liberal critique leads him to embrace a politics inspired by Machiavelli's conceptions of *virtù* (leadership)[15] and immoralism (political technique), the latter shrouded in the mediatic problem of the art of dissimulation. His political conception concedes victory to the democratic movement, but seeks the method to manipulate it, which he mediates through an active investment in the Bonapartist reaction and through the Machiavellianism of power. Furthermore, in opposition to the idea that Nietzsche's political position 'most closely resembles that of the anarchists' of his period, I argued that Nietzsche's political ideology (his conception of the masses derived from Machiavelli and Taine, his philosophy of social control) more closely resembles that of the anti-democratic neo-Machiavellians of his period. The neo-Machiavellians also incorporated aspects of the aristocratic liberal critique and, like Nietzsche, radicalized it through the Machiavellian conceptions of *virtù* and immoralism. I indicated that both Nietzsche and the neo-

Machiavellians seek the authoritarian potential within democracy, that they wish to provide incentive for a new aristocracy and prepare the ground for an active *reversal*, an active *legislation*. Even though Nietzsche may place his philosopher *above* the state, it is clear that, for Nietzsche (as with Bauer), 'philosophy must act in the political sphere'.

Many commentators today defend the stance that Nietzsche is political, given the extensive political commentary in his work, or that his philosophy has political consequences, but there is continuing disagreement regarding the extent to which Nietzsche's political commentary can be converted into a unified political position or theory. Deleuze, who represents another prominent reading formation in Nietzsche studies, sees in Nietzsche a philosopher of 'becoming' and, however sophistically such a term is employed or superficially invoked in pseudo-arguments, it means precisely for Deleuze, in 'Pensée nomade', that Nietzsche makes no attempt at recodification and thus achieves no unity of position.

My understanding of Nietzsche is that he wages, in Gramscian terms, both a war of position (against Christian and neo-Christian or democratic culture) and a war of manoeuvre (against the egalitarian state, or states making egalitarian compromises such as Bismarck's *Reich* in the aftermath of the revolution of 1848) and that he is politically coherent on both counts, even though he will manoeuvre as the moment demands, forming as he does, for example in *Human, All Too Human*, a convenient alliance with democracy against socialism, and elsewhere against anarchism, because, displaying the gist of his conclusions, democracy or democratic culture, by virtue of its atomistic tendency and its depreciation of war and the 'warrior spirit', generates weakness of will.

The Deleuzian reading misses something in Nietzsche in respect of tactics (which, for example, the Straussian reader does not) and thus obscures Nietzsche's strategic objectives. However, I disagree with Deleuze, because I think Nietzsche expresses a unified political position which can be seen once its tactical element is illuminated, and because I see in this position a proto-fascist nomadology, I want to remind the reader that this view should not lead to a simple political binary, as there is as much variety in fascism and protofascism as there is in democracy.[16]

I also disagree with the Deleuzian reading because I think that Nietzsche does begin to recodify in terms of laws, contracts and institutions. Nietzsche's various criticisms and affirmations of laws, contracts and institutions may be seen, essentially, to converge on a conception of right as special privilege, immunity or exception (degraded by the advent of egalitarian doctrine) and a conception of the masses or the multitude as 'criminal' and 'conspiratorial' and, ultimately, through Machiavellian and Bonapartist mediations, as passive material for manipulation and command. It is difficult to defend the Deleuzian thesis that Nietzsche is engaged in an exercise of 'absolute decodification' when, in fact, Nietzsche (through a genealogy of morals and a revaluation of all values) reasserts these instruments of codification; takes an administrative stance towards the multitude and reproduces a hybrid template for a state apparatus; all in the name of a radical *'aristokratischen Gesellschaft'*.

Nietzsche's political philosophy constitutes a return to Bonapartist subversions (*autocratic will in the guise of popular rule*). His political philosophy is imperial and is sharply opposed to the constituent political power of the multitude, their claim for political legitimacy. His political theory is grounded in a rejection of this claim and is activated against it. This antagonism for militant labour movements is an extension of the war Nietzsche wages against Christianity. Nietzsche begins to think the reversal or manipulation of the becoming a *political subject* of the multitude along Machiavellian parameters, through an authoritarian reading of *The Prince*. Recognizing this, we may recognize Nietzsche not as a philosopher of 'Pensée nomade' (in the Deleuzian sense, which reads Nietzsche's work as nothing but the self-conscious design of an arena of conflict and contradiction), but as a philosopher of 'Societies of Control' (Deleuze *cum* Foucault) inspired by the Bonapartist state mechanism.

Notes

Introduction

1. Peter Bergmann, *Nietzsche, 'The Last Antipolitical German'* (Bloomington: Indiana University Press, 1987), p. 4. It is not unique in the literature on Nietzsche to attribute such a position to him given his antistatist and individualistic doctrines. But these doctrines are often only superficially examined.
2. See David S. Thatcher, *Nietzsche in England 1890–1914: The Growth of a Reputation* (Toronto: University of Toronto Press, 1970), pp. 61–2.
3. Randolph Bourne, 'Trans-National America', *Atlantic Monthly*, June 1917, 778–86.
4. See Jules Harmand, *Domination et colonisation* (Paris: Ernest Flammarion, 1910), and Ernest Seillière, *La Philosophie de l'impérialisme* (Paris: Plon-Nourrit, 1905).
5. Alfred Bäumler, 'Nietzsche and National Socialism', *Nazi Culture: Intellectual, Cultural and Social Life in the Third Reich*, ed. George L. Mosse, trans. Salvator Attanasio (New York: Grosset & Dunlop, 1966), p. 99. See also *Nietzsche, der Philosoph und Politiker* (Leipzig: Reclam, 1931).
6. See, for example, Ernst Jünger, 'Die Totale Mobilmachung', *Ernst Jünger Werke*, Band 5, Essays I (Stuttgart: Ernst Klett Verlag), and Oswald Spengler, *Man and Technics*, trans. Charles Francis Atkinson (Westport: Greenwood Press, 1976).
7. Martin Heidegger, *Nietzsche*, Vols. II–IV, trans. David Farrell Krell (San Francisco: Harper & Row Publishers, 1984, 1987, 1982). This quotation is taken from Ernst Behler, *Confrontations: Derrida/Heidegger/Nietzsche*, trans. Steven Taubeneck (Stanford: Stanford University Press, 1991), p. 101.
8. For example, Benito Mussolini and Julius Evola.
9. See Pierre-André Taguieff, 'The Traditional Paradigm – Horror of Modernity and Antiliberalism: Nietzsche in Reactionary Rhetoric', *Why We Are Not Nietzscheans*, ed. Luc Ferry and Alain Renaut, trans. Robert de Loaiza (Chicago: The University of Chicago Press, 1997), p. 204.
10. Gyorgy Lukács, *The Destruction of Reason*, trans. Peter Palmer (Englewood Cuffs, NJ: Humanities Press, 1981), pp. 321, 371.
11. See Douglas Smith, *Transvaluations: Nietzsche in France 1872–1972* (Oxford: Clarendon Press, 1996).
12. Mark Warren, *Nietzsche and Political Thought* (Cambridge, Mass: The MIT Press, 1988), p. 247.
13. Ibid., p. 142.
14. See Charles Andler, *Nietzsche: sa vie et sa pensée*, Vol. II (Paris: Librairie Gallimard, 1958), p. 538.
15. As Nietzsche has been described. See James A. Gregor, *The Ideology of Fascism: The Rationale of Totalitarianism* (New York: The Free Press, 1969), p. 127.

1   Wills to Power, Genealogy: Which Ones Are At War?

1. See, for example, Werner J. Dannhauser, 'Friedrich Nietzsche', *History of Political Philosophy*, ed. Leo Strauss and Joseph Cropsey (Chicago: University of Chicago Press, 1981), p. 794; and Nancy Love, *Marx, Nietzsche and Modernity* (New York: Columbia University Press, 1986), who writes, Nietzsche 'understands the creation of social values, indeed society itself, in terms of political domination', p. 10.
2. Tracy Strong, *Friedrich Nietzsche and the Politics of Transfiguration* (Berkeley: University of California Press, 1975, 1988), pp. 106, 189.
3. By the same token, any treatment of Nietzschean psychology should not be detached from his account of institutions, as it may perpetuate the very individualistic abstractions Nietzsche repudiates.
4. See Ernst Bloch, *Natural Law and Human Dignity*, trans. Dennis J. Schmitt (Cambridge, Mass.: The MIT Press, 1996), p. 62.
5. As Strong writes, 'Nietzsche's genealogical investigations do not undermine all values and all modes of evaluation equally. There are past tendencies, as well as present ones . . . that Nietzsche esteems highly, and it is out of these estimations that his own ideal of the future emerges' (*Friedrich Nietzsche and the Politics of Transfiguration*, p. 116).
6. Ansell-Pearson comments that 'It would be mistaken, as well as misleading, to infer from Nietzsche's construction of a typology of morals that he is simply *for* master morality and *against* slave morality. Such an assessment would fail to appreciate the historical basis of Nietzsche's attempt to trace the evolution of humanity as a moral species' (Keith Ansell-Pearson, *An Introduction to Nietzsche as Political Thinker: The Perfect Nihilist*, Cambridge: Cambridge University Press, 1994, p. 132). None the less, once the aforesaid 'historical basis' is appreciated, as it should be, that master and slave moralities are intertwined, that sometimes they occur 'within a *single* soul', it is important to note that Nietzsche's typology is about 'two basic types and one basic difference' (BGE 260), and that he is attempting to recover this 'difference', no doubt with a decided preference, over and against the 'tyranny' of the Christian moral interpretation which 'has *educated* the spirit' (BGE 188). Second, while these moralities may occur 'within a *single* soul', Nietzsche says it is a '*higher nature*' who realizes itself as 'a genuine battleground of these opposed values'. In short, 'today there is perhaps no more decisive mark of a '*higher nature*', than that of being . . . a genuine battleground of these opposed values' (GM I 16).
7. Of *amor fati*, this 'highest state of affirmation' that can be attained, Nietzsche writes, 'It is part of this state to perceive not merely the necessity of those sides of existence hitherto denied, but their desirability . . . as the more powerful, more fruitful, *truer* sides of existence. It is also part of this state to depreciate that side of existence which alone has been affirmed hitherto' (WP 1041 Nachlaß 1888 KSA 13 16[32]).
8. It should be said that Nietzsche does not completely reject the ascetic ideal, which is to say, its disciplinary aspect, for he considers it necessary for 'the education of the will' (WP 916 Nachlaß 1887 KSA 12 10[165]). 'To grant oneself the right to exceptional actions; as an experiment in self-overcoming and freedom. . . . To create control and certainty in regard to

one's strength of will through asceticism of every kind' (WP 921 Nachlaß 1887–88 KSA 13 11[146]). See, also, BGE 61.

9. See also *On the Genealogy of Morals*: 'The ascetic ideal has a *goal* . . . it interprets epochs, nations, and men inexorably with a view to this one goal; it permits no other interpretation, no other goal; it rejects, denies, affirms, and sanctions solely from the point of view of *its* interpretation . . . it submits to no power, it believes in its own predominance over every other power' (GM III 23).

10. Eugen Dühring (1833–1921) and Adolf Stöcker (1835–1909), founder of the Christian Socialist Workers' Party in 1878. On Dühring and Stöcker as 'intellectual forerunners of the Third Reich', see Weaver Santaniello, 'A Post-Holocaust Re-Examination of Nietzsche and the Jews: *Vis-à-Vis* Christendom and Nazism', *Nietzsche & Jewish Culture*, ed. Jacob Golomb (London: Routledge, 1997) and, *Nietzsche, God and the Jews: His Critique of Judeo-Christianity in Relation to the Nazi Myth* (Albany: State University of New York Press, 1994). Among the anarchists, Nietzsche refers to Mikhail Bakunin (1813–76) in an 1873 notebook entry: 'Bakunin, who out of hatred for the present wants to destroy history and the past . . . he . . . wants to destroy all prior *cultivation*, our intellectual inheritance in its entirety' (UW 26[14] 1873 KSA 7).

11. See also 'they make the ruling classes responsible for their character' (WP 765 Nachlaß 1888 KSA 13 15[30]). See also WP 98 Nachlaß 1887 KSA 12 9[146]: Rousseau sought the 'cause of his wretchedness in the ruling classes'.

12. In *The Politics*, Aristotle writes, 'That one should command and another obey is both necessary and expedient. Indeed, some things are so divided right from birth, some to rule, some to be ruled . . . that by nature some are free others slaves' (1254a17) (Aristotle, *The Politics*, trans. T. A. Sinclair, Harmondsworth: Penguin Books, 1986). Nietzsche recovers the Aristotelian justification of a natural division of labour, of natural slavery. A theory of natural slavery is also held by Herodotus, Plato and the Roman Republicans.

13. This process is evident in a notebook entry from 1885–86: 'The Body as a Political Structure. The aristocracy in the body, the majority of the rulers (struggle between cells and tissues). Slavery and division of labor: the higher type possible only through the subjugation of the lower. . . . Inference concerning the evolution of mankind: perfecting consists in the production of the most powerful individuals, who will use the great mass of people as their tools (and indeed the most intelligent and most pliable tools)' (WP 660 Nachlaß 1885–86 KSA 12 2[76]).

14. See letter to Georg Brandes, 2 December 1887. *The Selected Letters of Friedrich Nietzsche*, ed. Christopher Middleton (Chicago: University of Chicago Press, 1969), p. 279: 'The expression "aristocratic radicalism", which you use, is very good. That is, if I may say so, the shrewdest remark that I have read about myself till now.' Brandes was the first to lecture on Nietzsche. In his correspondence with Nietzsche Brandes says he finds Nietzsche's 'aristocratic radicalism' and his distaste for 'democratic mediocrity' harmonious with his own ideas, but does not agree with Nietzsche's views on women, his 'contempt for the morality of pity' (26 November 1887), nor his 'impetuous pronouncements against . . . socialism and anarchism' (17 December 1887). See also Georg Brandes, 'An Essay on Aristocratic Radicalism' (1889), *Friedrich Nietzsche*, trans. A. G. Chater (New York: The MacMillan Co., 1915).

15. As Casey writes, 'For Nietzsche, the strong exercise of the will is in itself good, and essential to what is noble in man' (John Casey, *Pagan Virtue: An Essay on Ethics*, Oxford: Clarendon Press, 1990, p. 141).

16. Ishay Landa, 'Nietzsche, the Chinese Worker's Friend', *New Left Review*, No. 236, July/August 1999, 3–23, p. 9.

17. See, Antonio Negri, *Insurgencies: Constituent Power and the Modern State*, trans. Maurizia Boscagli (Minneapolis: University of Minnesota Press, 1999), p. 324.

18. Peter Kropotkin, *Selected Writings on Anarchism and Revolution* (Cambridge: MIT Press, 1970), pp. 293–307. Max Horkheimer, *Dawn & Decline: Notes 1926–1931 and 1950–1969*, trans. Michael Shaw (New York: The Seabury Press, 1978), pp. 32–3. Though Horkheimer adds that a creative reading of Nietzsche might contribute to 'proletarian *praxis*'.

19. Peter Bergmann, *Nietzsche, 'The Last Antipolitical German'* (Bloomington: Indiana University Press, 1987), p. 120. See also Marc Sautet, *Nietzsche et la Commune* (Paris: Éditions Le Sycomore, 1981), and Geoff Waite, 'The Politics of Reading Formations: the case of Nietzsche in Imperial Germany (1870–1919)', *New German Critique*, 29, Spring/Summer 1983, 185–209. Waite writes that 'Nietzsche's polemic is directed [against] . . . proletarian class consciousness *circa* 1870–1890', p. 202.

20. 'A declaration of war on the masses by *higher men* is needed! Everywhere the mediocre are combining in order to make themselves master! Everything that makes soft and effeminate, that serves the ends of the "people" . . . works in favour of *suffrage universel*. . . . But we should take reprisal and bring the whole affair (which in Europe commenced with Christianity) to light and to the bar of judgment' (WP 861 Nachlaß 1884 KSA 11 25[174]).

21. See, for example, Ansell-Pearson, *An Introduction to Nietzsche as Political Thinker*.

22. Thomas H. Brobjer, 'Nietzsche's Knowledge, Reading, and Critique of Political Economy', *Journal of Nietzsche Studies* 18, Fall 1999, 56–70.

23. See Friedrich Engels, *The Condition of the Working Class in England* (Moscow: Progress Publishers, 1973).

24. In his fine analysis of this passage from *Daybreak*, Landa correctly remarks that Nietzsche's 'attack on the dictatorship of machines and capital . . . [is] swiftly transformed into a meditation on the best way of supplying the very same capital, the very same machines, with [a] new labour force, with fresh slaves' (Ishay Landa, 'Nietzsche, the Chinese Worker's Friend', p. 21).

25. In a note regarding the theologian, David Strauss (1808–74), Nietzsche associates 'an ethics of the *bellum omnium* and of greater utility and power' with Darwinism (UW 27[2] 1873 KSA 7).

26. For example, in *The Greek State*, Nietzsche writes, 'Now, after States have been established almost everywhere, that bent of the *bellum omnium contra omnes* concentrates itself from time to time into a terrible gathering of war-clouds and discharges itself as it were in rare but so much the more violent shocks. . . . But in consequence of the effect of that *bellum* . . . society is given time during the intervals to germinate and burst into leaf . . . to let the shining blossoms of genius sprout forth' (12–13).

27. Aristotle, *The Politics*, 1318b1. See, also, WP 784 Nachlaß 1887 KSA 12 10[82].

28. Leo Strauss comments, in his study of Hobbes, that Spinoza 'relinquishes the distinction between might and right and teaches the natural right of all passions' and thus possesses a view of right more naturalistic than that of Hobbes. Leo Strauss, *The Political Philosophy of Hobbes: Its Basis and Its Genesis*, trans. Elsa M. Sinclair (Chicago: The University of Chicago Press, 1952), p. 169.
29. See Chapter 2, section 8. *The Chief Works of Benedict de Spinoza*, Vol. II, trans. R. H. M. Elwes (London: George Bell and Sons, 1883).
30. In *The Greek State*, Nietzsche refers to the ideas of the 'dignity of man' and the 'dignity of labour' as 'the needy products of slavedom' (4). Furthermore, Nietzsche writes, ' "man in himself", the absolute man possesses neither dignity, nor rights, nor duties' (17).
31. See Ludwig Gumplowicz, *Outlines of Sociology*, ed. Irving L. Horowitz (New York: Paine-Whitman Publishers, 1963). Other conflict theorists include Franz Oppenheimer (1864–1943), Gustav Ratzenhofer (1842–1904) and Lester Ward (1841–1913).
32. (1194–1250). Emperor of the Holy Roman Empire, he was considered by the Church to be the Anti-Christ. See, for example, David G. Einstein, *Emperor Frederick II* (New York: Philosophical Library, 1949).
33. I borrow this expression from Conway. Daniel W. Conway, *Nietzsche & the Political* (London: Routledge, 1997), p. 98.
34. Ibid., p. 32.
35. *Briefe und Berichte*, pp. 417–19. See *The Selected Letters of Friedrich Nietzsche*, ed. Middleton, p. 276, n116.
36. Treitschke writes: 'All civil society is . . . aristocratic by nature . . . while all democracy is rooted in a contradiction of nature, because it premises a universal equality which is nowhere actually existent' (Heinrich von Treitschke, *Politics*, ed. Hans Kohn, New York: Harcourt, Brace & World, Inc. 1963, p. 31).
37. I borrow this expression from Honig who writes that Nietzsche 'has a deep reverence for institutions (of particular kinds) as well as an abiding interest in the way they function to produce and maintain a variety of forms of life and excellence' (Bonnie Honig, *Political Theory and the Displacement of Politics*, Ithaca: Cornell University Press, 1993, p. 69).
38. See Treitschke, *Politics*, p. 13.
39. Josef Chytry, *The Aesthetic State: A Quest in Modern German Thought* (Berkeley: University of California Press, 1989), p. 349.
40. At the time Nietzsche wrote this, in 1888, Russia was ruled by Tsar Alexander III who represented a return to a more rigid form of autocratic government. See, for example, Hugh Seton-Watson, *The Decline of Imperial Russia 1855–1914* (London: Methuen & Co., 1952).
41. Paul Deussen was a scholar of Indian philosophy and religion. *The Selected Letters of Friedrich Nietzsche*, ed. Middleton, p. 311.
42. Nietzsche, rather, wishes to rekindle 'that greatest of all conflicts of ideals. . . . Must the ancient fire not some day flare up much more terribly. . . . More: must one not desire it with all one's might? even will it? even promote it?' (GM I 17).
43. In German the term, *die große Politik*, as Peter Bergmann explains, 'has a . . . majestic ring, one rooted in the . . . conviction of the primacy of

foreign policy, of a higher form of politics specifically addressing European and world power conflicts in contradistinction to a presumably lesser form of politics dealing with internal matters' (*Nietzsche, 'The Last Antipolitical German'*, p. 162).

44. Nietzsche associates correctly; for in 1887 Bismarck had written, in the spirit of opposing the idea of the annihilation of the enemy, that 'France's continued existence as a great power is just as needful to us as that of any other of the great powers'. *Die große Politik der europäischen Kabinette*, VII, pp. 177–8. Quoted in Edward Mead Earle, 'Hitler: The Nazi Concept of War', *Makers of Modern Strategy: Military Thought from Machiavelli to Hitler*, ed. Edward Mead Earle (Princeton: Princeton University Press, 1943), p. 510.

45. Bergmann, *Nietzsche, 'The Last Antipolitical German'*, p. 163.

46. Strong writes that *Die große Politik* means 'international politics', and refers to Nietzsche's *Geisterkrieg* as 'ideological warfare'. *Friedrich Nietzsche and the Politics of Transfiguration*, pp. 210, 169.

47. The *Übermensch* is he who will *'remain true to the earth'* (Z Prologue); 'a type of supreme achievement', anti-Christian and antimodern (EH WGB 1). See, also, A 3: 'The problem I raise here is . . . what type of human being one ought to breed, ought to *will*. . . . out of fear the reverse type has been willed . . . the Christian'.

48. Ansell-Pearson, *An Introduction to Nietzsche as Political Thinker*, p. 44.

49. 49. Ibid., pp. 90, 96–7.

50. Gyorgy Lukács, *The Destruction of Reason*, trans. Peter Palmer (Englewood Cliffs, NJ: Humanities Press, 1981), pp. 326, 332. This point is basically repeated in Bruce Detwiler, *Nietzsche and the Politics of Aristocratic Radicalism* (Chicago: The University of Chicago Press, 1990), p. 180. Detwiler says 'bulwark' rather than 'counterpoise'. Nietzsche also sees democracy as a counterpoise to anarchism (BGE 202).

51. In Nietzsche's notebooks there is an entry which provides some elucidation: 'there will always be too many who have possessions for socialism to signify more than an attack of sickness . . . "one must possess something in order to *be* something" . . . But this is the oldest and healthiest of all instincts: I should add, "one must want to have more than one has in order to *become* more". For this is the doctrine preached by life itself' (WP 125 Nachlaß 1885 KSA 11 37[11]). This is important to note, too, in the transposition or conversion of Nietzschean 'general economy' into political economy.

52. See also, for example, Nietzsche's reference to the 'rotted ruling classes', who 'have ruined the image of the ruler' (WP 750 Nachlaß 1884 KSA 11 25[349]) and, 'Whoever still wants to retain power flatters the mob, works with the mob, must have the mob on its side' (WP 864 Nachlaß 1888 KSA 13 14[182]).

53. I direct these comments against those who would appear to protect Nietzsche from his politics with the word, 'spiritual'. See Leslie Paul Thiele, 'Twilight of Modernity: Nietzsche, Heidegger and Politics', *Political Theory* 22(3), August 1994, 468–90: Nietzsche's 'doctrine of the will to power . . . remains fundamentally within the governance of a spiritual regime', p. 485.

54. The *Laws of Manu* are the earliest known *Dharma Sastras*. They are a code of laws which provide a quasi-legal justification of a caste system. See George J. Stack, 'Nietzsche and the Laws of Manu', *Sociology and Social Research* 51,

October, 1966, 94–106. On Manu Nietzsche had in his library, Louis Jacol-
liot, *Les législateurs religieux. Manou-Moise-Mahomet*, Paris, 1876. See Max
Oehler, ed. *Nietzsches Bibliothek*, Nietzsche Archivs, 1942.
55. As Stack writes, this 'theory of caste . . . appears to have emerged out of [a]
fundamental distinction between . . . Aryans and . . . non-Aryans'. 'It is precisely the racist aspect of the *Laws of Manu* which Nietzsche found unac-
ceptable.' Stack, 'Nietzsche and the Laws of Manu', pp. 96, 103. Nietzsche
acknowledges that the law-book is 'racially purest' (WP 143 Nachlaß 1888
KSA 13 14[204]). Ric Brown has pointed out to me that the Sanskrit for 'caste'
is *varna* which means 'colour'. The caste system primarily reflects 'colour',
the invading Aryans being light-skinned, conquering the indigenous, dark-
skinned Dravidians.
56. Eric Voegelin remarks that Nietzsche's is a 'vitiated Platonism' since 'the light
of the transcendental idea and faith in the social substance is missing'. Eric
Voegelin, 'Nietzsche, the Crisis and the War', *Journal of Politics*, Vol. 6, 1944,
p. 202.
57. Stack, 'Nietzsche and the laws of Manu', p. 102.

2 The Radical Liberal Democratic Reading of Nietzsche

1. Most notably in the works of William Connolly, Lawrence Hatab, Bonnie
Honig, Alan D. Schrift and Mark Warren. For criticism of this reading see,
for example, Frederick Appel, *Nietzsche contra Democracy* (Ithaca: Cornell
University Press, 1999); Mark Fowler, 'Nietzschean Perspectivism: "How
Could Such a Philosophy – Dominate?" ', *Social Theory and Practice* 16 (2),
Summer 1990, pp. 119–62; Ishay Landa, 'Nietzsche, the Chinese Worker's
Friend', *New Left Review* 236, July/August 1999, pp. 3–23; Ted Sadler, 'The
Postmodern Politicization of Nietzsche', *Nietzsche, Feminism and Political
Theory*, ed. Paul Patton (London: Routledge, 1993); Pierre-André Taguieff,
'The Traditional Paradigm – Horror of Modernity and Antiliberalism: Niet-
zsche in Reactionary Rhetoric', *Why We Are Not Nietzscheans*, ed. Luc Ferry
and Alain Renaut, trans. Robert de Loaiza (Chicago: The University of
Chicago Press, 1997); and Geoff Waite, *Nietzsche's Corps/e: Aesthetics, Politics,
Prophecy, or, The Spectacular Technoculture of Everyday Life* (Durham, NC and
London: Duke University Press, 1996).
2. Gyorgy Lukács, *The Destruction of Reason*, trans. Peter Palmer (Englewood
Cliff, NJ: Humanities Press, 1981), p. 343.
3. See, for example, Thomas H. Brobjer, 'The Absence of Political Ideals in Niet-
zsche's Writings', *Nietzsche-Studien* 27, 1998, 300–19; and Brian Leiter,
Nietzsche on Morality (New York: Routledge, 2002).
4. As Behler has succinctly stated it. See Ernst Behler, *Confrontations:
Derrida/Heidegger/Nietzsche*, trans. Steven Taubeneck (Stanford: Stanford
University Press, 1991), p. 104.
5. Walter Kaufmann, *Nietzsche: Philosopher, Psychologist, Anti-Christ* (Princeton,
NJ: Princeton University Press, 1974), pp. 123, 418. This view of Nietzsche
as Perfectionist is more recently argued for in Stanley Cavell, *Conditions
Handsome and Unhandsome: The Constitution of Emersonian Perfectionism*
(Chicago: University of Chicago Press, 1990), p. 50; and in James Conant,

'Nietzsche's Perfectionism: A Reading of *Schopenhauer as Educator*', *Nietzsche's Postmoralism*, ed. Richard Schacht (Cambridge: Cambridge University Press, 2001).

6. Karl Jaspers, *Nietzsche: An Introduction to the Understanding of His Philosophical Activity*, trans. Charles F. Wallraft and Frederick J. Schmitz (Tucson: University of Arizona Press, 1965). For this apt paraphrasing of Jasper's position see Behler, *Confrontations*, p. 20.
7. Georges Bataille, 'Nietzsche and the Fascists', *Visions of Excess*, ed. Allan Stoekl, trans. Allan Stoekl, Carl R. Lovitt and Donald M. Leslie Jr. (Minneapolis: University of Minnesota Press, 1985), p. 184.
8. See Gilles Deleuze, 'Pensée nomade', *Nietzsche aujourd'hui* (Paris: Union Générale d'Editions, 1973) or 'Nomad Thought', *The New Nietzsche*, ed. David B. Allison (New York: Dell Publishing Co., 1977).
9. Deleuze, 'Nomad Thought', p. 146. Italics mine.
10. Benito Mussolini, *The Political and Social Doctrine of Fascism*, trans. Jane Soames (London: The Hogarth Press, 1933), p. 19.
11. Quoted in Mark Neocleous, *Fascism* (Minneapolis: University of Minnesota Press, 1977), p. 54.
12. For example, Alan Schrift who writes, 'while much interpretive work is needed to show Nietzsche as a supporter of democratic pluralism, such work can be done'. Alan D. Schrift, *Nietzsche's French Legacy: A Genealogy of Poststructuralism* (New York: Routledge, 1995), p. 124. See also Alan D. Schrift, 'Nietzsche *for* Democracy?', *Nietzsche-Studien* 29, 2000, 220–33; and my response to Schrift in *Nietzsche-Studien* 31, 2002, 278–90.
13. Henry S. Kariel, 'Nietzsche's Preface to Constitutionalism', *Journal of Politics* 25:2, May 1963, 211–25.
14. Mark Warren, *Nietzsche and Political Thought* (Cambridge, Mass.: The MIT Press, 1988), p. 205.
15. I borrow this expression from Tracy Strong, *Friedrich Nietzsche and the Politics of Transfiguration* (Berkeley: University of California Press, 1975), p. 301.
16. David Owen, *Nietzsche, Politics and Modernity: A Critique of Liberal Reason* (London: SAGE Publications, 1995), p. 138.
17. Lawrence J. Hatab, *A Nietzschean Defense of Democracy* (Chicago: Open Court, 1995), p. 30.
18. William E. Connolly, *Political Theory and Modernity* (Ithaca: Cornell University Press, 1988, 1993), p. 190.
19. William E. Connolly, *Identity/Difference: Democratic Negotiations of Political Paradox* (Ithaca: Cornell University Press, 1991), p. 185.
20. Ibid.
21. Hatab, *A Nietzschean Defense of Democracy*, p. 3.
22. Warren, *Nietzsche and Political Thought*, p. 247.
23. Ibid., p. 211.
24. Hatab, *A Nietzschean Defense of Democracy*, p. 45.
25. Warren, *Nietzsche and Political Thought*, p. 201.
26. Ibid., pp. 113, 208.
27. Connolly, *Political Theory and Modernity*, p. 140.
28. William E. Connolly, *The Augustinian Imperative: A Reflection on the Politics of Morality* (Newbury Park: SAGE Publications, 1993), pp. 37–8.
29. Ibid., p. 143.

30. Connolly, *Political Theory and Modernity*, p. 140.
31. Connolly, *Identity/Difference*, p. 185.
32. Ibid., p. 187. By way of demonstrating nuances within the radical liberal democratic reading, Schrift, in contrast to Connolly, says that the *Übermensch* 'does not designate an ontological state or a way of being that a subject could instantiate'. Schrift, 'Nietzsche *For* Democracy?', p. 225.
33. Warren, *Nietzsche and Political Thought*, p. 208.
34. Following Deleuze. Gilles Deleuze, *Nietzsche and Philosophy*, trans. Hugh Tomlinson (New York: Columbia University Press, 1983), p. 17.
35. Keith Ansell-Pearson, *An Introduction to Nietzsche as Political Thinker: The Perfect Nihilist* (Cambridge: Cambridge University Press, 1994), p. 55. Ansell-Pearson does not espouse the radical liberal democratic appropriation of Nietzsche but, like Deleuze, assumes the position that Nietzsche resists political codification. Josef Chytry also fails to see a 'satisfactory link' between the Dionysian and Nietzsche's caste-state idea. Josef Chytry, *The Aesthetic State: A Quest in Modern German Thought* (Berkeley: University of California Press, 1989), p. 347.
36. Reiner Schürmann, 'Political Thinking in Heidegger', *Social Research*, Spring 1978, Vol. 45, No. 1, 191–221.
37. Alfred Bäumler, 'Nietzsche and National Socialism', *Nazi Culture: Intellectual, Cultural and Social Life in the Third Reich*, ed. George L. Mosse, trans. Salvator Attansio (New York: Grosset & Dunlop, 1966), p. 99.
38. On Bäumler's reading of Nietzsche, and the Radical Right's 'disregard for systems and . . . emphasis on dynamic movement . . . "living dangerously" and "overcoming" ', see Steven E. Aschheim, *The Nietzsche Legacy in Germany: 1890–1990* (Berkeley: University of California Press, 1992). Bauemler writes that Nietzsche's values 'exist only so long as we make ourselves responsible for them'. Bäumler, 'Nietzsche and National Socialism', p. 99.
39. See, for example, John Farrenkopf, 'Nietzsche, Spengler, and the Politics of Cultural Despair', *Interpretation* 20(2), Winter 1992–93, 165–85.
40. As Heidegger rightly recognizes, 'the will to power is the fluctuating nexus of preservation and enhancement of power'. This means that the will to power fixates into complex forms or constructs of domination (*Herrschaftsgebilde*) which are, to be sure, finite in their 'positions and configurations', but which may, nevertheless, prevail for a long time. Martin Heidegger, *Nietzsche: The Will to Power as Knowledge*, Vol. III, trans. David Farrell Krell (San Francisco: Harper & Row Publishers, 1987), pp. 199, 211.
41. 'How far off may that . . . be? What do I care! But I am not less certain of it on that account – I stand securely with both feet upon . . . this eternal foundation' (Z Honey Offering). See also Nietzsche's reference to the 'new aristocracy' which would 'endure for millennia' (WP 960 Nachlaß 1885–86 KSA 12 2[57]).
42. Randolph Bourne, 'Denatured Nietzsche', *The Dial*, October 1917, 389–91. For a similar viewpoint, see also Havelock Ellis, *Affirmations* (1898) (London: Constable, 1915).
43. See, also, GM I 4 and WP 51 Nachlaß 1888 KSA 13 14[6] where Nietzsche writes: 'everywhere the Christian nihilistic value standard still has to be pulled up and fought under every work . . . in present day sociology,

in present day music'. In place of 'democratic' sociology Nietzsche proposes 'a theory of the forms of domination' (WP 462 Nachlaß 1887 KSA 12 9[8]).

44. This has been recognized as 'the most revolutionary aspect of Nietzsche's psychology, his idea of a multiple soul' or psyche. See Graham Parkes, *Composing the Soul: Reaches of Nietzsche's Psychology* (Chicago: University of Chicago Press, 1994), p. 18. Nevertheless, a similar description may be found in Bernard Mandeville's *The Fable of the Bees* (1714).

45. Hatab, *A Nietzschean Defense of Democracy*, p. 36.

46. Warren, *Nietzsche and Political Thought*, pp. 190–212.

47. See *Thus Spoke Zarathustra*, Of the Afterworldsmen: 'I teach mankind a new will', and Of the Bestowing Virtue 1: 'When you are the willers of a single will . . . that is when your virtue has its origin . . . It is power, this new virtue' (which is to say, *virtù*, as Nietzsche's ethics is a *virtù* ethics, not a virtue ethics).

48. Compare Nietzsche's description with Lawrence Hatab's, who writes, the 'postmodern self should be understood as an agonistic complex of forces and meanings that are in continual oscillation, that cannot be "located" in any stable site'. Hatab, *A Nietzschean Defense of Democracy*, p. 209. The final clause is the operative one. Nietzsche would consider this 'disgregation of the will'.

49. Tracy Strong, 'Texts and Pretexts: Reflections on Perspectivism in Nietzsche', *Political Theory* 13(2), May 1985, 164–82, p. 165.

50. Owen, *Nietzsche, Politics and Modernity*, p. 160.

51. Bonnie Honig, *Political Theory and the Displacement of Politics* (Ithaca: Cornell University Press, 1993), p. 247, n. 40.

52. Hatab, *A Nietzschean Defense of Democracy*, pp. 12, 66.

53. Honig, *Political Theory and the Displacement of Politics*, p. 262, n. 9.

54. There is a certain frustration and consequently the desire to discipline Nietzsche in the radical liberal democratic reading because Nietzsche 'did not develop the pluralistic implications of his philosophy of truth'. But Nietzsche's philosophy *should* have led 'to the radical openness and pluralism of democracy'. See Warren, *Nietzsche and Political Thought*, p. 237, and Hatab, *A Nietzschean Defense of Democracy*, p. 73.

55. Schrift, *Nietzsche's French Legacy*, p. 124.

56. Schrift, 'Nietzsche *For* Democracy?', p. 223.

57. Sarah Kofman expresses it well when she says that will to power 'implies repression and a return of repressed forces'. Sarah Kofman, *Nietzsche and Metaphor*, trans. Duncan Large (Stanford: Stanford University Press, 1993), p. 24.

58. Connolly, *Political Theory and Modernity*, p. 194.

59. Hatab, *A Nietzschean Defense of Democracy*, p. 67.

60. See, for example, Hannah Arendt, *The Origins of Totalitarianism* (New York: The World Publishing Company, 1958), pp. 462–63; and, *Fascism*, ed. Roger Griffin (Oxford: Oxford University Press, 1995), p. 5: Fascism 'lacks a genuine metaphysical dimension'.

61. See Ernst Basch, *The Fascist: His State and His Mind* (New York: William Morrow & Co., 1972), p. 133.

62. Or, like Mussolini, even though he would agree that there is no 'doctrine of unquestioned efficacy for all times and all peoples'.

63. Hatab, *A Nietzschean Defense of Democracy*, p. 137.
64. The *Second Reich* was founded in 1871. Such concessions were made incrementally, if not discontinuously, in the aftermath of the revolutions of 1848.
65. The Social Democratic Party of Germany; formed out of an alliance between Ferdinand Lasalle's General German Worker's Association and August Bebel's and Wilhelm Liebknecht's Social Democratic Worker Party at Gotha in 1875. The antisocialist laws continued until 1890. They made all union activity illegal.
66. In *Beyond Good and Evil* Nietzsche writes, 'I found that certain features recurred regularly together and were closely associated – until I finally discovered two basic types and one basic difference. There are *master* morality and *slave* morality' (BGE 260). Nietzsche's earlier intention was to 'compare *many* moralities' and 'to collect and arrange a vast realm of subtle feelings of value and differences of value ... and ... to present vividly some of the more frequent and recurring forms of such living crystallizations' (BGE 186). What Nietzsche does, in fact, is locate the 'recurring forms' without the groundwork of 'comparing *many* moralities'.
67. As Fowler has pointed out. Fowler, 'Nietzschean Perspectivism: "How Could Such a Philosophy – Dominate?" ', p. 143.
68. *The Selected Letters of Friedrich Nietzsche*, ed. Christopher Middleton (Chicago: University of Chicago Press, 1969), p. 311.
69. In support of this point see WP 936 Nachlaß 1887–88 KSA 11[140–42]: 'The presupposition inherent in an aristocratic society for preserving a high degree of freedom among its members is the extreme tension that arises from the presence of an antagonistic drive in all its members: the will to dominate.'
70. See Bonnie Honig, 'The Politics of Agonism', *Political Theory* 21(3), August 1993, 528–33.
71. Connolly, *The Augustinian Imperative*, pp. 155–6.
72. Owen, *Nietzsche, Politics and Modernity*, p. 163.
73. Connolly, *The Augustinian Imperative*, pp. 155–6.
74. Hatab, *A Nietzschean Defense of Democracy*, p. 122.
75. Connolly, *The Augustinian Imperative*, p. 142.
76. Owen, *Nietzsche, Politics and Modernity*, p. 163.
77. Honig, *Political Theory and the Displacement of Politics*, p. 209.
78. Honig, *The Politics of Agonism*, p. 530.
79. Hatab, *A Nietzschean Defense of Democracy*, p. 65.
80. See Carl Schmitt, *The Concept of the Political*, trans. George Schwab (New Jersey: Rutgers University Press, 1976). As Nietzsche writes, 'A society that preserves a regard ... for freedom must feel itself to be an exception and must confront a power from which it distinguishes itself, toward which it is hostile, and on which it looks down' (WP 936 Nachlaß 1887–88 KSA 13 11[140]).
81. When Nietzsche criticizes Herbert Spencer (1820–1903), the originator of Social Darwinism, it is to criticize the ascendency in social theory of the idea of 'adaptation' over 'aggressive, expansive ... forces that give new interpretations and directions' (GM II 12). In other words, the liberal democratic element in Spencer's Social Darwinism.
82. For comments on Nietzsche and Social Darwinism, see Lukács, *The Destruc-*

tion of Reason, pp. 369, 686; and Arno Mayer, *The Persistance of the Old Regime: Europe to the Great War* (New York: Pantheon Books, 1981).

83. See Frantz Fanon, *Black Skin White Masks*, trans. Charles Lam Markmann (New York: Grove Press, 1967), pp. 216–22.

84. Connolly, *The Augustinian Imperative*, p. 88.

85. Thus it is misleading to characterize the will to power simply as a 'becoming driven by *conflicting* tensions' or as an 'agonistic force field'. See Hatab, *A Nietzschean Defense of Democracy*, pp. 9, 68.

86. Think, for example, of the National Socialist architect Albert Speer and his 'law of ruins' which, as Kenneth Frampton writes, conceived 'of the State in such terms as to anticipate its own eclipse'. Kenneth Frampton, 'A Synoptic View of the Architecture of the Third Reich', *Oppositions: A Journal for Ideas and Criticism in Architecture*, Spring 1978: 12.

87. Alan D. Schrift, 'Response to Don Dombowsky', *Nietzsche-Studien* 31, 2002, 291–7, p. 296.

88. See, for example, Marcus Paul Bullock, *The Violent Eye: Ernst Jünger's Visions and Revisions of the European Right* (Detroit: Wayne State University Press, 1992), p. 11. The Italian Fascist, Alfredo Rocco, writing against liberal democracy, also makes the conservation of 'competitiveness and conflicts' between 'various human societies' the basis of his agonistic conception. Alfredo Rocco, 'The *Politica* Manifesto', *Italian Fascisms: From Pareto to Gentile*, ed. Adrian Lyttelton (London: Jonathan Cape, 1973), p. 258.

89. *Fascism*, ed. Griffin, p. 7. Nietzsche possesses six of the ten features of generic fascism, and arguably eight, that Griffin enumerates in his General Introduction. Another could apply to Nietzsche not enumerated: the politics of the demobilization of militant labour.

90. For example, 'In Italy even Gentile, the philosophical idealist, called for a continual progression of the "new spirit" . . . which should not be allowed to harden into a credo or a system of dogma . . . French fascist intellectuals were apt to reject Hegelianism itself as blurring and reconciling differences in a bourgeois fashion, opting for a simple Nietzschean dynamic instead.' See George L. Mosse, 'Fascism and the Intellectuals', *The Nature of Fascism*, ed. S. J. Woolf (London: Weidenfeld and Nicolson, 1968), p. 217.

91. Gentile writes that 'from the Fascist standpoint, the nation itself is realized in the spirit and is not a mere presupposition. The nation is never complete and neither is the state, which is the nation itself expressed in concrete political form. The state is always becoming.' Gentile, 'The Origins and Doctrine of Fascism', *Italian Fascisms*, p. 310.

92. Schrift, 'Response to Don Dombowsky', p. 295.

93. Julius Evola, 'Four Excerpts from *Pagan Imperialism: Fascism before the Euro-Christian Peril* (1928)', *A Primer of Italian Fascism*, ed. Jeffrey T. Schnapp (Lincoln: University of Nebraska Press, 2000). Evola (1898–1974) was an Italian Fascist, Nietzschean, anti-Christian. *Pagan Imperialism* affirms a 'will to difference', reorientation towards pagan values and autonomous individuality.

94. Schrift, 'Response to Don Dombowsky', p. 292, n. 4.

95. Martin Heidegger, *Nietzsche: The Will to Power as Knowledge*, Vol. III, pp. 199, 211.

96. I am following Laclau and Mouffe here, to whom the radical liberal democratic reader often appeals, who write: '– it is equally wrong to propose as an alternative, either pluralism or the total diffusion of power within the social, as this would blind the analysis to the presence of nodal points and to partial concentrations of power existing in every concrete social formation'. Ernesto Laclau and Chantal Mouffe, *Hegemony & Socialist Strategy: Towards a Radical Democratic Politics* (London: Verso, 1985), p. 142. This is exactly what radical liberal democratic readers like Schrift appear to do, which is why they see in Nietzsche 'evasion of fixed identity'.
97. Ibid., pp. 111–12.
98. Such as Appel, *Nietzsche contra Democracy*.

3 Nietzsche and Aristocratic Liberalism

1. See, Alan D. Schrift, 'Nietzsche *For* Democracy?', *Nietzsche-Studien* 29, 2000, 220–33.
2. As maintained by S. Kahan. Alan S. Kahan, *Aristocratic Liberalism: The Social and Political Thought of Jacob Burckhardt, John Stuart Mill, and Alexis de Tocqueville* (Oxford: Oxford University Press, 1992), p. 163. Kahan identifies Aristocratic liberalism as 'a distinct discourse within the European liberal movement in the period 1830–70', p. 135.
3. *The Selected Letters of Friedrich Nietzsche*, ed. Christopher Middleton (Chicago: University of Chicago Press, 1969), p. 225.
4. For his part, Burckhardt wrote to Nietzsche on 26 September 1886: 'What I find easier to understand in your work are your historical judgments and, more particularly, your views on the present age; on the will of nations, and its periodic paralysis; on the antithesis between the great security given by prosperity, and the need for education through danger; on hard work as the destroyer of religious instincts; on the herd man of the present day, and his claims; on democracy as the heir of Christianity; and . . . on the powerful on earth of the future! On this point you define and describe their probable formation and the conditions of their existence in a manner which ought to arouse the highest interest'. Burckhardt is responding to Nietzsche's *Beyond Good and Evil*. See *The Letters of Jacob Burckhardt*, trans. Alexander Dru (New York: Pantheon Books, 1955), p. 212.
5. According to Marti. See Urs Marti, 'Nietzsches Kritik der Französischen Revolution', *Nietzsche-Studien* 19, 1990, 312–35.
6. See Hippolyte Taine, 'Napoléon Bonaparte', *Revue des deux mondes* 15 February, Vol. 79, 721–52, and 1 March, Vol. 80, 5–49.
7. See also Burckhardt's remarks in a letter to von Preen (1871) against Rousseau's 'doctrine of the goodness of human nature'. *The Letters of Jacob Burckhardt*, p. 147.
8. *The Selected Letters of Friedrich Nietzsche*, ed. Middleton, p. 261.
9. Alexis de Tocqueville, *Democracy in America*, trans. George Lawrence, ed. J. P. Mayer (New York: Anchor Books, 1969), p. 702. Mill expressed a similar concern. See, for example, John Stuart Mill, *On Liberty* (New York: The Liberal Arts Press, 1956).
10. Kahan, *Aristocratic Liberalism*, p. 140. As Kahan writes, for the aristocratic

liberals the 'worst of all worlds . . . would be a society dominated by the lower class . . . [through] Universal Suffrage', p. 37.

11. To borrow the words of Burckhardt. Jacob Burckhardt, *Force and Freedom: Reflections on History*, ed. James Hastings Nichols (New York: Pantheon Books, 1943), p. 224.
12. Ibid., p. 179.
13. Ibid., p. 226.
14. Ibid., p. 152.
15. Ibid., p. 182.
16. See Richard F. Sigurdson, 'Jacob Burckhardt: The Cultural Historian as Political Thinker', *Review of Politics* 52, 3, Summer 1990, 417–40, 420–1. See, also, Burckhardt's remarks in a letter to von Preen (1882) against the 'participation of the masses on any and every question'. *The Letters of Jacob Burckhardt*, p. 207.
17. Ibid., p. 432.
18. As Sigurdson says, unlike the liberals of his period. Ibid., p. 429.
19. Nietzsche also cites the preoccupation with 'power, grand politics, economic affairs, world commerce, parliamentary institutions [and] military interests', in short, the preoccupations of the new *Reich*, as contributing to this decline (TI Germans 4).
20. Thomas Mann remarks that there is a tradition in German conservative political thought, in particular, and I think it applies to Nietzsche, which recognizes the identity of politics and democracy, of politicization and democratization (85). 'When one sees things in a conservative way, one sees them antipolitically' or antidemocratically (191). 'But anti-politics is also politics' (303). Thomas Mann, *Reflections of a Nonpolitical Man* (1918), trans Walter D. Morris (New York: Frederick Ungar Publishing Co., 1983).
21. For comments against 'public opinion' and newspapers as 'repulsive verbal swill', see, for example, *Thus Spoke Zarathustra*, Of Passing By.
22. 'Chinese' is a common slur in the aristocratic liberal canon.
23. See Hippolyte Taine, *History of English Literature* (New York: Colonial Press, 1900), p. 175.
24. Italics mine.
25. See Burckhardt, *Force and Freedom*, Introduction.
26. De Tocqueville, *Democracy in America*, p. 675.
27. In a note from 1883, Nietzsche says that Napoleon 'lost *noblesse* of character' through 'the means', probably militaristic, 'he *had* to employ' (WP 1026 Nachlaß 1883 KSA 10 7[27]). However, in subsequent notes Nietzsche refers to Napoleon as a 'commander' type (WP 128 Nachlaß 1884 KSA 11 26[449]) and a 'higher' human being (WP 544 Nachlaß 1887 KSA 12 10[159]). The criticism contained in the note from 1883 is, none the less, effectively tempered by Nietzsche's commentary in a note from 1887 where, in reference to Napoleon, he states that the 'higher' and 'terrible' belong together, adding that Napoleon represents 'the most powerful instinct, that of life itself, the lust to rule, affirmed' (WP 1017 Nachlaß 1887 KSA 12 10[5]). Nietzsche praises Napoleon because he represents a 'synthesis of the *inhuman* and *superhuman*' (GM I 16); in this sense Napoleon is a man of *virtù*. Finally, Nietzsche has no objection to the militarism of Napoleon, who overcame the eighteenth century by again 'awakening . . . the soldier' (WP 104 Nachlaß

1888 KSA 13 15[68], citing his militarism as a 'cure' for decadence (WP 41 Nachlaß 1888 KSA 13 15[31]).

28. Gyorgy Lukács, *The Young Hegel: Studies in the Relations between Dialectics and Economics*, trans. Rodney Livingstone (Cambridge, Mass.: The MIT Press, 1976), p. 451.

29. Mark Warren's view that Nietzsche's critique of the state is 'consistently antitotalitarian' and that it suggests 'that all politically sustained hierarchies . . . are inconsistent with the intersubjective space of individuation' is simply wrong. First, Nietzsche is not concerned with the *individuation* of *all* individuals, for example, in terms of equality of opportunity. Second, Nietzsche says just the opposite: that the 'ingrained difference between strata' is necessary for the 'enhancement of the human type' (BGE 257); the maximization of individual power implies oppression (as Peter Kropotkin recognized and criticized in Nietzsche). And third, Nietzsche's own ideal regime is arguably totalitarian, given its internal coordination, and does not eschew the use of control. Nietzsche does say, in his notes, that everything 'a man does in the service of the state is contrary to his nature', but he may have something very specific in mind here when he says 'the state'. For elsewhere in his notes, during the same period, he writes that the 'maintenance of the military state is the last means of all of acquiring . . . the great tradition with regard to the supreme type of man, the strong type'. See Mark Warren, *Nietzsche and Political Thought* (Cambridge Mass.: The MIT Press, 1988), p. 223. See, also, WP 718 Nachlaß 1887–88 KSA 13 11[252] and WP 729 Nachlaß 1887–88 KSA 13 11[407].

30. On this aspect of Burckhardt's view of the state, see Sigurdson, 'The Cultural Historian as Political Thinker', p. 433.

31. See also: 'the democratization of Europe is at the same time an involuntary arrangement for the cultivation of *tyrants* – taking that word in every sense, including the most spiritual' (BGE 242).

32. It is not surprising that Nietzsche approved in an early *Germania* club paper (*Napoleon III as President*, 1862) of the *coup d'état* of Louis Bonaparte in 1851 which, as Marx put it, 'annihilated' parliament and overturned the French constitution. Later in life, Nietzsche prided himself on reading only one newspaper, the *Journal des Debats*, principle organ of the counterrevolutionary bourgeosie in France (EH WGB 1). See, also, Karl Marx, *The Eighteenth Brumaire of Louis Bonaparte* (New York: International Publishers, 1963).

33. As Tombs comments, 'Napoleon popularized the idea of a conflict of superstates for world domination'. Robert Tombs, *France 1814–1914* (London: Longman, 1996), p. 201.

34. De Tocqueville, *Democracy in America*, p. 436.

35. Ibid., p. 705.

36. Which, as Kahan writes, the aristocratic liberals viewed 'as outside the pale of valuable diversities'. Kahan, *Aristocratic Liberalism*, p. 109. For de Tocqueville's ambivalence regarding universal suffrage, see *Democracy in America*, pp. 199–201.

37. This difference between Nietzsche and the aristocratic liberals, namely, the remedy for *décadence*, is missed by readers such as James Conant, who think that Nietzschean 'perfectionism' is compatible with democratic theory. But,

as Nietzsche writes, 'perfecting consists in the production of the most powerful individuals, who will use the great mass of people as their tools' (WP
660 Nachlaß 1885–86 KSA 12 2[76]). Such readers not only lack a coherent
historical account, but obscure Nietzsche's conceptual processes. Nietzsche
wanted to develop a theory of the forms of domination. To put it briefly, he
did not view the *self* as separate from the mediations of social and political
organization. Therefore, in order to show that Nietzschean 'perfectionism'
does not conflict with democratic theory, it would have to be shown that
Nietzsche sets his account of 'perfectionism' within democratic institutions.
Indeed, Nietzsche does so in *Beyond Good and Evil* (242), but the point
is: they are to be infiltrated in order to be subverted. See James Conant,
'Nietzsche's Perfectionism: A Reading of *Schopenhauer as Educator*', *Nietzsche's
Postmoralism: Essays on Nietzsche's Prelude to Philosophy's Future*, ed. Richard
Schacht (Cambridge: Cambridge University Press, 2001).

38. See, for example, Taine: 'they demolish all that remains of social institutions,
and push on equalisation until everything is brought down to a dead level'.
Hippolyte Taine, *The Origins of Contemporary France*, ed. Edward T. Gargan
(Chicago: University of Chicago Press, 1974), p. 147.

39. See de Tocqueville, *Democracy in America*: the 'taste for well-being is the most
striking . . . characteristic of democratic ages', p. 448.

40. The full passage reads: 'For this is how things are: the diminution and levelling of European man constitutes *our* greatest danger, for the sight of him
makes us weary. – We can see nothing today that wants to grow greater, we
suspect that things will continue to go down . . . to become thinner, more
good natured, more prudent, more comfortable, more mediocre, more indifferent, more Chinese, more Christian'. See also 'The more I relinquish my
rights and level myself down, the more I come under the dominion of the
average and finally of the majority' (WP 936 Nachlaß 1887–88 KSA 13
11[140]).

41. See de Tocqueville, *Democracy in America*, p. 548.

42. See ibid., pp. 508, 705.

43. See ibid., p. 257.

44. Nietzsche's comments in this note are not made in the interests of human
dignity. Rather, he sees in the abolition of slavery, for example, the 'destruction of a fundamentally different type', meaning, that some human beings
are, typologically speaking, slaves. It is arguable that Nietzsche did not
entirely cast off all racist sentiments.

45. It is relevant to recall here Albert Camus' discerning remark that 'for Nietzsche nature is to be obeyed to subjugate history', meaning, proletarian
revolt. Albert Camus, *The Rebel: An Essay on Man in Revolt*, trans. Anthony
Bower (New York: Vintage Books, 1956), p. 79.

46. Italics mine. Cf. Z Of the Tarantulas, BGE 202, GS 377, A 57.

47. See Burckhardt to von Preen (1888). *The Letters of Jacob Burckhardt*, p. 215.

48. See, also, WP 890 Nachlaß 1887 KSA 12 9[17]: 'The dwarfing of man must
for a long time count as the only goal, because a broad foundation has first
to be created so that a stronger species of man can stand upon it'. In *The
Anti-Christ(ian)* Nietzsche writes that every higher culture must stand upon
the 'broad base' of a 'soundly consolidated mediocrity' (A 57). So Nietzsche
does not reject the mediocre per se. But they require a 'justification', and
that 'lies in serving a higher sovereign species'.

49. Kahan, *Aristocratic Liberalism*, p. 101.
50. De Tocqueville, *Democracy in America*, p. 506.
51. Ibid., p. 444. See, also, pp. 507, 527.
52. Ibid., pp. 500, 639.
53. As Kahan writes, the aristocratic liberals viewed political participation as a 'good in itself'. Their ideals of liberty and individuality 'implied the value of community'; they 'did not include a concentration on the self to the exclusion of society'. Kahan, *Aristocratic Liberalism*, pp. 100, 102.
54. As Nietzsche writes, 'Christianity has taught best . . . the soul atomism . . . the belief which regards the soul as something indestructible, eternal, indivisible, as a monad, as an *atomon*' (BGE 12). See, also, WP 765 Nachlaß 1888 KSA 13 15[30]: 'With this idea, the individual is made transcendent; as a result he can attribute a senseless importance to himself . . . play the judge of everything and everyone'.
55. To become what one is 'means to discharge it in works and actions' (H 263).
56. Burckhardt concurs with Nietzsche regarding the 'necessity of great men'. See Burckhardt, *Force and Freedom*, 'The Great Men of History', p. 345.
57. Letter to Franz Overbeck (1882). *The Selected Letters of Friedrich Nietzsche*, ed. Middleton, p. 195.
58. As Nietzsche writes to Malwida von Meysenbug (1883). Ibid., p. 216.
59. See Burckhardt to Ludwig von Pastor (1896), *The Letters of Jacob Burckhardt*. See also Burckhardt, *Force and Freedom*, Introduction, and Peter Heller, *Studies on Nietzsche*.
60. See, also, WP 753 Nachlaß 1885 KSA 11 34[177]: 'I am opposed to . . . socialism, because it dreams quite naively of "the good, true and beautiful" and of "equal rights" . . . parliamentary government and the press, because these are the means by which the herd animal becomes master'.
61. Mill, *On Liberty*, p. 95.
62. See, for example, 'The Claims of Labour' (1845), *The Collected Works of John Stuart Mill: Essays on Politics and Society*, Vol. V (Toronto: University of Toronto Press, 1967). On Nietzsche and Mill, see, for example, Gerald M. Mara and Suzanne L. Dovi, 'Mill, Nietzsche, and the Identity of Post-Modern Liberalism', *Journal of Politics* 57 (1), February 1995, 1–23. Mill, incidentally, is very well represented in Nietzsche's library.

4 Nietzsche and Machiavellianism

1. See, for example, Raymond Aron, *L'Homme contre les tyrans* (New York: Éditions de la Maison Française, 1944).
2. Nietzsche owned a French translation of *The Prince: Le Prince*, trans. C. Ferrari (Paris, 1873). See *Nietzsches Bibliothek*, ed. Max Oehler (Nietzsche Archivs, 1942). I have found no further references to C. Ferrari. Perhaps Nietzsche's French edition was, in fact, translated by G. (or Giuseppe) Ferrari (1812–76), the author of *Machiavel juge des revolutions de notre temps* (1849). It has been reported that Nietzsche read *The Prince* as early as 1862. Ronald Hayman, *Nietzsche: A Critical Life* (New York: Penguin Books, 1987), p. 44.
3. For commentary on Nietzsche's reading of Machiavelli and sources on Machiavelli see Thomas H. Brobjer, *Nietzsche's Ethics of Character: A Study of*

Nietzsche's Ethics and its Place in the History of Moral Thinking (Uppsala: Uppsala University, 1995), p. 81, n. 37.

4. Jacob Burckhardt, *The Civilization of the Renaissance in Italy*, Vols. I and II (New York: Harper Colophon Books, 1958), p. 472.

5. Emile Gebhart, *Les Origines de la Renaissance en Italie* (Paris: Librairie Hachette, 1923), p. 151.

6. Pasquale Villari, *Machiavelli and His Times*, trans. Linda Villari (London: Kegan Paul, 1883). In July 1879, Nietzsche cited Villari's book as one of many books to read. KSA 8 39[8].

7. Ibid., p. 271.

8. Ibid., p. 329.

9. F. A. Lange, *The History of Materialism*, trans. Ernest Chester Thomas (London: Truber & Co., 1877), pp. 222–3.

10. Frederick Ueberweg, *A History of Philosophy*, Vol. I, trans. George S. Morris (London: Hodder & Stoughton, 1865), pp. 29–30. Ueberweg writes, 'Machiavelli measures the value of the means exclusively with reference to their adaptation to the ends proposed.'

11. Of whom Machiavelli writes, 'I know of no better precepts for a new prince to follow than may be found in his actions', and refers to him as 'an example to be imitated' (P VII).

12. For a discussion of the elite theorists see, for example, Walter Struve, *Elites against Democracy: Leadership Ideals in Bourgeois Political Thought in Germany 1890–1933* (Princeton, NJ: Princeton University Press, 1972).

13. Peter Bergmann, *Nietzsche, 'The Last Antipolitical German'* (Bloomington: Indiana University Press, 1987), p. 4. Curious, since Bergmann later says 'Nietzsche . . . would remain strictly a Machiavellian in his approach to politics' (123). Had Bergmann continued this line of thought he might have been led to the position I will articulate in this chapter.

14. For other commentary on the relation between Nietzsche and Machiavelli, see Charles Andler, *Nietzsche: sa vie et sa pensée*, Vol. II (Paris: Librairie Gallimard, 1958), pp. 538–42; Keith Ansell-Pearson, *Nietzsche contra Rousseau: A Study of Nietzsche's Moral and Political Thought* (Cambridge: Cambridge University Press, 1991); Peter Bünger, *Nietzsche als Kritiker des Sozialismus* (Aachen: Shaker Verlag, 1997); Werner Dannhauser, *Nietzsche's View of Socrates* (Ithaca: Cornell University Press, 1974); Bruce Detwiler, *Nietzsche and the Politics of Aristocratic Radicalism* (Chicago: The University of Chicago Press, 1990); Robert Eden, *Political Leadership and Nihilism: A Study of Weber and Nietzsche* (Tampa: University Presses of Florida, 1983), and 'To What Extent Has the World of Concern to Contemporary Man Been Created by Nietzschean Politics?', *Nietzsche Heute*, ed. S. Bauschinger (Stuttgart: Francke, 1988); Martin Heidegger, *Nietzsche: Nihilism*, Vol. IV, trans. David Farrell Krell (San Francisco: Harper & Row, Publishers, 1982); Bonnie Honig, *Political Theory and the Displacement of Politics* (Ithaca: Cornell University Press, 1993); Samuel Lublinski, *Machiavelli und Nietzsche* (Zukunft, 1901); Conor Cruise O'Brien, *The Suspecting Glance* (London: Faber and Faber, 1972); N. Prostka, *Nietzsches Machtbegriff in Beziehung zu den Machiavellis* (Münster: Lit. Verlag, 1989); Stanley Rosen, *The Mask of Enlightenment: Nietzsche's Zarathustra* (Cambridge: Cambridge University Press, 1995); Hans Dieter Stell, *Machiavelli und Nietzsche* (Munich, 1987); Bernhard H. F. Taureck, *Nietzsche und der*

Faschismus, Eine Studie über Nietzsches politische Philosophie und ihre Folgen (Hamburg: Junius Verlag, 1989); and Geoff Waite, 'Zarathustra or the Modern Prince: The Problem of Nietzschean Political Philosophy', *Nietzsche Heute*, ed. S. Bauschinger (Stuttgart: Francke, 1988).

15. Heidegger, *Nietzsche*, Vol. IV, p. 165.
16. Andler, *Nietzsche: sa vie et sa pensée*, p. 538.
17. Karl Jaspers, *Nietzsche: An Introduction to the Understanding of His Philosophical Activity*, trans. Charles F. Walraff and Frederick J. Schmitz (Tucson: University of Arizona Press, 1965), pp. 252–3. This point is repeated by Simone Goyard-Fabre, *Nietzsche et la question politique* (Paris: Édition Sirey, 1977), p. 19, n. 15.
18. Ansell-Pearson, *Nietzsche contra Rousseau*, pp. 40, 193. Ansell-Pearson derives his characterization of Machiavelli from Wolin. See Sheldon S. Wolin, *Politics and Vision: Continuity and Innovation in Western Political Thought* (Boston: Little, Brown, 1960).
19. In this passage from *Human, All Too Human*, Nietzsche appears to be quoting Machiavelli, but he is more likely paraphrasing a secondary source since there is no such quotation to be found in Machiavelli. Or, perhaps, Nietzsche is simply presenting a composite of views that may be found in *The Prince*, for example, in chapters XVIII and XXV.
20. Machiavelli writes, 'It is . . . necessary for a prince to know well how to use both the beast and the man. This was . . . taught to ancient rulers by ancient writers, who relate how Achilles and many others of those ancient princes were given to Chiron the centaur to be brought up and educated under his discipline. The parable of this semi-animal, semi-human leader is meant to indicate that a prince must know how to use both natures, and that the one without the other is not durable'.
21. In a letter to Franz Overbeck (1882). *The Selected Letters of Friedrich Nietzsche*, ed. Christopher Middleton (Chicago: University of Chicago Press, 1969), p. 195.
22. As John Casey rightly avers. John Casey, *Pagan Virtue: An Essay in Ethics* (Oxford: Clarendon Press, 1990), p. 141.
23. For a discussion of Nietzsche's knowledge and use of the term *virtù*, see Brobjer, *Nietzsche's Ethics of Character*. My disagreement with Brobjer is very slight. Nietzsche was certainly aware of the concept of *virtù* prior to 1885, but he used the German word *Tüchtigkeit* which stands for it and continued to do so. See, for example, WP 127 Nachlaß 1884 KSA 11 26[417] and compare with WP 75 Nachlaß 1885 KSA 11 34[161] and A 2.
24. Honig, *Political Theory and the Displacement of Politics*, pp. 69–73.
25. Letter to Malwida von Meysenbug (1883). *The Selected Letters of Friedrich Nietzsche*, ed. Middleton, p. 216.
26. Louis Althusser, *Machiavelli and Us*, ed. Francois Matheron, trans. Gregory Elliott (London: Verso, 2000), p. 94.
27. Nietzsche read Niebuhr's *Römische Geschichte* and *Geschichte des Zeitalters der Revolution*.
28. Prezzolini, for example, also locates the tenet in Machiavelli that 'no single political system can claim superiority over another. The aim of the state is to survive'. Giuseppe Prezzolini, *Machiavelli* (New York: Farrar, Strauss & Giroux, 1967), p. 37.

29. As Nietzsche writes, 'destructive . . . frightful energies – those which are called evil – are the cyclopean architects and road-makers of humanity' (H 246). And so as not to be mistaken about where Nietzsche situates himself, read: 'We investigators are, like all conquerors, discoverers . . . of an audacious morality and must reconcile ourselves to being considered on the whole evil' (D 432).

30. See Nietzsche's references to 'Bismarck's Machiavellism' (GS 357) and to the German 'addiction' to *Realpolitik* (BGE 11). A. L. von Rochau coined the expression *Realpolitik* in his *Foundations of Realistic Policy as Applied to the Conditions of the German State* (1853).

31. See, also, GM II 14: 'actions practiced in the service of justice and approved with a good conscience: spying, deception, bribery, setting traps, the whole cunning and underhand art of police'.

32. Ansell-Pearson, *Nietzsche contra Rousseau*, p. 42.

33. See Laurence Lampert, *Leo Strauss and Nietzsche* (Chicago: University of Chicago Press, 1996), p. 119, and O'Brien, *The Suspecting Glance*, p. 58.

34. Waite, 'Zarathustra or the Modern Prince', p. 236.

35. Frederick II (King of Prussia), *The Refutation of Machiavelli's* Prince *or Anti-Machiavel*, trans. Paul Sonnino (Athens: Ohio University Press, 1981).

36. Prezzolini, *Machiavelli*, p. 216.

37. Ibid., pp. 272–3.

38. Ibid., pp. 277–8.

39. G. W. F. Hegel, 'The German Constitution', *Hegel's Political Writings*, trans. T. M. Knox (Oxford: Clarendon Press, 1964), p. 220.

40. Friedrich Meinecke, *Machiavellism: The Doctrine of Raison d'État and its Place in Modern History*, trans. Douglas Scott (New Haven: Yale University Press, 1957), p. 410.

41. Ibid., pp. 358, 369.

42. Ibid., p. 406.

43. As has been pointed out by Josef Chytry. Josef Chytry, *The Aesthetic State: A Quest in Modern German Thought* (Berkeley: University of California Press, 1989), p. 339.

44. Ansell-Pearson correctly asserts that 'Nietzsche's political theory makes the classic move of resting a theory of the political on a theory of nature . . . the noble *lie* disguised as a natural *law*'. Keith Ansell-Pearson, *An Introduction to Nietzsche as Political Thinker: The Perfect Nihilist* (Cambridge: Cambridge University Press, 1994), p. 41. Lukács expresses quite plainly that Nietzsche 'projected the main principles of his social philosophy on to natural phenomena'. Gyorgy Lukács, *The Destruction of Reason*, trans. Peter Palmer (Englewood Cliffs, NJ: Humanities Press, 1981), p. 375.

45. Plato, *The Republic*, trans. Desmond Lee (Harmondsworth: Penguin Books, 1974), p. 324.

46. Ibid., pp. 152–3.

47. Laurence Lampert, 'Nietzsche, The History of Philosophy, and Esotericism', *Nietzsche: Critical Assessments*, Vol. IV, *Between The Last Man and The Overman: The Question of Nietzsche's Politics*, ed. Daniel W. Conway with Peter S. Groff (London and New York: Routledge, 1998).

48. Ernst Bloch, *Natural Law and Human Dignity*, trans. Dennis J. Schmitt (Cambridge, Mass.: The MIT Press, 1996), p. 182.

49. As it has been by Geoff Waite and myself. See Geoff Waite, *Nietzsche's Corps/e: Aesthetics, Politics, Prophecy, or, The Spectacular Technoculture of Everyday Life* (Durham, NC and London: Duke University Press, 1996), p. 383, and Don Dombowsky, 'The Rhetoric of Legitimation: Nietzsche's "Doctrine" of Eternal Recurrence', *Journal of Nietzsche Studies*, Issue 14, Autumn 1997, 26–45. Lukács refers to Nietzsche's doctrine as a 'mythical counterpart . . . to the class struggle', which makes it appear as if the class struggle were ordained by 'nature'. Lukács, *The Destruction of Reason*, pp. 394, 691.

50. Nietzsche notes Blanqui's treatise in 1883. KSA 10, 17[73].

51. Louis Blanqui (1805–81) was a revolutionary socialist and prominent symbol for the adherents of the Paris Commune. See Alan B. Spitzer, *The Revolutionary Theories of Louis Auguste Blanqui* (New York: Columbia University Press, 1957).

52. As Ernst Bloch refers to it. Bloch, *Natural Law and Human Dignity*, p. 272.

53. The Jewish priesthood, as Nietzsche writes, 'translated their own natural past *into religious terms*', falsified history and constructed the '*lie* of a "moral world-order" ' (A 26), while the Christian Church 'falsified the history of Israel over again so as to make this history seem the pre-history of *its* act' (A 42).

54. Ansell-Pearson, *Nietzsche contra Rousseau*, p. 40. However, Ansell-Pearson will later remark that 'it is difficult to see how Nietzsche's aristocrats could maintain their rule without recourse to the deployment of the most oppressive instruments of political control and manipulation' (p. 211). And elsewhere, he writes that Nietzsche 'reduces politics to no more than an instrument of social control'. Ansell-Pearson, *An Introduction to Nietzsche as Political Thinker*, p. 79. See also Wolin, *Politics and Vision*, p. 216.

55. Daniel W. Conway, *Nietzsche's Dangerous Game: Philosophy in the Twilight of the Idols* (Cambridge: Cambridge University Press, 1997), p. 230. This point also finds general agreement in Andler, *Nietzsche: sa vie et sa pensée*, and Ofelia Schutte, *Beyond Nihilism: Nietzsche without Masks* (Chicago: University of Chicago Press, 1984).

56. Quoted in Waite, 'Zarathustra or the Modern Prince', p. 235. See Nachlaß 1881 KSA 9 11[221].

57. Vilfredo Pareto, *The Mind and Society: A Treatise on General Sociology*, Vols. I–IV, trans. Andrew Bongiorno and Arthur Livingston (New York: Dover, 1935), sections 545–626.

58. Ibid., section 1157.

59. Ibid., sections 1859–68.

60. In the same vein, in his essay 'Trasformazione della Democrazia', Pareto writes that the 'upper classes . . . have become gutless and demoralised'. In his essay 'Les Systèmes Socialistes', it is clear that this 'decadence' is due to the 'intrusion of humanitarian feelings'. Vilfredo Pareto, *Sociological Writings*, trans. Derick Mirfin (Totowa, NJ: Rowman and Littlefield, 1976), pp. 321, 135.

61. Pareto, *Mind and Society*, see sections 2183, 2244, 2250, 2454 and 2518.

62. Pareto, 'Les Systèmes Socialistes', *Sociological Writings*, p. 132.

63. Ibid., p. 135.

64. Gaetano Mosca, *The Ruling Class: Elementi di Scienza Politica*, trans. Hannah D. Kahn (New York: McGraw-Hill, 1939), p. 88.

65. Ibid., p. 492.
66. Ibid., pp. 493–4.
67. Ibid., p. 326.
68. Ibid., p. 397.
69. Ibid., p. 447.
70. Gustave Le Bon, *The French Revolution and the Psychology of Revolution* (New Brunswick: Transaction Inc., 1980), pp. 65–6.
71. Ibid., p. 300.
72. Ibid., p. 189.
73. Ibid., p. 104.
74. Gustave Le Bon, *The Crowd: A Study of the Popular Mind* (London: Ernest Benn, 1952). For these points, see pp. 66–118.
75. Ibid., p. 102.
76. Ibid., p. 183.
77. Ibid., p. 165.
78. See, for example, Mosca, *The Ruling Class*, p. 96 and Pareto, *Mind and Society*, section 2047.
79. Gustave Le Bon, *The Psychology of Socialism* (Vermont: Fraser Publishing Company, 1965), p. 112.
80. In this regard, Le Bon quotes Napoleon: 'It was by becoming a Catholic that I terminated the Vendéen war, by becoming a Mussalman that I obtained a footing in Egypt, by becoming an Ultramontane that I won over the Italian priests, and had I to govern a nation of Jews I would rebuild Solomon's temple.' *The Crowd*, p. 69.
81. On Le Bon, see Serge Moscovici, *The Age of the Crowd: A Historical Treatise on Mass Psychology*, trans. J. C. Whitehouse (Cambridge: Cambridge University Press, 1985).
82. See H. Stuart Hughes, *Consciousness and Society: The Reorientation of European Social Thought 1890–1930* (New York: Alfred A. Knopf, 1958), p. 253. Nevertheless, the early work of Mosca remains 'a vehicle for restoring the self-confidence of the European ruling classes, whose will to govern has been sapped by the Rousseauist dogmas of democracy and social equality'. See H. Stuart Hughes, 'Gaetano Mosca and the Political Lessons of History', *Pareto & Mosca*, ed. James H. Meisel (Englewood Cliffs, NJ: Prentice-Hall, Inc., 1965), p. 149.
83. As Nye says. Robert A. Nye, *The Anti-Democratic Sources of Elite Theory: Pareto, Mosca, Michels* (London: SAGE Publications, 1977), p. 20.
84. Ettore A. Albertoni, *Mosca and the Theory of Elitism*, trans. Paul Goodrick (Oxford: Basil Blackwell, 1987), pp. viii, ix.
85. Nye observes that Taine 'elaborated the arguments that later nourished both collective psychology and elite theory'. Nye, *The Anti-Democratic Sources of Elite Theory*, p. 10.
86. Le Bon, *The Psychology of Socialism*, p. 411.
87. Hippolyte Taine, *The Origins of Contemporary France*, ed. Edward T. Gargan (Chicago: The University of Chicago Press, 1974), pp. 108, 126, 255–67.
88. Nye, *The Anti-Democratic Sources of Elite Theory*, p. 8. Gramsci also makes this point in his, *Note sul Machiavelli*. See James H. Meisel, *The Myth of the Ruling Class: Gaetano Mosca and the Elite* (Ann Arbor: The University of Michigan Press, 1962), p. 315.

89. As Nietzsche writes, who 'could overturn with reasons what the mob has once learned to believe without reasons?' (Z Higher Men 9). Le Bon writes, in order to 'manipulate' a crowd, never speak to 'their reason, for they have none'. Rather, speak to their 'sentiments' and especially their 'unconscious sentiments'. Le Bon, *The Psychology of Socialism*, p. 412.
90. Le Bon, *The Crowd*, p. 146.
91. See, for example, Eugene Pyziur, *The Doctrine of Anarchism of Michael A. Bakunin* (Milwaukee: The Marquette University Press, 1955). See also Michael Bakunin, *God and State* (New York: Dover, 1970).

Epilogue

1. Thomas H. Brobjer, 'The Absence of Political Ideals in Nietzsche's Writings', *Nietzsche-Studien* 27, 1998, 300–19. My response to Brobjer above appears in a slightly revised version in *Nietzsche-Studien* 30, 2001, 387–93.
2. Italics mine.
3. Michel Foucault, *Power/Knowledge: Selected Interviews and Other Writings 1972–1977*, ed. Colin Gordon, trans. Colin Gordon, Leo Marshall, John Mepham and Kate Soper (Brighton: The Harvester Press, 1980), p. 53.
4. See Frederick Appel, *Nietzsche contra Democracy* (Ithaca: Cornell University Press, 1999).
5. Karl Löwith, *From Hegel to Nietzsche: The Revolution in Nineteenth-Century Thought*, trans. David E. Green (London: Constable, 1965), and Zvi Rosen, *Bruno Bauer and Karl Marx: The Influence of Bruno Bauer on Marx's Thought* (The Hague: Martinus Nijhoff, 1977).
6. Ibid., p. 176.
7. Ibid., pp. 186–7.
8. Following Löwith's description of Stirner. Ibid., p. 249.
9. Ibid., pp. 298, 244.
10. *The Selected Letters of Friedrich Nietzsche*, ed. Christopher Middleton (Chicago: University of Chicago Press, 1969), pp. 268, 279.
11. Bauer quoted in Rosen, *Bruno Bauer and Karl Marx*, p. 118.
12. Ibid., p. 110.
13. Ibid., pp. 117–22. Ernst Barnikol, however, writes that 'After the failures of 1848, Bauer no longer holds that the future is one of democratic progress. He now, like Nietzsche, foresees an age of multinational or global imperialism, in which Russia will play a prominent part. This change of position brings the late Bauer into much closer proximity with Nietzsche.' Ernst Barnikol, *Bruno Bauer, Studien und Materialen*, ed. P. Riemer and H. M. Sass (Assen: van Gorcum, 1972), pp. 310–424. I am grateful to Douglas Moggach for this reference.
14. Löwith, *From Hegel to Nietzsche*, p. 256.
15. Nietzschean *virtù* ethics are politically appointed in so far as they are personified in the 'genuine philosophers' who are 'legislators' and 'commanders' and, evidently, over political formations.
16. Nietzsche, conceptually and philosophically, exhibits clear complicity with intellectual variants within fascism. Putting his anti-anti-Semitism aside, his antinationalism (although, in its place he asserts European hegemony over the earth) and his antistatism (which needs to be qualified), and aside from

the evident proximity of his antidemocratic doctrine and his 'warrior ethos', and then other particulars with respect to vocabulary, he is complicit with generic fascism in his argument for the demobilization of militant labour, his conception of the 'soldier-worker', his idea of perpetual war (he transforms the Hobbesian state of nature into the concept of the political), and in his idea of law (against 'rule of law'), that legal conditions are exceptional conditions.

Bibliography

Albertoni, Ettore A. *Mosca and the Theory of Elitism*. Trans. Paul Goodrick: Oxford: Basil Blackwell, 1987.

Althusser, Louis. *Machiavelli and Us*. Ed. François Matheron. Trans. Gregory Elliott. London: Verso, 1999.

Andler, Charles. *Nietzsche: sa vie et sa pensée*. Paris: Librairie Gallimard, 1958.

Ansell-Pearson, Keith. *An Introduction to Nietzsche as Political Thinker: The Perfect Nihilist*, Cambridge: Cambridge University Press, 1994.

——. *Nietzsche contra Rousseau: A Study of Nietzsche's Moral and Political Thought*. Cambridge: Cambridge University Press, 1991.

Appel, Frederick. *Nietzsche contra Democracy*. Ithaca: Cornell University Press, 1999.

Aristotle. *The Politics*. Trans. T. A. Sinclair. Harmondsworth: Penguin Books, 1957.

Aron, Raymond. *L'Homme contre les tyrans*. New York: Éditions de la Maison Française, 1944.

Aschheim, Steven E. *The Nietzsche Legacy in Germany: 1890–1990*. Berkeley: University of California Press, 1992.

Bakunin, Michael. *God and the State*. New York: Dover, 1970.

Barnikol, Ernst. *Bruno Bauer, Studien und Materialen*, ed. P. Riemer and H. M. Sass. Assen: van Gorcum, 1972.

Basch, Ernst. *The Fascist: His State and His Mind*. New York: William Morrow & Co., 1972.

Bataille, Georges. 'Nietzsche and the Fascists' and 'The Obelisk'. *Visions of Excess*. Ed. Allen Stoekl. Trans. Allan Stoekl, Carl R. Lovitt and Donald M. Leslie Jr. Minneapolis: University of Minnesota Press, 1985.

Bäumler, Alfred. *Nietzsche, der Philosoph und Politiker*. Leipzig: Reclam, 1931.

——. 'Nietzsche and National Socialism'. *Nazi Culture: Intellectual, Cultural and Social Life in the Third Reich*. Ed. George L. Mosse. Trans. Salvator Attanasio. New York: Grosset & Dunlop, 1966.

Behler, Ernst. *Confrontations: Derrida/Heidegger/Nietzsche*. Trans. Steven Taubeneck. Stanford: Stanford University Press, 1991.

Bentham, Jeremy. *The Principles of Morals and Legislation*. New York: Haffner Publishing Co., 1948.

Bergmann, Peter. *Nietzsche, 'the last Antipolitical German'*. Bloomington: Indiana University Press, 1987.

Biddiss, Michael. 'Hippolyte Taine and the Making of History'. *The Right in France: 1789–1997*. Ed. Nicholas Atkin and Frank Tallet. London: Tauris Academic Studies, 1997.

Bloch, Ernst. *Natural Law and Human Dignity*. Trans. Dennis J. Schmitt. Cambridge, Mass.: The MIT Press, 1996.

Bourne, Randolph. 'Denatured Nietzsche'. *The Dial*. October 1917, 389–91.

——. 'Trans-National America'. *Atlantic Monthly*, June 1917, 778–86.

Brandes, Georg. *Friedrich Nietzsche*. Trans. A. G. Chater. New York: Macmillan, 1915.

Brobjer, Thomas H. 'The Absence of Political Ideals in Nietzsche's Writings'. *Nietzsche-Studien.* 27, 1998, 300–19.

——. *Nietzsche's Ethics of Character: A Study of Nietzsche's Ethics and its Place in the History of Moral Thinking.* Uppsala: Uppsala University, 1995.

——. 'Nietzsche's Knowledge, Reading, and Critique of Political Economy'. *Journal of Nietzsche Studies.* 18, Fall 1999, 56–70.

Bullock, Marcus Paul. *The Violent Eye: Ernst Jünger's Visions and Revisions of the European Right.* Detroit: Wayne State University Press, 1992.

Bünger, Peter. *Nietzsche als Kritiker des Sozialismus.* Aachen: Shaker Verlag, 1997.

Burckhardt, Jacob. *The Civilization of the Renaissance in Italy.* Vols. I and II. Trans. S. G. C. Middlemore. New York: Harper & Row, 1958.

——. *Force and Freedom: Reflections on History.* Ed. James Hastings Nichols. New York: Pantheon Books, 1943.

——. *The Letters of Jacob Burckhardt.* Ed. and Trans. Alexander Dru. New York: Pantheon Books, 1955.

Burke, Edmund. *Reflections on the Revolution in France.* Harmondsworth: Penguin Books, 1981.

Burnham, James. *The Machiavellians: Defenders of Freedom.* New York: John Day Co., 1943.

Camus, Albert. *The Rebel: An Essay on Man in Revolt.* Trans. Anthony Bower. New York: Vintage Books, 1956.

Casey, John. *Pagan Virtue: An Essay in Ethics.* Oxford: Clarendon Press, 1990.

Cavell, Stanley. *Conditions Handsome and Unhandsome: The Constitution of Emersonian Perfectionism.* Chicago: University of Chicago Press, 1990.

Chytry, Josef. *The Aesthetic State: A Quest in Modern German Thought.* Berkeley: University of California Press, 1989.

Conant, James. 'Nietzsche's Perfectionism: A Reading of *Schopenhauer as Educator*'. *Nietzsche's Postmoralism.* Ed. Richard Schacht. Cambridge: Cambridge University Press, 2001.

Connolly, William E. *The Augustinian Imperative: A Reflection on the Politics of Morality.* Newbury Park: SAGE Publications, 1993.

——. *Identity/Difference: Democratic Negotiations of Political Paradox.* Ithaca: Cornell University Press, 1991.

——. *Political Theory and Modernity.* Ithaca: Cornell University Press, 1993.

Conway, Daniel W. *Nietzsche's Dangerous Game: Philosophy in the Twilight of the Idols.* Cambridge: Cambridge University Press, 1997.

——. *Nietzsche & the Political.* London: Routledge, 1997.

Dannhauser, Werner J. 'Friedrich Nietzsche'. *History of Political Philosophy.* Ed. Leo Strauss, Joseph Cropsey. Chicago: University of Chicago Press, 1981.

Deleuze, Gilles. *Nietzsche and Philosophy.* Trans. Hugh Tomlinson. New York: Columbia University Press, 1983.

——. 'Nomad Thought'. *The New Nietzsche: Contemporary Styles of Interpretation.* Ed. David B. Allison. New York: Dell, 1977.

——. 'Pensée nomade'. *Nietzsche aujourd'hui.* Paris: Union Générale d'Editions, 1973.

Detwiler, Bruce. *Nietzsche and the Politics of Aristocratic Radicalism.* Chicago: The University of Chicago Press, 1990.

Dombowsky, Don. ' "Agitation anarchiste dans l'Empire" '. *Conjonctures.* No. 35, Autumn 2002, 155–60.

——. 'A Response to Alan D. Schrift's "Nietzsche *For* Democracy?" '. *Nietzsche-Studien*. 31, 2002, 278–90.

——. 'A Response to Thomas H. Brobjer's "The Absence of Political Ideals in Nietzsche's Writings" '. *Nietzsche-Studien*. 30, 2001, 387–93.

——. 'Nietzsche, Justice and the Critique of Liberal Democracy'. *Eidos*. XIV, 2, June 1997, 105–25.

——. 'The Rhetoric of Legitimation: Nietzsche's "Doctrine" of Eternal Recurrence'. *Journal of Nietzsche Studies*. 14, Autumn 1997, 26–45.

Earle, Edward Mead, Ed. *Makers of Modern Strategy: Military Thought from Machiavelli to Hitler*. Princeton, NJ: Princeton University Press, 1943.

Eden, Robert. *Political Leadership and Nihilism: A Study of Weber and Nietzsche*. Tampa: University Presses of Florida, 1983.

——. 'To What Extent Has the World of Concern to Contemporary Man Been Created by Nietzschean Politics?'. *Nietzsche Heute*. Ed. Sigrid Bauschinger et al. Stuttgart: Francke, 1988, 211–25.

Einstein, David G. *Emperor Frederick II*. New York: Philosophical Library, 1949.

Ellis, Havelock. *Affirmations*. London: Constable, 1915.

Engels, Friedrich. *The Condition of the Working Class in England*. Moscow: Progress Publishers, 1973.

Evola, Julius. 'Four Excerpts from *Pagan Imperialism: Fascism before the European Christian Peril* (1928)'. *A Primer of Italian Fascism*. Ed. Jeffrey T Schnapp. Lincoln: University of Nebraska Press, 2000.

Eyck, Erich. *Bismarck and the German Empire*. London: George Allen & Unwin, 1958.

Fanon, Frantz. *Black Skin White Masks*. Trans. Charles Lam Markmann. New York: Grove Press, 1967.

Farrenkopf, John. 'Nietzsche, Spengler, and the Politics of Cultural Despair'. *Interpretation*. 20 (2), Winter 1992–93, 165–85.

Femia, Joseph. 'Pareto's Concept of Demagogic Plutocracy'. *Government and Opposition*. 30, 3, Summer 1995, 370–92.

Foucault, Michel. *Power/Knowledge: Selected Interviews and Other Writings 1972–1977*. Ed. Colin Gordon. Trans. Colin Gordon, Leo Marshall, John Mepham and Kate Soper. Brighton: The Harvester Press, 1980.

Fowler, Mark. 'Nietzschean Perspectivism: "How Could Such a Philosophy – Dominate?" ' *Social Theory and Practice*. 16 (2), Summer 1990, 119–62.

Frampton, Kenneth. 'A Synoptic View of the Architecture of the Third Reich'. *Oppositions: A Journal for Ideas and Criticism in Architecture*. Spring 1978: 12.

Frederick II (King of Prussia). *The Refutation of Machiavelli's Prince or Anti-Machiavel*. Trans. Paul Sonnino. Athens: Ohio University Press, 1981.

Garner, Roberta. 'Jacob Burckhardt as a Theorist of Modernity: Reading *The Civilization of the Renaissance in Italy*'. *Sociological Review*. 1990, 48–57.

Gebhart, Emile. *Les Origines de la Renaissance en Italie*. Paris: Librairie Hachette, 1923.

Gentile, Giovanni. 'The Origins and Doctrine of Fascism'. *Italian Fascisms: From Pareto to Gentile*. Ed. Adrian Lyttelton. London: Jonathan Cape, 1973.

Golomb, Jacob, and Wistrich, Robert S. Eds. *Nietzsche, Godfather of Fascism?: On the Uses and Abuses of a Philosophy*. Princeton, NJ: Princeton University Press, 2002.

Goyard-Fabre, Simone. *Nietzsche et la question politique*. Paris: Éditions Sirey, 1977.

Gregor, James A. *The Ideology of Fascism: The Rationale of Totalitarianism*. New York: The Free Press, 1969.

Griffin, Roger. Ed. *Fascism*. Oxford: Oxford University Press, 1995.

Gumplowicz, Ludwig. *Outlines of Sociology*. Ed. Irving L. Horowitz. New York: Paine-Whitman Publishers, 1963.

Harmand, Jules. *Domination et colonisation*. Paris: Ernest Flammarion, 1910.

Hatab, Lawrence J. *A Nietzschean Defense of Democracy: An Experiment in Postmodern Politics*. Chicago: Open Court, 1995.

Hayman, Ronald. *Nietzsche: A Critical Life*. New York: Penguin Books, 1987.

Hegel, G. W. F. 'The German Constitution', *Hegel's Political Writings*. Oxford: Clarendon Press, 1964.

Heidegger, Martin. *Nietzsche*. Vols. I–IV. Trans. David Farrell Krell. San Francisco: Harper & Row, 1979, 1984, 1987, 1982.

Heller, Peter. *Studies on Nietzsche*. Bonn: Bouvier Verlag Herbert Grundmann, 1980.

Hobbes, Thomas. *Leviathan: or The Matter, Forme and Power of a Commonwealth Ecclesiastical and Civil*. Ed. Michael Oakeshott. Oxford: Basil Blackwell, 1955.

Honig, Bonnie. *Political Theory and the Displacement of Politics*. Ithaca: Cornell University Press, 1993.

——. 'The Politics of Agonism'. *Political Theory*. 21 (3), August 1993, 528–33.

Horkheimer, Max. *Dawn & Decline: Notes 1926–1931 and 1950–1969*. Trans. Michael Shaw. New York: The Seabury Press, 1978.

Hughes, H. Stuart. *Consciousness and Society: The Reorientation of European Social Thought 1890–1930*. New York: Alfred A. Knopf, 1958.

——. 'Gaetano Mosca and the Political Lessons of History'. *Pareto & Mosca*. Ed. James H. Meisel. Englewood Cliffs, NJ: Prentice-Hall, 1965. 141–60.

Hulliung, Mark. *Citizen Machiavelli*. Princeton: Princeton University Press, 1983.

Hunt, Lester H. *Nietzsche and The Origin of Virtue*. Routledge: London, 1991.

Jameson, Frederic. *The Political Unconscious: Narrative as a Socially Symbolic Act*. Ithaca: Cornell University Press, 1981.

Jaspers, Karl. *Nietzsche: An Introduction to the Understanding of His Philosophical Activity*. Trans. Charles F. Walraff and Frederick J. Schmitz. Tucson: University of Arizona Press, 1965.

Jünger, Ernst. 'Die Totale Mobilmachung'. *Ernst Jünger Werke*. Band 5, Essays I. Stuttgart: Ernst Klett Verlag.

Kahan, Alan S. *Aristocratic Liberalism: The Social and Political Thought of Jacob Burckhardt, John Stuart Mill, and Alexis de Tocqueville*. Oxford: Oxford University Press, 1992.

Kariel, Henry S. 'Nietzsche's Preface to Constitutionalism'. *Journal of Politics*. 25:2, May 1963, 211–25.

Kaufmann, Walter. *Nietzsche: Philosopher, Psychologist, Anti-Christ*. Princeton, NJ: Princeton University Press, 1950.

Kofman, Sarah. *Nietzsche and Metaphor*. Trans. Duncan Large. Stanford: Stanford University Press, 1993.

Kropotkin, Peter. *Selected Writings on Anarchism and Revolution*. Cambridge, Mass.: MIT Press, 1970.

Laclau, Ernesto and Mouffe, Chantal. *Hegemony & Socialist Strategy: Towards a Radical Democratic Politics*. London: Verso, 1985.

Lampert, Laurence. *Leo Strauss and Nietzsche*. Chicago: The University of Chicago Press, 1996.

——. 'Nietzsche, The History of Philosophy, and Esotericism'. *Nietzsche: Critical Assessments*. Vol. IV. Ed. Daniel W. Conway with Peter S. Groff. London: Routledge, 1998.

——. *Nietzsche and Modern Times: A Study of Bacon, Descartes, and Nietzsche*. New Haven: Yale University Press, 1993.

Landa, Ishay. 'Nietzsche, the Chinese Worker's Friend'. *New Left Review*. Number 236, July/August 1999, 3–23.

Lange, F. A. *The History of Materialism*. Trans. Ernest Chester Thomas. London: Truber & Co., 1877.

Le Bon, Gustave. *The Crowd: A Study of the Popular Mind*. London: Ernest Benn, 1952.

——. *The French Revolution and the Psychology of Revolution*. New Brunswick: Transaction Inc., 1980.

——. *The Psychology of Socialism*. Vermont: Fraser Publishing Company, 1965.

Leiter, Brian. *Nietzsche on Morality*. New York. Routledge, 2002.

Lively, Jack. *The Social and Political Thought of Alexis de Tocqueville*. Oxford: Clarendon Press, 1962.

Love, Nancy S. *Marx, Nietzsche and Modernity*. New York: Columbia University Press, 1986.

Löwith, Karl. *From Hegel to Nietzsche: The Revolution in Nineteenth-Century Thought*. Trans. David E. Green. London: Constable, 1965.

Lublinski, Samuel. *Machiavelli und Nietzsche*. 1901.

Lukács, Gyorgy. *The Destruction of Reason*. Trans. Peter Palmer. Englewood Cliffs, NJ: Humanities Press, 1981.

——. *The Young Hegel: Studies in the Relations between Dialectics and Economics*. Trans. Rodney Livingstone. Cambridge, Mass.: The MIT Press, 1976.

Machiavelli, Niccolò. *Discourses On The First Ten Books of Titus Livius*. Trans. Christian E. Detmold. New York: The Modern Library, 1950.

——. *The Prince*. Trans. Luigi Ricci. New York: The Modern Library, 1950.

Mann, Thomas. *Reflections of a Nonpolitical Man* (1918). Trans. Walter D. Morris. New York: Frederick Ungar, 1983.

Mannheim, Karl. *Ideology and Utopia: An Introduction to the Sociology of Knowledge*. Trans. Louis Wirth and Edward Shils. New York: Harcourt, Brace & World, 1936.

Mansfield, Harvey C., Jr. 'Machiavelli's Political Science'. *The American Political Science Review*. Vol. 75, June 1981, 2, 293–305.

——. *Machiavelli's Virtue*. Chicago: The University of Chicago Press, 1996.

Mara, Gerald M. and Dovi, Suzanne L. 'Mill, Nietzsche, and the Identity of Post-Modern Liberalism'. *Journal of Politics*. 57(1), February 1995, 1–23.

Marti, Urs. 'Nietzsches Kritik der Französischen Revolution'. *Nietzsche-Studien*. 19, 1990, 312–35.

Martin, Alfred von. *Nietzsche und Burckhardt: zwei Geistige Welten im Dialog*. München: Verlag Ernst Reinhardt, 1941.

Marx, Karl. *The Eighteenth Brumaire of Louis Bonaparte*. New York: International Publishers, 1963.

Mayer, Arno. *The Persistance of the Old Regime: Europe to the Great War*. New York: Pantheon Books, 1981.

McGrath, William J. *Dionysian Art and Populist Politics in Austria*. New Haven: Yale University Press, 1974.

McIntyre, Alex. ' "Virtuosos of Contempt": An Investigation of Nietzsche's Political Philosophy Through Certain Platonic Political Ideas'. *Nietzsche-Studien*. 21, 1992, 184–210.

Meinecke, Friedrich. *Machiavellism: The Doctrine of Raison d'État and its Place in Modern History*. Trans. Douglas Scott. New Haven: Yale University Press, 1957.

Meisel, James H. *The Myth of the Ruling Class: Gaetano Mosca and the Elite*. Ann Arbor: The University of Michigan Press, 1962.

Mill, John Stuart. 'Chapters on Socialism'. *Collected Works of John Stuart Mill: Essays on Politics and Society*. Volume V. Toronto: University of Toronto Press, 1967.

——. 'The Claims of Labour'. *Collected Works of John Stuart Mill: Essays on Politics and Society*. Volume IV. Toronto: University of Toronto Press, 1967.

——. 'De Tocqueville on Democracy in America', Vols. I and II. *Collected Works of John Stuart Mill: Essays on Politics and Society*. Vol. XVIII. Toronto: University of Toronto Press, 1977.

——. *On Liberty*. New York: The Liberal Arts Press, 1956.

Mosca, Gaetano. *The Ruling Class: Elementi de Scienza Politica*. Trans. Hannah D. Kahn. New York: McGraw-Hill Book Company, 1939.

Moscovici, Serge. *The Age of the Crowd: A Historical Treatise on Mass Psychology*. Trans. J. C. Whitehouse. Cambridge: Cambridge University Press, 1985.

Mosse, George L. 'Fascism and the Intellectuals'. *The Nature of Fascism*. Ed. S. J. Woolf. London: Weidenfeld and Nicolson, 1968.

Müller, Herbert J. *Freedom in the Ancient World*. New York: Harper & Row, Publishers, 1961.

Mussolini, Benito. *The Political and Social Doctrine of Fascism*. Trans. Jane Soames. London: The Hogarth Press, 1933.

Negri, Antonio. *Insurgencies: Constituent Power and the Modern State*. Trans. Maurizia Boscagli. Minneapolis: University of Minnesota Press, 1999.

Neocleous, Mark. *Fascism*. Minneapolis: University of Minnesota Press, 1997.

——. 'Perpetual War, or "War and War Again" '. *Philosophy and Social Criticism*. Vol. 22, no. 2, 1996, 47–66.

Nietzsche, Friedrich. *The Anti-Christ*. Trans. R. J. Hollingdale. Harmondsworth: Penguin Books, 1968.

——. *Beyond Good and Evil: Prelude to a Philosophy of the Future*. Trans. Walter Kaufmann. New York: Vintage Books, 1966.

——. *The Birth of Tragedy Out of the Spirit of Music or: Hellenism and Pessimism*. Trans. Walter Kaufmann. New York: Vintage Books, 1967.

——. *The Case of Wagner: A Musician's Problem. Turinese Letter of May 1888*. Trans. Walter Kaufmann. New York: Vintage Books, 1967.

——. *Daybreak: Thoughts on the Prejudices of Morality*. Trans. R. J. Hollingdale. Oxford: Cambridge University Press, 1982.

——. *Ecce Homo: How One Becomes What One Is*. Trans. Walter Kaufmann. New York: Vintage Books, 1969.

——. 'On The Future of Our Educational Institutions'. *The Complete Works of Friedrich Nietzsche*. Vol. 3. Ed. Oscar Levy. Trans. J. M. Kennedy. Edinburgh: T. N. Foulis, 1909.

——. *The Gay Science*. Trans. Walter Kaufmann. New York: Vintage Books, 1974.

——. *On The Genealogy of Morals: A Polemic*. Trans. Walter Kaufmann. New York: Vintage Books, 1969.

——. 'The Greek State' and 'Homer's Contest'. *Early Greek Philosophy and Other*

Essays. The Complete Works of Friedrich Nietzsche. Ed. Dr. Oscar Levy. Trans. Maximilian A. Mügge. Edinburgh: T. N. Foulis, 1909.
——. *Human, All Too Human: A Book for Free Spirits.* Vols. I and II (*Assorted Opinions and Maxims* and *The Wanderer and His Shadow*). Trans. R. J. Hollingdale. Cambridge: Cambridge University Press, 1996.
——. *Nietzsche Werke: Kritische Gesamtausgabe.* Ed. Colli and Montinari. Berlin: Walter de Gruyter.
——. *Philosophy in the Tragic Age of the Greeks.* Trans. Marianne Cowen. Washington D.C.: Regnery Gateway, 1962.
——. *Sämtliche Werke: Kritische Studienausgabe.* Ed. Colli and Montinari. Berlin: Walter de Gruyter.
——. *The Selected Letters of Friedrich Nietzsche.* Ed. Christopher Middleton. Chicago: University of Chicago Press, 1969.
——. *Thus Spoke Zarathustra: A Book for Everyone and No One.* Trans. R. J. Hollingdale. Harmondsworth: Penguin Books, 1969.
——. *Twilight of the Idols: or How to Philosophize with a Hammer.* Trans. R. J. Hollingdale. Harmondsworth: Penguin Books, 1968.
——. *Unpublished Writings: from the period of Unfashionable Observations.* Trans. Richard T. Gray. Stanford: Stanford University Press, 1995.
——. *Untimely Meditations.* Trans. R. J. Hollingdale. Oxford: Cambridge University Press, 1983.
——. *The Will to Power.* Trans. Walter Kaufmann and R. J. Hollingdale. New York: Vintage Books, 1968.
Nye, Robert. *The Anti-Democratic Sources of Elite Theory: Pareto, Mosca, Michels.* London: SAGE Publications, 1977.
——. *The Origins of Crowd Psychology: Gustave Le Bon and the Crisis of Mass Democracy in the Third Republic.* London: SAGE Publications, 1975.
O'Brien, Conor Cruise. *The Suspecting Glance.* London: Faber and Faber, 1972.
Oehler, Max. Ed. *Nietzsches Bibliothek.* Nietzsche Archivs, 1942.
Owen, David. *Nietzsche, Politics and Modernity: A Critique of Liberal Reason.* London: SAGE Publications, 1995.
Paine, Thomas. *The Rights of Man.* London: J. M. Dutton & Sons, 1941.
Pangle, Thomas L. 'The Roots of Contemporary Nihilism and Its Political Consequences According to Nietzsche'. *Review of Politics.* 45, 1, January 1983, 45–70.
Pareto, Vilfredo. *The Mind and Society: A Treatise on General Sociology.* Vols. I–IV. Trans. Andrew Bongiorno and Arthur Livingston. New York: Dover, Inc., 1935.
——. *The Rise and Fall of the Elites: An Application of Theoretical Sociology.* New Jersey: The Bedminster Press, 1968.
——. *Sociological Writings.* Trans. Derick Mirfin. New Jersey: Rowman and Littlefield Totowa, 1976.
Parkes, Graham. *Composing the Soul: Reaches of Nietzsche's Psychology.* Chicago: University of Chicago Press, 1994.
Paton, H. J. *The Moral Law: Kant's Groundwork of the Metaphysic of Morals.* London: Hutchinson University Library, 1966.
Patton, Paul. 'Politics and the Concept of Power in Hobbes and Nietzsche'. *Nietzsche, Feminism and Political Theory.* Ed. Paul Patton. London: Routledge, 1993.
Plato. *The Republic.* Ed. Trans. I. A. Richards. Cambridge: Cambridge University Press, 1966.

Prezzolini, Giuseppe. *Machiavelli*. New York: Farrar, Straus & Giroux, 1967.

Prostka, N. *Nietzsches Machtbegriff in Bezeihung zu den Machiavellis*. Münster: 1989.

Pyziur, Eugene. *The Doctrine of Anarchism of Michael A. Bakunin*. Milwaukee: The Marquette University Press, 1955.

Read, James H. 'Nietzsche: Power as Oppression'. *Praxis International*. 9 (1–2), April 1989, 72–87.

Rémond, René. *The Right Wing in France: From 1815 to de Gaulle*. Trans. James M. Laux. Philadelphia: University of Pennsylvania Press, 1966.

Rocco, Alfredo. 'The *Politica* Manifesto'. *Italian Fascisms: From Pareto to Gentile*. Ed. Adrian Lyttelton. London: Jonathan Cape, 1973.

Rosen, Stanley. *The Ancients and the Moderns: Rethinking Modernity*. New Haven: Yale University Press, 1989.

——. *The Mask of Enlightenment: Nietzsche's Zarathustra*. Cambridge: Cambridge University Press, 1995.

Rosen, Zvi. *Bruno Bauer and Karl Marx: The Influence of Bruno Bauer on Marx's Thought*. The Hague: Martinus Nijhoff, 1977.

Rousseau, Jean-Jacques. *A Discourse on the Origin of Inequality*. Trans. G. D. H. Cole. London: J. M. Dent, 1993.

——. *Du Contrat Social*. Ed. Ronald Grimsley. Oxford: Clarendon Press, 1972.

Rudé, George. *The Crowd in the French Revolution*. Oxford: Clarendon Press, 1959.

Sadler, Ted. 'The Postmodern Politicization of Nietzsche'. *Nietzsche, Feminism and Political Theory*. Ed. Paul Patton. London: Routledge, 1993.

Santaniello, Weaver. 'A Post-Holocaust Re-Examination of Nietzsche and the Jews: *Vis-à-Vis* Christendom and Nazism'. *Nietzsche & Jewish Culture*. Ed. Jacob Golomb. London: Routledge, 1997.

——. *Nietzsche, God and the Jews: His Critique of Judeo-Christianity in Relation to the Nazi Myth*. Albany: SUNY Press, 1994.

Sautet, Marc. *Nietzsche et la Commune*. Paris: Editions Le Sycomore, 1981.

Sax, Benjamin C. 'Cultural Agonistics: Nietzsche, the Greeks, Eternal Recurrence'. *Agonistics: Arenas of Creative Contest*. Ed. Janet Lungstrum and Elizabeth Sauer. Albany: State University of New York Press, 1997.

Schmitt, Carl. *The Concept of the Political*. Trans. George Schwab. New Brunswick: Rutgers University Press, 1976.

——. *The Crisis of Parliamentary Democracy*. Trans. Ellen Kennedy. Cambridge, Mass.: The MIT Press, 1985.

Schrift, Alan D. 'Nietzsche For Democracy?'*Nietzsche-Studien*. 29, 2000, 220–33.

——. *Nietzsche's French Legacy: A Genealogy of Poststructuralism*. New York: Routledge, 1995.

——. 'Response to Don Dombowsky'. *Nietzsche-Studien*. 31, 2002, 291–7.

Schürmann, Reiner. 'Political Thinking in Heidegger'. *Social Research*. Spring 1978, Vol. 45, No. 1, 191–221.

Schutte, Ofelia. *Beyond Nihilism: Nietzsche without Masks*. Chicago: University of Chicago Press, 1984.

Seillière, Ernest. *La Philosophie de l'impérialisme: vol. 2, Apollon ou Dionysos, étude critique sur Frédérick Nietzsche et l'utilitarisme impérialiste*. Paris: Plon-Nourrit, 1905.

Seton-Watson, Hugh. *The Decline of Imperial Russia 1855–1914*. London: Methuen, 1952.

Sigurdson, Richard F. 'Jacob Burckhardt: The Cultural Historian as Political Thinker'. *Review of Politics*. 52, 3, Summer 1990, 417–40.
——. 'Jacob Burckhardt's Liberal-Conservatism'. *History of Political Thought*. Vol. XIII, No. 3, Autumn 1992, 489–511.
Smith, Douglas. *Transvaluations: Nietzsche in France 1872–1972*. Oxford: Clarendon Press, 1996.
Sokel, W. H. 'Political Uses and Abuses of Nietzsche in Walter Kaufmann's Image of Nietzsche'. *Nietzsche-Studien*. 12, 1983, 436–42.
Spengler, Oswald. *Man and Technics*. Trans. Charles Francis Atkinson. Westport: Greenwood Press, 1976.
Spinoza, Benedict de. *Tractatus Politicus. The Chief Works of Benedict de Spinoza*. Vol. I. Trans. R. H. M. Elwes. London: George Bell and Sons, 1883.
Spitzer, Alan B. *The Revolutionary Theories of Louis Auguste Blanqui*. New York: Columbia University Press, 1957.
Stack, George J. 'Nietzsche and the Laws of Manu'. *Sociology and Social Research*. 51, October, 1966, 94–106.
Stell, Hans Dieter. *Machiavelli und Nietzsche*. Munich: 1987.
Stern, J. P. *A Study of Nietzsche*. Cambridge: Cambridge University Press, 1979.
Sternhill, Zeev. 'Fascist Ideology'. *Fascism: A Reader's Guide*. Ed. Walter Laquer. Berkeley: University of California Press, 1976, 315–76.
Strauss, Leo. 'Note on the Plan of *Beyond Good and Evil*'. *Interpretation*. 3 (2–3), 1973.
——. *The Political Philosophy of Hobbes: Its Basis and Its Genesis*. Trans. Elsa M. Sinclair. Chicago: The University of Chicago Press, 1952.
——. *Thoughts on Machiavelli*. Seattle: University of Washington Press, 1958.
Strong, Tracy B. *Friedrich Nietzsche and the Politics of Transfiguration*. Berkeley: University of California Press, 1975.
——. 'Texts and Pretexts: Reflections on Perspectivism in Nietzsche'. *Political Theory*. 13 (2), May 1985, 164–82.
Struve, Walter. *Elites Against Democracy: Leadership Ideals in Bourgeois Political Thought in Germany 1890–1933*. Princeton, NJ: Princeton University Press, 1972.
Taguieff, Pierre-André. 'The Traditional Paradigm – Horror of Modernity and Antiliberalism: Nietzsche in Reactionary Rhetoric'. *Why We Are Not Nietzscheans*. Ed. Luc Ferry and Alain Renaut. Trans. Robert de Loaiza. Chicago: The University of Chicago Press, 1997.
Taine, Hippolyte. *History of English Literature*. New York: Colonial Press, 1900.
——. 'Napoléon Bonaparte'. *Revue des deux mondes*. 15 February, Vol. 79, 721–52, and 1 March, Vol. 80, 5–49.
——. *The Origins of Contemporary France*. Ed. Edward T. Gargan. Chicago: The University of Chicago Press, 1974.
Taureck, Bernhard H. F. *Nietzsche und der Faschismus: Eine Studie über Nietzsche politische Philosophie und ihre Folgen*. Hamburg: Junius Verlag, 1989.
Taylor, Quentin P. *The Republic of Genius: A Reconstruction of Nietzsche's Early Thought*. Rochester, NJ: University of Rochester Press, 1997.
Thatcher, David S. *Nietzsche in England 1890–1914: The Growth of a Reputation*. Toronto: University of Toronto Press, 1970.
Thiele, Leslie Paul. 'Nietzsche, Heidegger and Politics'. *Political Theory*. 22 (3), August 1994, 468–90.

Thomas, R. Hinton. *Nietzsche in German Politics and Society: 1890–1918*. Manchester: Manchester University Press, 1983.

Thompson, J. M. *Napoleon Bonaparte*. New York: Oxford University Press, 1952.

Tocqueville, Alexis de. *Democracy in America*. Trans. George Lawrence. Ed. J. P. Mayer. New York: Anchor Books, 1969.

——. *The Old Régime and the French Revolution*. Trans. Stuart Gilbert. Garden City, NY: Doubleday, 1955.

Tombs, Robert. *France: 1814–1914*. London: Longman, 1996.

Treitschke, Heinrich von. *Politics*. Ed. Hans Kohn. New York: Harcourt, Brace & World, Inc. 1963.

Ueberweg, Frederick. *A History of Philosophy*. Vol. I. Trans. George S. Morris. London: Hodder & Stoughton, 1865.

Villari, Pasquale. *Machiavelli and His Times*. Trans. Linda Villari. London: Kegan Paul, 1883.

Voegelin, Eric. 'Nietzsche, the Crisis and the War'. *Journal of Politics*. Vol. 6, 1944, 177–211.

Waite, Geoff. 'On Esotericism: Heidegger and/or Cassirer at Davos'. *Political Theory*. 26, 5, October 1998, 603–51.

——. *Nietzsche's Corps/e: Aesthetics, Politics, Prophecy, or, The Spectacular Techno-culture of Everyday Life*. Durham, NC and London: Duke University Press, 1996.

——. 'The Politics of Reading Formations: The case of Nietzsche in Imperial Germany (1870–1919)'. *New German Critique*. 29, Spring/Summer 1983, 185–209.

——. 'Zarathustra or the Modern Prince: The Problem of Nietzschean Political Philosophy'. *Nietzsche Heute*. Ed. Sigrid Bauschinger et al. Stuttgart: Francke, 1988, 227–50.

Warren, Mark. 'Nietzsche and Political Philosophy'. *Political Theory*. 13, May 1985, 183–212.

——. *Nietzsche and Political Thought*. Cambridge, Mass.: The MIT Press, 1988.

——. 'The Politics of Nietzsche's Philosophy: Nihilism, Culture and Power'. *Political Studies*. 33, 1985, 418–38.

Weinstein, Leo. *Hippolyte Taine*. New York: Twayne Publishers, 1972.

Wolin, Sheldon S. *Politics and Vision: Continuity and Innovation in Western Political Thought*. Boston: Little, Brown, 1960.

Yack, Bernard. *The Longing for Total Revolution: Philosophic Sources of Social Discontent from Rousseau to Marx and Nietzsche*. Princeton, NJ: Princeton University Press, 1986.

Yovel, Yirmiyahu. 'Nietzsche and the Jews: The Structure of an Ambivalence'. *Nietzsche & Jewish Culture*. Ed. Jacob Golomb. London: Routledge, 1997.

Index

Printed in the United States
70672LV00002B/1

9 781403 933676